BLOOD OF THE
VIKINGS

BLOOD OF THE
VIKINGS

Julian Richards

Hodder & Stoughton

In memory of Ali Borthwick,
archaeologist and friend

Copyright © 2001 by Julian Richards

By arrangement with the BBC

The BBC logo and "The Blood of the Vikings" logos are trademarks
of the British Broadcasting Corporation and are used under licence.
BBC logo © BBC 1996
"The Blood of the Vikings" logo © BBC 2001

Executive Producer – Caroline van den Brul
Series Producer – Paul Bradshaw
Assistant Producer and Book contributor – Nicola Cook

First published in Great Britain in 2001 by Hodder and Stoughton
A division of Hodder Headline

2 4 6 8 10 9 7 5 3

A CIP catalogue record for this title is available from the British Library

ISBN 0 340 73385 3

Typeset in Adobe Minion by Palimpsest Book Production Limited,
Polmont, Stirlingshire
Printed and bound in Great Britain
by Butler & Tanner, Frome, Somerset

Hodder and Stoughton
A division of Hodder Headline
338 Euston Road
London NW1 3BH

CONTENTS

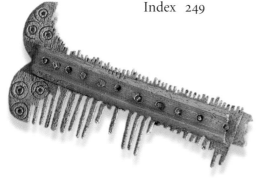

CHAPTER 1

THE VIKING MYTH

The Vikings active in the West during the reigns of Alfred the Great and Aethelred the Unready were decidedly unfriendly, unpleasant and unwelcome . . .

SIMON KEYNES

I think they've been unfairly treated by history actually. The problem is that the people who wrote about them were primarily monks, and they had every reason to portray the Vikings as wicked and evil because, of course, the Vikings were pagans.

OLWYN OWEN

The popular image of the Vikings has definitely stayed blood and thunder down throughout the centuries and I don't think we'll eradicate that.

ANNA RITCHIE

LEFT | *This nineteenth century stained-glass window portrays a traditional image of the Vikings – bravely sailing violent seas.*

Three Viking experts, three differing opinions. Which one do we believe?

The Vikings have one of the most powerful images of any people from the past, an image of seafaring warriors in horned helmets, of battleaxes, flowing locks and majestic longships. But how much truth is there in this image?

Growing up in the 1950s with a boy's inevitable obsessions, the first image of a Viking that I recall was on the badge of my headmaster's car. Here was a classic 'sea rover', a picture strengthened by my childhood history books and finally confirmed as accurate by Kirk Douglas and Tony Curtis in the 1958 film *The Vikings*. This image stayed with me for many years until I discovered archaeology. Over the thirty or so years that I have been an archaeologist I have spent most of my time studying and digging on prehistoric sites and it was only when I started work on *Blood*

The 1958 film The Vikings *portrayed these Scandinavian adventurers in typical Hollywood fashion.*

of the Vikings that I sat down and took stock of what my experience of the Vikings had been. This was when I realised that the first dig that I ever worked on, and for which I was paid five shillings a day as an 'inexperienced volunteer living at home', had a Viking connection.

Home then was Nottingham, and the site lay in the old Lace Market area of town where narrow medieval streets and Victorian warehouses were being torn down to create the sort of soulless development that is now itself being demolished and replaced. I vividly remember digging out the sandy soil that filled a huge ditch, cut into the soft sandstone on which Nottingham sits. I also remember the sides of our cutting collapsing, nearly burying the digging team; this was in the days when health and safety rules were largely ignored. The ditch that nearly ended my archaeological career just as it was getting started was in fact part of the town defences during the Viking period. Home today is Shaftesbury in Dorset, another burgh where somewhere there is another huge ditch awaiting discovery . . .

A few years after that first dig, as an archaeology student at Reading University, I was lucky enough to be sent off to Trondheim in Norway to work on a Viking-period excavation over the summer break. This was my first experience of working on a waterlogged site, slow to excavate and record but incredibly rewarding and one that has created some lasting memories. It was enough to be able to expose the entire wooden floor of a Viking house, but to turn over the last bit of stray 'plank' and find that it was a beautifully carved chair-back was a moment that I will always treasure. Little did I know that twenty-five years later I would be back in Trondheim to quiz some of my Norwegian fellow diggers about their distant Vikings ancestors.

Over the years I learnt that my original picture of the Vikings was maybe only partly true, and that there was a much stranger truth lurking somewhere in the archaeological and historical records. This book is about my search for that truth, a search that has taken me from the fjords of the Viking homelands in Scandinavia to the most remote islands of the British Isles. I have talked to archaeologists as they excavate evidence that challenges some of our most long-held ideas about the Vikings. I have come face to face with the written words and the wonderful objects that paint such a vivid picture of raiders and traders. And I have had some very strange experiences . . . Imagine riding through the streets of Dublin in an orange Second World War amphibious vehicle, driven by a 'Viking' complete with flaxen plaits and a horned helmet. This is the 'Viking Splash Tour' that, true to its name, does involve a short trip on the water, although I'm sure that the Dublin Vikings would have found the idea of lifejackets a bit soft. The intentions are good and, as well as giving open-topped tour buses and traffic wardens an authentic Viking 'roar', the tour is genuinely educational. But the Viking image, despite being instantly recognisable to tourists from Denmark or Japan, comes straight out of my forty-year-old history book. So where does this image have its origins? Just who is responsible?

The story of the Vikings has been passed down through history for

In Dublin, the Viking Splash Tour takes tourists round the Viking sites – and teaches them an authentic Viking roar!

over one thousand years. Time and again they turn up in records kept throughout Europe, and nearly every time they are portrayed as violent thugs. The story of the first Viking footstep on British soil is a perfect illustration of their almost universally bad press. It occurred on Portland, a small island on the south coast of Dorset, the county where I now live, in the late eighth century.

One day, ships were spotted approaching Portland beach. At that time Dorset lay within the kingdom of Wessex which was ruled by King Beorhtric and so the king sent Beaduheard, reeve of Dorchester, to greet the new arrivals. The reeve was a royal official, the king's representative responsible for collecting taxes and for making sure that any merchants' ships paid the fees due to the king for trading on his land. As he made his way to the beach Beaduheard was probably expecting a fairly routine transaction but when he arrived he was greeted by three ships full of unfamiliar sailors. The reeve's attempts to direct them to Dorchester, the nearest royal outpost, failed and the discussion ended when these strange sailors killed him on the spot.

Perhaps they objected to being taxed, maybe they simply did not understand what the reeve wanted them to do, or it may have been a deliberate attempt to threaten the kingdom of Wessex. We will never know, but a century later a scribe, with the benefit of hindsight, describes these three ships as the 'first ships of the Danish men which sought out the land of the English race'. Although the name was not in use at that time, these 'Danish men' were Vikings, and the late-lamented reeve had had the dubious honour of being the first Englishman to meet them.

This initial encounter fits well with the Vikings' subsequent image as intrepid but violent explorers, the beginnings of which can be traced back through the years to the twelfth and thirteenth centuries. It was then that the first sagas and skaldic poems were written, celebrating the lives of Scandinavian adventurers at the turn of the first millennium. Up until this time, the only written descriptions of the Vikings were in the annals and chronicles, all of which were penned by people who had been the victims of Viking raids, the English, the French, or Arabs. They were hardly likely to describe their attackers in favourable terms and so the

Vikings appear as heathen barbarians. But the sagas were written by fellow Scandinavians who wished to elevate their ancestors to the heights of respect which the Roman Empire had enjoyed. The authors of the Norse sagas, writing just a few centuries later, already regarded the Viking Age as a golden era, when exploring heroes settled new lands. Many were written in Iceland, no doubt in an attempt to create a history for this relatively new land. In some ways these sagas were much like today's Hollywood version of history. The bare bones of the stories probably have some truth to them, but there will have been much invention and exaggeration to carry the story along.

There are two authors in particular who might be given the most credit for passing the Viking story on to future generations. These are Saxo Grammaticus and Snorri Sturluson. Snorri was an Icelandic poet and historian who wrote the history of the Norwegian kings, the *Heimskringla*. Despite its use of folk tales to build up the stories, the *Heimskringla* is written in such a factual, impartial way that for many centuries it was accepted as a historically accurate record. Saxo was a Danish historian who went one step further in his attempt to convince the rest of Europe that his Danish ancestors were honourable heroes despite their pagan beliefs. He wrote *Gesta Danorum*, a history of Denmark, in which, drawing on Roman models for his characters, he presents the Viking chiefs as honourable statesmen.

Gesta Danorum had a big influence on historians and artists in the sixteenth and seventeenth centuries. Being written in Latin, it had the benefit of being easily understood by a wider audience than Snorri Sturluson's Old Norse text. Shakespeare even derived the story of Hamlet from Saxo's great work. Scandinavian historians continued to recreate their past, and as the Old Norse works were gradually translated, some historians were subject to flights of fancy. The Swedish historian Olof Rudbeck, in his quest to outdo the Danes, went so far as to suggest that Sweden was the true location of Atlantis, the mythical island paradise which had sunk into the sea.

In their desire to portray a noble and worthy race, fit to stand alongside the Romans as a conquering culture, both historians and artists sometimes went for effect rather than accuracy. In one edition of Saxo Grammaticus' *Gesta Danorum* Odin is pictured in a full suit of armour and a plumed helmet, while Thor is given a crown and sceptre. The illus-

Standard Viking costume often seems to include horned helmets – although there is no evidence that the real Vikings ever wore them.

trator clearly decided that he could get his point across best by using the symbols of power which were common when the book was produced in the sixteenth century.

This attempt to create a civilised and refined image for the Vikings was ultimately in vain. During the eighteenth century the Romantic Movement was searching for ways to portray the wild beauty of nature and thought the Vikings fitted the bill perfectly. Here was a noble yet savage race, who had tamed the violent seas in their majestic boats. The change in image is most obvious in the work of Paul-Henri Mallet, a professor of French at the University of Copenhagen in the 1750s. In the 1755 edition of his *Introduction to the History of Denmark,* Mallet stressed the complex nature of Old Norse poetry and the intellectual satisfaction which his readers could gain from studying it. But by 1763, when the book was republished, Mallet's opinion had changed: the Vikings were now a 'rude and uncultivated' people who had managed to harness the power of nature in their poetry, without needing any degree of intellectual understanding.

During this period the national identity of both Denmark and Sweden was taking a battering. Denmark had suffered a humiliating defeat at the hands of the British who bombarded and invaded Copenhagen during the Napoleonic Wars, and in 1809 the Swedes had lost Finland to Russia. The Swedish response, designed to encourage patriotism, was the formation of the Gothic Society. Its members drank mead from horns, addressed each other by Nordic names, and published a magazine named after the Norse goddess Iduna. *Iduna* published poems and other literary work, but also featured a smattering of archaeology.

This interest in folk culture spread across society. The fashionable aristocracy attended fancy-dress Viking balls and a 'Viking style' became popular with architects. Old Norse gods and saga heroes featured in the works of many artists, and in Denmark there was even a series of 'folk high schools' established to teach the lessons of the Viking Age. In Norway the desire to claim the Vikings as belonging more to their country than to any other in Scandinavia was enhanced by the fact that Norway had been part of the Danish kingdom until 1814, after which it joined Sweden where it would remain until 1905. All official documents had been written in Danish, so reclaiming their own language from the countryside dialects was fundamental to the Norwegian sense of national identity. These dialects, which had continued to be spoken despite the changing nation-

In Sweden, the Vikings became a popular theme for fancy-dress balls. This one took place in Stockholm in 1869.

alities of Norwegian rulers, were closest to the Old Norse and Icelandic which the Vikings themselves might have used. Snorri Sturluson's *Heimskringla* became a classic text, portraying the great kings who had ruled Norway in the distant past.

During the nineteenth century archaeology began to contribute to this growing Viking awareness, and new discoveries were widely publicised. At Tune, the sparse remains of a Viking ship were unearthed in 1867 and three years later, the discovery of another ship at Gokstad further ignited that country's passion for its Viking past. These boats provided inspiration for many artists, and in 1893 a full-size replica was sailed across the Atlantic to the World Columbian Exposition in Chicago.

The *Viking* sailed to New York and then around the Great Lakes, in a trip designed to popularise the notion that Leif Eriksson discovered America long before Columbus. This trip fanned the flames of Viking enthusiasm not only in Scandinavia but across Europe and the United States. A second, even better-preserved ship was revealed at Oseberg in Norway, a burial ship that contained the greatest array of Viking objects yet found.

In 1893 a Viking ship crossed the Atlantic, on its way to the World Columbian Exposition in Chicago. It was a replica of the Gokstad ship, discovered in Norway in 1880.

In Britain, enthusiasm for the Vikings grew during Victoria's reign. The queen herself took a keen interest in Norse mythology, the moral tales found in the sagas particularly appealing to her. The stars of these stories, Scandinavian warriors who return home from dangerous expeditions wiser and more mature, to become upstanding members of the community, were just the sort of men Victorian England would have been happy to welcome. One of the first English translations of *Frithiof's Saga*, subtitled 'A Scandinavian Legend of Royal Love', was dedicated to the young Princess Victoria by William Strong, a Windsor chaplain.

Indeed the enthusiasm for the Vikings spread to the genealogy of the queen herself. Not only was her court physician, Sir Henry Holland, a keen Icelandic enthusiast; claims were made that Victoria was descended from Odin, and that the entire Hanoverian royal family were the progeny of a bloodthirsty Viking chief. One family tree suggested that Alexandra, daughter of Christian IX of Denmark, who became Princess of Wales on her marriage to Victoria's son Edward in 1863, was descended from the tenth-century Danish king, Harald Bluetooth. There was even an Icelandic peasant who insisted that two of his rural friends were closely related to the queen.

The Vikings probably also appealed to the Victorians as daring explorers, who used their superior knowledge of ships and navigation to roam the world and found their own empire. This fitted well with the Victorians' image of themselves as intrepid, all-conquering adventurers in the days when Britain's empire stretched around the globe. It is hardly surprising that one British saga-translator wrote:

They [the Vikings] were like England in the nineteenth century: fifty years before all the rest of the world with her manufactories and firms – and twenty years before them in railways. They were foremost in the race of civilisation and progress; well started before all the rest had thought of running. No wonder therefore that both won.

Another notable Victorian who found the Vikings fascinating was the great craftsman, writer and Socialist, William Morris. As a poet, Morris was greatly influenced by the Scandinavian sagas, which he read in the original Old Norse. His interest in Viking crafts developed through a love of medieval art and, although Nordic art rarely featured prominently in art and design, he was asked to undertake one commission with a very Norse theme. Miss Catharine Wolfe, a wealthy American living on the eastern seaboard of the United States, hired Morris to design stained-glass windows depicting the discovery of Vinland (America) by the Vikings.

It was during Queen Victoria's reign that the word Viking first came into common use. Although it had appeared in a few historical documents well before this, it was the Victorians who made it a household name. Although listed in the *Oxford English Dictionary* in 1807, thirty years before Queen Victoria's coronation, the word was at this point used primarily by scholars studying the Anglo-Saxon manuscripts in which it originally occurred. Fifty years later scores of book titles featuring the word Viking appeared, including poetry, fiction, saga translations and plays. The popularity of the Viking myth in the Victorian era was given intellectual credence when both Oxford and Cambridge universities started Old Norse programmes.

The Viking myth was also being perpetuated in Germany where, in 1876, Richard Wagner's *Ring des Nibelungen* was first performed in Bayreuth. This was a dramatic musical recreation of Norse mythology, following the story of Siegfried and his mistress, the Valkyrie Brunnhilde. Siegfried is a character who also appeared in Early Germanic mythology and so provided the perfect opportunity to merge German nationalism with the heroic Viking past. The original performance of the *Ring* cycle was sponsored by the King of Bavaria, and it soon became an annual national ritual.

By the end of the nineteenth century the mystique of the myth which Wagner had created met with the elitist philosophy of the superhuman, and a more ominous form of nationalism was born. The German people were suggested as being the descendants of the Aryans, a race of superior people who were responsible for all mankind's great achievements. It was only a small step to identify the already mythologised Vikings with this pure Germanic race. This association was developed further by Adolf Hitler and the Nazi Party after the German defeat in World War I. The

FOR DANMARK!
MOD BOLCHEVISMEN!

Meld Dig hos ⚡⚡-Ersatzkommando Dänemark
København V., Jernbanegade 7

*The Nazis used Viking imagery
in their recruitment posters*

Nazis were particularly keen to create new cultural rituals, and majestic outdoor arenas were designed to resemble the venues of the great meetings or *Things*, described in the Norse sagas. Here a new form of drama would be performed, including much parading and chanting of political slogans. The name Viking was co-opted for a Nazi regiment of Norwegian volunteers and Nazi propaganda often featured the Viking image. Posters calling for Scandinavian help in the battle against Bolshevism used an SS soldier against a ghostly backdrop of Viking images, warrior or longship.

But the Viking image had not been entirely subsumed into Nazi ideology. Denmark boasted a Resistance movement that rallied around the name of Holger Danske, an Old Norse saga hero. However, at the end of World War II, popular interest in Viking heritage diminished, both in Germany and in Scandinavia. Perhaps the Vikings had become tainted by their association with the horrors of modern warfare, and it took a while for their popularity to re-emerge. Now a new fascination with Norse culture has developed and the old image of bold explorers can once again be seen in films and in the use of the Viking name. In 1976, when America's National Air and Space Administration (NASA) chose a name for its expedition to Mars, it was Viking, in a deliberate celebration of their courageous explorations of the New World. The mission was devised in 1966, just after a site at L'Anse Aux Meadows in Newfoundland had been confirmed as the first and only Viking settlement in continental North America.

So this is the Viking myth, a strong and sometimes contradictory image developed over twelve centuries, the most pervasive element of which is still the fearsome heathen attacker. But the Vikings' influence on the culture and language of the British Isles suggests that they were more than this; that they traded rather than just raided, settled and farmed rather than just paid flying visits. Some now see them as misunderstood and emphasise their artistic achievements although one Dublin primary school pupil has no doubts about just how bad they were. According to him, 'the Vikings drank blood', elevating them to new heights of nastiness.

But what *is* the truth about the Vikings? If we can find the truth about a people from such a distant time, then it lies somewhere in a combination of history (taken with a pinch of salt), archaeology, where new discoveries are made each year, and science, particularly the field of genetics. This is the start of our journey to seek that truth.

CHAPTER 2

THE TERRIBLE TRUTH?

*Here terrible portents came about over the land of Northumbria, and
miserably frightened the people: these were immense flashes of lightning
and fiery dragons were seen flying in the air.*

ANGLO-SAXON CHRONICLE, 793

LEFT | *The Vikings raided
monasteries looking for
valuable treasures. This
beautiful manuscript was
probably begun by Irish monks
at the monastery on the
Scottish island of Iona, and
finished in Kells, in County
Meath. The monastery was
forced to move here after a
number of Viking attacks.*

The starting point in our search for the real Vikings, in contrast to the
mythical peoples portrayed by Wagnerian opera and Hollywood,
should logically be what has been written about them. But who do you
believe? The Vikings themselves whose sagas are full of epic deeds and
great triumphs, or the Anglo-Saxons who were on the other end of those
great victories and, in consequence, did not have quite such a rosy view
of them?

In Britain much of our knowledge of the Viking Age comes from the
annals and chronicles compiled and kept at monasteries throughout the
British Isles and Ireland. These works, which recorded the most significant events of their times, could be considered the newspapers of the day,
but just like today's newspapers, a story can appear very different
depending on who is reporting on it. The most famous of these 'newspapers' is the Anglo-Saxon Chronicle.

Today there are seven surviving manuscripts, each with a slightly
different perspective on the reported events. In the Anglo-Saxon period it
was normal practice for copies of significant documents to be widely circu-
lated to important regional centres, usually the monasteries. In the case
of the Chronicle, several copies of the original document were distributed
and the monks then continued to update their own copy as time went by.
So the manuscripts that survive today contain the local and national news
from such diverse locations as Canterbury, Worcester and Peterborough.

The original document, which formed the basis for all the subsequent
versions of the Anglo-Saxon Chronicle, was begun in the 890s as an attempt
to trace the heritage of the 'English' people. The author's intention was

to chart the history of Britain right back to the beginning of the first century AD, basing his work on earlier written records. So he was not simply relying on his own memory, nor was he inventing historical events. After the initial documents had been distributed, later authors in each of the regional centres continued to make entries. From this point onwards the prime concern of the authors was to detail the passage of time, providing markers to remember what happened in each year. The entries grow in length and detail as time progresses; hardly surprising as the authors of these later entries are now writing about contemporary events rather than historical incidents. The entries also seem to vary in their significance, some recording obviously important events while others detail incidents that must have seemed significant to the authors, even if their relevance is not entirely clear to the modern reader.

The Chronicle begins with a genealogy of King Alfred, most likely because the author was a member of his court. For the same reason it is also particularly good at recording the battles between the English and the Vikings during the last decade of the ninth century, battles fought by Alfred and his ancestors. So while it gives us an interesting perspective on the Danish Vikings who were active in the ninth century, it offers a much less detailed account of the raids that had taken place a hundred years before the Chronicle was written.

These early Viking raids were still clearly regarded as important and the picture painted by the Chronicle, of Christian sites across the British Isles suffering at the hands of heathen men, helped to create a lasting image of the Vikings as godless raiders. When these raids took place, in the late eighth century, England was not yet a unified land, so it was the individual kingdoms of Wessex, Mercia, Sussex, East Anglia, Essex, Kent and Northumbria that all fell prey to raiding and looting.

As well as the individual reports of actual assaults, there are other clues which suggest that the threat from these pirates of the north was being taken very seriously by the rulers of the English kingdoms. In 792 Offa, the powerful king of Mercia, insisted that the Church of Kent contributed to sea defences against the attacking pagans. The Church was a good source of funds for Offa's protective measures and had more reason than most to be concerned about the raids. The main victims of the looting that was taking place were the rich religious centres, the monasteries of the British Isles.

RIGHT | *Viking attacks on the early kingdoms of Britain in the late eighth-century.*

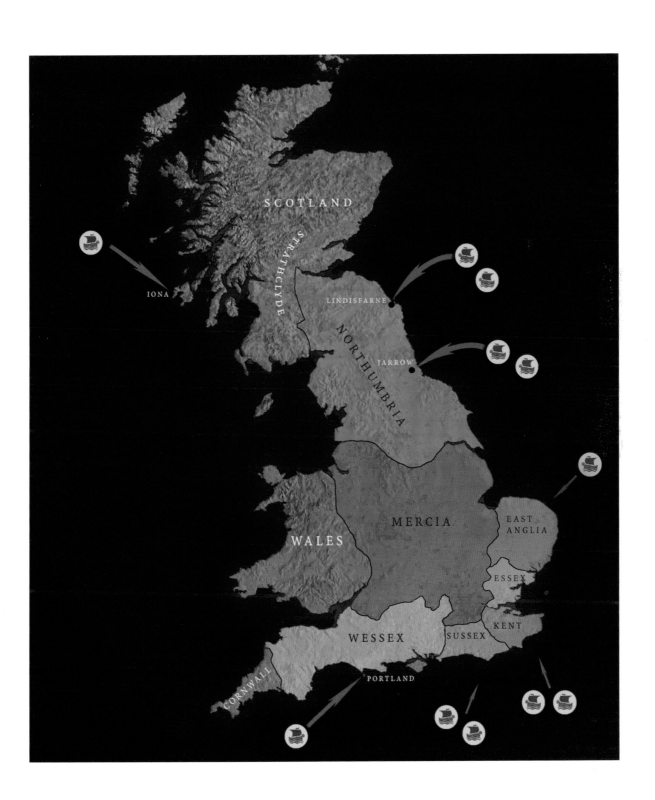

It is easy to see why the monasteries were such attractive targets. They were often in coastal locations vulnerable to seaborne raiders, were largely undefended, and contained all sorts of treasures. Sacred relics of the saints were housed in reliquaries of gold or silver, often encrusted with precious stones, while the covers of holy books were also splendidly and richly decorated. The best surviving example of the wealth of the monasteries is the jewel-encrusted gold cover of the Lindau Gospels. This book is actually a mishmash of parts from different places and times. The manuscript was produced in the late ninth century at the abbey of St Gall in Switzerland but the back cover, which may originally not even have been intended for a book, was already about a hundred years old by the time the manuscript was written. Dated by its elaborate artwork, the cover has a strange mixture of styles, some similar to the Lindisfarne Gospels of around 700 but including Viking animal ornaments of a century later and enamel animals resembling art produced in France in the middle of the eighth century.

The glittering front cover, which may also not have been intended for the manuscript it now protects, is thought to come from the court of the Emperor Charles the Bald, grandson of Charlemagne. The spectacular raised gold figures of Christ and the Virgin, surrounded by jewels, means the cover doesn't sit well with the manuscript itself. The text contains no evangelist portraits and, although finely written, is relatively modest by comparison to its bindings. In the Viking Age every important monastery would have had similar richly bound works of literature, irresistible pickings to a Viking raider.

So the Vikings had good reasons for raiding the monasteries, and, hardly surprisingly, the scribes saw the raids as events important enough to include in the Anglo-Saxon Chronicle. The Church was an immensely important part of the English kingdoms and attacking an important monastery must have been equivalent of a modern-day assault on the Houses of Parliament.

The first attack on a monastery recorded in the Anglo-Saxon Chronicle is that on Lindisfarne in 793.

Here terrible portents came about over the land of Northumbria, and miserably frightened the people: these were immense flashes of lightning, and fiery dragons were seen flying in the air. A great famine immediately followed these signs; and a

LEFT | *The lavishly decorated cover of the Lindau Gospels clearly demonstrates the riches of the monasteries in the Viking Age.*

little after that in the same year on 8 January the raiding of heathen men miserably devastated God's church in Lindisfarne island by looting and slaughter.

The Vikings had arrived. This was the most famous of all their attacks and is often regarded as the very beginning of the 'Viking Age'. The sacking of Lindisfarne resulted in the deaths of several monks, with others taken away as captives, the desecration of the altars, and the loss of some holy relics. The Lindisfarne Gospels no longer have their original binding, but a note inserted by a monk in the mid tenth century describes what would have been a rich prize to a Viking raider.

And Billfrith, the anchorite, wrought the ornaments on the outside and adorned it with gold and with gems and gilded silver, unalloyed metal.

This version of the Anglo-Saxon Chronicle describes the raid which took place on Lindisfarne in 793.

Most historians are used to dealing with historical documents like the Anglo-Saxon Chronicle in the user-friendly form of translations, printed, indexed and cross-referenced. Yet there is still something very inspiring about coming face to face with the original, sitting at a table and looking at the words written by a monastic scribe over a thousand years ago. I had this wonderful experience in the library of Corpus Christi College in Cambridge, courtesy of its enthusiastic Fellow Librarian Dr Christopher de Hamel. With strict instructions that I could 'look but not touch!' I was helped through the book by Professor Raymond Page, a leading authority on the Chronicle who just happened to be passing by. What I wanted most of all was to see for myself the magical date 793 and the description of the raid, in which 'heathen men miserably devastated God's church in Lindisfarne'. But I was to be disappointed. The copy of the Chronicle that I had in front of me was written in Winchester and this pivotal event was clearly not considered worthy of a mention down south in Hampshire.

But there is a more contemporary source we can turn to for this period. Numerous letters of an English monk who was alive at the turn of the eighth century have survived to this day. Alcuin was from York, but spent much of his life in Europe, at the court of Charlemagne, King of the Franks. He taught at the court at Aachen and often reported back to the King of Northumbria, as well as to many others in York. His most famous letter is that commenting on the raid at Lindisfarne in 793. He writes:

Never before has such terror appeared in Britain as we have now suffered from a pagan race, nor was it thought that such an inroad from the sea could be made. Behold the church of St Cuthbert, spattered with the blood of the priests of God, despoiled of all its ornaments; a place more venerable than all in Britain is given as prey to pagan peoples.

There can be no doubt which side Alcuin is on. He shared the distress of the religious community at the Vikings' disregard for the sanctity of their churches. Alcuin could not believe that 'pagans play where God was praised'. The Vikings are, in his opinion, a curse, which may have befallen the British people because of their sinful ways. He had issued 'warnings . . . of this calamity' to the people of Northumberland, but they had been ignored. There is also a more subtle reason for Alcuin to be firmly against the Vikings. His role at Aachen was probably a bit like that of foreign minister for the British government, cementing bonds with Charlemagne's own court. But at this time Charlemagne's empire was itself under threat from pagan Danes to the north and so Alcuin's strongly anti-Viking stance was certainly a wise political move. Maybe Alcuin's letter is the first example of the Vikings being used for propaganda purposes.

Not only was Alcuin clearly biased in his interpretation of events, but he cannot have been writing his vivid and bloody description from personal experience. At the time that the raid took place he was not in Northumbria, not even in Britain, but in Aachen. Given the second-hand nature of Alcuin's reporting and his obvious partiality, perhaps we would be better to return to the Anglo-Saxon Chronicle for our interpretation of these events, even if it was written in retrospect.

In comparison to Alcuin's writing, the tone of the Chronicle appears relatively unbiased. But it is inextricably linked to King Alfred, and the Vikings were bound to seem like a bad thing in his eyes. At the beginning of his reign Alfred had successfully defeated a Viking army but, at the time the Chronicle was started, the Vikings were once again becoming a threat. This would have been quite a good time for Alfred to remind his subjects just what he had achieved so far. The factual style of the work suggests to the modern reader that the authors were aware they were writing an historical document and should keep their personal opinions out of it. But as part of the English establishment that was under attack they cannot be assumed to be giving the whole story.

So both the Anglo-Saxon Chronicle and Alcuin may be guilty of over-dramatising events to suit their needs. In Irish sources, too, the Vikings are used as convincing villains. In the twelfth century the Vikings starred in a story designed to enhance the reputation of one of Ireland's most famous kings. The descendants of Brian Boru created a myth around him in the Cogadh Gáedhel re Gallaibh (The War of the Irish with the Foreigners), and here too the partiality of the author can be questioned. The story presents the Vikings as a singular threat, whose defeat required a man of incredible courage and strength. There are no prizes for guessing who succeeds against them: it is of course the great man himself, Brian Boru!

Although the Cogadh Gáedhel re Gallaibh gives an exaggerated and biased account of the Viking attacks in Ireland, there are other sources which appear to paint a fairer picture. Despite the amount of emphasis placed in English sources on recording Viking attacks on English kingdoms, the Vikings were also a significant threat in Ireland. The Irish Annals are not as well known as the Anglo-Saxon Chronicle. But they can reveal a lot about the Viking activity in North-West Europe, and they are probably a more reliable source than many of the English ones.

Perhaps because there are fewer translations of these annals from the original Irish, they have not been as popular with historians as their English counterparts. But annals written at various locations in Ireland record Viking attacks, reported simply and without the moralising tone often apparent in other records. There is another great difference between the Irish Annals and their English counterparts. In Ireland the records show it was not just the Vikings who attacked monasteries, and not Vikings who attacked them first. The Irish played their part, sacking monasteries in opposing kingdoms, understanding the powerful message this would send to their rivals. The unfortunate monastery at Clonmacnoise was attacked six times during the Viking era of 842 to 946 but in the same period there were at least eleven incidents of native violence. Seen through the eyes of the Irish scribes, the Viking leaders appear no different to many of the Irish kings. Violent certainly, but no more so than many of their contemporaries. The English too may have attacked monasteries before the Vikings arrived, but if they did it was not recorded.

The most potent image of the Vikings which history has handed down to us, reported in both England and Ireland, by Alcuin, the Anglo-Saxon Chronicle, and the Irish Annals, is of raiders without qualms about attacking religious sites. So how did the Vikings view themselves at this time? Did they give themselves a more sympathetic press?

The earliest documents to tell the story of the Viking Age from a Scandinavian perspective are the sagas, medieval writings from Iceland. Saga is the Icelandic word meaning 'what is said', or 'told' and the sagas are probably the first attempt to record stories, originally in Old Norse or skaldic verse, which had been passed down orally from one generation to another.

There are several different types of saga. The oldest are religious texts, mostly translations of Latin biographies of saints. The kings' sagas, written at the turn of the twelfth century, record the lives of Scandinavian rulers while the thirteenth-century family sagas present the stories of less noble individuals, often tracking events through several generations. These are the most well known, and read a bit like historical novels, written about two hundred years after the events they record.

Snorri Sturluson, the famous Icelandic saga writer, lived in Iceland during the late twelfth and early thirteenth centuries.

There are two other groups of sagas, the 'sagas of knights' which are adaptations of European romances for an Icelandic audience, and the 'legendary sagas' which recount mythical stories. But it is the first two groups which are of most historical interest, and are regarded as the finer works of literature.

The most famous of the kings' sagas is Heimskringla, in which the author, Snorri Sturluson, has attempted to document the history of Norway. It is written in a very straightforward and realistic style; his stories are always eminently plausible, but in reality the historical facts are used mainly to aid in characterisation of the kings. This means that they are often at odds with other accounts, the most noticeable example of this being in King Harald's saga. Here Snorri's account of the events of 1066 varies considerably from what the contemporary English sources report. But Snorri was trying to create a work of literature rather than a history text, so he can be forgiven some inaccuracies.

The family sagas tell the tales of Icelanders on an epic scale in which Njal, Egil, and Grettir are each given a saga to themselves. Grettir's saga is slightly unusual, portraying this historical figure in a world much more like that of legends. He has near superhuman strength, and gets into trouble with ghosts and trolls. His fatal weakness is being scared of the dark as the result of a ghost's curse, and his enemies eventually overcome him by witchcraft.

Unlike Grettir, Njal and Egil are both classic Viking heroes. They live in a much more realistic world, as mortals responsible for their own actions. Egil is a complex character, who starts the story as an adventurer and killer. His father was a beserker, one of a group of Viking warriors who worked themselves up into a frenzy of rage before going into battle. So it is not surprising that Egil inherited some of his violent tendencies. These surface at the tender age of six when Egil kills one of his playmates. But he is also a poet, and uses his lyrical skills to escape more than one tricky situation. Having exhausted his thirst for adventure, Egil eventually settles down on a farm in Iceland, and ends up as a blind and deaf old man sitting by the fire.

Njal's saga follows the intricate development of a blood feud. In contrast to Egil, Njal is a good and honest man who finds himself inescapably drawn into other people's disputes. At the start of the tale, Njal and his good friend Gunnar are maintaining good relations despite constant quarrelling between their wives. But their wives enlist the help of other relatives and, when Gunnar dies, the two families declare all-out war. Njal and his family end up trapped in their hall where they are burned alive.

There is a considerable cross-over of characters and stories from one saga to the next, maybe because many of the events and people described are historical. But in the Vikings' eyes, historical characters could interact with ghosts and trolls in a world where superhuman power was entirely normal. It is also worth remembering that Iceland was in political turmoil at the time when the sagas were written and it must have been easy for the writers to look back on the Viking Age as a period of calm and prosperity. The feuds of honour and principle in the sagas, even if they often had destructive results, were usually resolved in a way that made a refreshing change from the political manoeuvring of the thirteenth century. The authors are creating a legend of a 'golden age'.

This makes it difficult to work out just what the sagas are telling us about life in the Viking Age. The authors rely on historical characters, but often alter events to make a better story. As a result, events are reported that simply cannot have happened. Egil apparently has a rather dramatic moment at the court of Erik Bloodaxe in York, when most modern scholars agree that he cannot possibly have been there.

Ultimately the sagas are historical fiction, rather than history books. But this does not mean they are of no use in understanding people and society in the Viking Age. Most importantly, the books tell us of the qualities that were considered valuable in a Viking hero. They can also be used as the starting point for other investigations, and may even provide clues that lead to remarkable archaeological discoveries.

The Greenlanders' Saga and Erik the Red's Saga are two versions of the same story. As usual they differ in the details, but in both works

explorers from Iceland make a momentous trip across the Atlantic Ocean to a new land, the exact location of which is never very clear. They arrive and set up small settlements in a land where the rivers are full of salmon and the land is rich with wild grapes. This is 'Vine land' or 'Vinland' and, from the description, it seems most likely to have been New England or Nova Scotia.

So, in 1961, when the Norwegian writer Helge Ingstad announced that he had found a Norse settlement, but in Newfoundland, few people believed him. However, when the site at L'Anse Aux Meadows was excavated by archaeologist Dr Anne Stine Ingstad there were indeed the remains of a Norse community. There is also evidence that these intrepid settlers went on expeditions even further south.

Evidence for Viking settlement was found at L'Anse Aux Meadows in the 1960s. This reconstructed turf house shows how the Vikings who made it to Newfoundland would have lived.

Even the sagas contain their grains of truth, as L'Anse Aux Meadows proves. So how much truth is there in the written records from England? Did that first attack on Lindisfarne, so vividly described in the Anglo-Saxon Chronicle (or at least in some versions of it), really happen? The best way to find out seemed to be to head off to Northumberland, wait for low tide and then splash across the causeway to Holy Island to find out for myself.

Lindisfarne today is a peaceful island that, despite the inroads of tourism, still manages to retain an air of spirituality. In the summer the holiday cottages fill up and a constant stream of cars crosses the tidal causeway to the mainland. In the winter the island seems almost deserted and, sitting on a windswept beach facing the grey North Sea, it is obvious what drew the first monks to this place. The sea that sweeps round the island would have provided the isolation which the spiritual life demanded, would perhaps have been seen as protection, but it was the sea that brought the Vikings. It is easy to imagine the monks sighting strange ships out to sea, wondering what fate they might bring, but unable to stop them.

Today on Lindisfarne tourism has largely replaced fishing and many of the old wooden boats now lie upturned on the shore, their bottoms tarred against the weather rather than the sea, with doors in their sterns and even the occasional window. The boats have become sheds and it is

On the island of Lindisfarne, these modern-day upturned boats – used as sheds – look remarkably like Viking houses.

not difficult to see the connection between these 'boat sheds' and the curved sides of the houses built by the seafaring Vikings. How many of their fine ships, once their roving days were over, lay upturned on a beach to provide shelter for Vikings far from home?

The monastery at Lindisfarne was founded in 635 by the first bishop of the northern Northumbrians, an Irish monk called Aidan. It housed the shrine of St Cuthbert, whose body had been placed in the church in 698, and the ruins that can be seen today are of a twelfth-century cathedral, built by monks from Durham to keep Cuthbert's memory alive.

By the eighth century, Lindisfarne was a bustling community with an international reputation for learning. It is impossible to know how the monks reacted to the terror that arrived so unexpectedly in 793, but a ninth-century gravestone from the island gives hints about how the events were viewed in hindsight. Carved on the stone are scenes suggesting that the Vikings may have been regarded as agents of divine retribution. On one side the sculptor has carved a cross reaching up to the sun and the moon, with two worshippers kneeling and praying at its base. This is undoubtedly the Day of Judgement, when a cross in heaven will darken the sun and the moon, nation will rise against nation, and mankind will mourn. But on the other side appears a less literal interpretation. A troop of warriors, swords and axes raised aloft, may well represent a general scene of warfare and destruction. But maybe the sculptor is making a direct reference to the horde of Vikings who sacked Lindisfarne in 793,

A troop of warriors, swords and axes raised aloft, depicted on the Lindisfarne Stone, might represent the Viking attack on the monastery of Lindisfarne.

portraying them as the instruments of God's wrath – a punishment for the sins of the British people, a view that was widespread in the Church at the time.

So the chronicles and annals are emphatic that the Vikings were responsible for many such attacks around Britain and Ireland. But where is the confirmation of the attacks from archaeological evidence? On Lindisfarne itself, the Vikings cannot be blamed for the ruinous state of the ecclesiastical buildings that can be seen today, because they were built long after the Viking raids.

What has been so exciting about working on Blood of the Vikings has been the opportunity to closely question all of the evidence and theories. As an archaeologist, and a prehistoric archaeologist to boot, I have a healthy scepticism of history, convinced that there is a hidden agenda behind everything that is written. I was convinced that if there had been more Viking attacks on Britain, there should be more archaeological evidence. But where was it?

The answer lay, at least partly, a couple of days' sail along the east coast from Lindisfarne, on a site which has done what archaeology is so good at – sprung a huge surprise. At Tarbat, on the east coast of Scotland about thirty miles north of Inverness, Martin Carver from the University of York has found the site of an eighth-century monastery which is not mentioned in the sparse historical records. The archaeology suggests a religious centre and, what is more, Martin believes that all the evidence points to a Viking attack.

Tarbat today is a small and peaceful village – that is, until the jets from the nearby Lossiemouth air base start screaming overhead. When Martin began the excavation he was not expecting to find any evidence for a religious settlement. There is a now redundant church standing on the site, but this dates back only to the twelfth century. What Martin thought that he would find would be some sort of secular establishment, probably spanning the sixth to eighth centuries. Such a site would have supported a small community of men, women and children, perhaps farmers under the control of a local lord. Given the location of the site, it would not have been unexpected if the settlement had been taken over by Norse settlers in the ninth or tenth centuries and turned into a beach market, for many coastal sites in Eastern England came under Danish rule at this time.

The initial stage of Martin's project involved excavation under the twelfth-century church, as part of works to convert it into a local heritage centre. The fact that there were burials inside the church was not a surprise; this was a common practice, as walking over ledger stones set into the floor of almost any church will show. What was a surprise was that of the sixty-seven skeletons removed from the interior of the church, fifty-seven of them were men. This was the first evidence that the site Martin and his team were looking at was not the home of the mixed community they had assumed it to be. Then, just down slope from the low rise on which the church sits, Martin's team found evidence for work-shops and of metalworking, including moulds and crucibles. Close by, in the bottom of a small valley, was a mill and traces of what appeared to be other farm buildings. But the most interesting part of the site lay between the church and the valley bottom.

Here, showing up as a strong contrast to the pale soils on the site, the archaeologists found a thin layer of jet-black soil, full of lumps and rusting nails. This looked like strong evidence for a large-scale fire, and not just a bonfire; the nails suggested that it may have been timber buildings that were burning. Layers like this are a great help in trying to establish the sequence of events that took place on a site. Rather than the gradual accumulation of silts and soils that can sometimes only be distinguished one from the other by means of a microscope, here was a layer that showed a huge contrast and identified one very different event. But it was what lay within the ashes that was even more exciting. As more of the layer was exposed and it could be seen to extend further across the site, fragments of sculpture began to appear.

Some of the sculpture fragments were large, and all were extremely beautiful. Much of the carving, depicting crosses and the figures of saints as well as inscriptions, appeared as fresh as if it had just been completed. The style of script on the stones is known as insular magiscules, and was used in contemporary religious manuscripts like the Book of Kells and the Lindisfarne Gospels. There was only one type of community which

At Tarbat, archaeologist Martin Carver has discovered fragments of beautifully engraved sculpture. It may have been destroyed during a Viking raid.

could have produced not only sculpture like this, but also metalwork. Martin was now sure that he had accidentally stumbled across an ancient religious site, a hitherto unknown monastery.

But the sculpture had more of a tale to tell. The excavated fragments showed no signs of erosion, and all of the broken edges were clean and sharp. Some fragments could be fitted back together to give a clearer impression of the stone's original beauty. They look like new sculptures that have been deliberately smashed, perhaps with a tool like a sledge-hammer. Combined with the charcoal, ash and nails, most likely the remains of burnt buildings, the evidence all seems to point to some sort of violent attack.

More evidence came from the detailed study of the skeletons from under the church. Several of them seem to have suffered blade injuries, and two had cuts that looked very like that of a sword. One man had been sliced across the head, a classic sword blow. The question in everyone's mind was, who could have been responsible for all this death and destruction?

There were a few possibilities. The casualties may have been from a battle that took place at Tarbat Ness in 1035. The stones may have been smashed by another group of Christians. Arriving at the site at a later date, they may have decided they didn't like what was already there, so pulled it down and started again. But Martin thinks that the most likely culprits were the Vikings. The men with sword-wounds could easily have been monks cut down by the raiders and the hostility shown by smashing up the sculpture would fit perfectly with a Viking attack. The monastery would have been a centre of power and the Vikings might have been attempting to assert their authority as well as take whatever wealth they could find.

One way to resolve the question, to see if Martin's idea was right, was to date the burnt layer and the skeletons with sword-wounds to see if they fell within the time of known Viking activity. The likely solution lay in radiocarbon dating. This dating method works on the principle that, while alive, all living organisms absorb carbon, including a radioactive isotope, carbon 14. When the organism finally dies, the radioactive carbon 14 starts to decay at a steady rate. Half will have disappeared in 5,568 years (the 'half life') so if the amount of remaining radioactivity is measured, then the length of time since the organism died can be calculated. Charcoal is a very good sample material for carbon 14 dating as it is almost pure carbon and will survive well when buried. The burnt layer contained lots of charcoal, but there was a problem. The charcoal was in large lumps, most probably from timbers, perhaps the beams of a house. So a radiocarbon date from one of these lumps would not indicate the date of the fire and the possible raid; instead it would show when the tree was felled to make the original beam. This could be decades, or even centuries before the beam, and the building of which it was part, was destroyed by fire. What was needed was something from the burnt layer that only had a short life, a piece of thin twig for example, or a nut shell, that would have have been formed only a year or so before the fire.

While the search for suitable material went on in the samples taken from the burnt layer, there were no problems in taking small samples of bone from some of the skeletons found buried under the church. Three were dated and the preliminary results, although showing a wider range of dates than had perhaps been expected, did include one that lay right in the middle of the period of Viking activity.

Further radiocarbon dates may help to clarify the dating of Martin Carver's site at Tarbat, a site that may provide the first bit of archaeological evidence that really backs up what the history books say about the Vikings. These were written by monks who suffered at 'heathen' hands and who wanted to make sure their descendants would not forget that religious houses were plundered across Ireland and England. But from Martin's evidence, it seems as if the reputation of the Vikings as violent and destructive heathens may well be justified.

What still seems strange is that this evidence isn't repeated at site after site throughout Ireland and England. If the raids were really as bad as the Anglo-Saxon Chronicle suggests, then wouldn't we expect to find more archaeological evidence for them? And wouldn't the monasteries that were attacked simply cease to exist? This does not seem to be the case at Tarbat where, despite the evidence of violence, the community appears to have continued after the attack. Admittedly the monastery was probably not reoccupied; all the sculpture and ecclesiastical activity seems to end with the layer of burnt material. But crafts like metalworking were still practised and the mill and farm all continued in use.

At Lindisfarne, too, things are not quite as awful as Alcuin would have us believe. Despite the recorded death and destruction, the greatest

The remains of St Cuthbert were exhumed from the monastery at Lindisfarne to protect them from Viking attack. The monastery was re-established at a safer location in Durham.

monastic treasures, including the Lindisfarne Gospels and the relics of St Cuthbert, were hidden from the marauding Vikings. We know that these treasures survived this first raid because, when the Vikings attacked again in 875, some of the monks escaped with them to Chester-le-Street, near Durham. The monastery eventually moved to within the city walls of Durham when it was threatened by further Viking attacks. The monks' evasive manoeuvres paid off – the beautifully illustrated manuscript of the Lindisfarne Gospels can still be seen today in the British Library. Other precious relics from St Cuthbert's tomb are preserved in Durham Cathedral, where the body of the wandering saint was finally laid to rest.

Archaeologist Graeme Young believes that he has located the site of the original monastery on Lindisfarne. In the summer of 2000, Graeme was called in to carry out a preliminary investigation of a site in the heart of the present-day village on Holy Island. As the site lay within the medieval village the rubbish deposits containing pottery and other domestic debris were hardly surprising; it was what lay underneath that was far more exciting. There was a cobbled street, which Graeme believes was part of the original layout of the settlement. There were also remains of timber buildings, and indications of metalworking, an activity that would have been a part of everyday life in a monastery.

This site lies 50 to 100 metres from the ruins of the later religious buildings. If this is the first glimpse of the original monastery, then there are also hints of its size. Graeme now thinks that it would have been much bigger than the later priory, probably encompassing the entire modern village from the sea at one end to the inlet on the other.

Graeme's excavations at Lindisfarne also seem to suggest that the results of the Viking raid were not as dramatic as they have been portrayed. The monastery was certainly moved, and it had been thought that the island was left completely abandoned. However, the new archaeological evidence shows a continuation of secular settlement and Graeme thinks there was likely to have been a continuation of religious life, even after the monks had gone. The present parish church contains masonry that dates to the eleventh century, so life perhaps went on much as it had before the Viking raid. For the ordinary person in Britain, the raids might have had relatively little impact.

These archaeological discoveries are helping to illuminate the Viking

The ruins visible at Lindisfarne today date to the twelfth century, but the original monastery was founded in the seventh century. This was the site of the first recorded Viking attack on a monastery.

Age in England. They can help us to decide just which historical sources to trust and to fill in the gaps the authors have left in their stories. But even history and archaeology combined can only paint part of the picture. There is another dimension to the Vikings, a legacy they left behind in the genes of the British population. A team of scientists at University College London (UCL), led by David Goldstein, think they may have found a way to trace the Vikings' footsteps across the British Isles by using our DNA.

In July 2000 Goldstein's team began to collect samples for a nationwide genetic survey, the foundations for which are to be found in the growing field of study known as population genetics. Previously, historical documents, fossils and archaeological findings were the only way to reveal the way that different populations spread out across the globe. Now, by analysing the genetic code of living humans, it is possible to begin to understand what happened to their ancestors many thousands of years ago.

The genetic code of humans is contained within their DNA, three very familiar letters that are an abbrevation of deoxyribonucleic acid. DNA contains some of the longest molecules in the human body, interlocking spirals that resemble a twisted ladder and which contains a crucial chemical called a base. Within each ladder there are only four different types of bases, known by the letters A, C, G and T. These bond to make 'base pairs' and it is their order, the sequence of those four letters A, C, G and T, that determines the genetic makeup of any living thing. Human DNA is made up of about 3 billion of these base pairs, so to write out that sequence would fill a telephone directory 200,000 pages long. Just to read it would take about twenty-six years, reading twenty-four hours a day!

Because the DNA contains so much information, the genetic scientists at UCL will look at just one small part of it, a section that does not have an important function. These sections of 'junk' DNA are likely to be different in different individuals. So the scientists look here for markers which might reveal a person's ancestry.

The long chain of human DNA is split up into smaller units called chromosomes. Females have two X chromosomes, males have both the X and Y versions. The Y is the one that contains the genes for 'maleness'. David Goldstein and his team decided to look at the Y chromosome, as it has a large block of 'junk' material on it that is passed directly from father to son and changes very little over generations. This was the clue the geneticists needed to unlock the key to the Viking heritage of the British Isles.

The Y chromosome is passed down from father to son in the same way as a surname. My own Y chromosome has come down from my grandfather Charles, through my father Albert and I, in turn, have passed it on to my son Barnaby. This has been going on for countless generations and will continue as long as the male line remains unbroken, as long as there are male Richards's. But how does this help to find Vikings? The answer lies back in the Viking homelands, in the Y chromosomes of modern Norwegians. If we find a Y chromosome in a British man which is very similar to that of a Norwegian man there is a strong chance that they share a common ancestor, who could well have been a Viking. But the study will only reveal one very small part of an individual's ancestry. The test traces the male line back through the generations, but cannot detect any of the hundreds of other ancestors who will have contributed to that person's genetic code.

The results of this survey could provide us with another clue in our search for the Vikings in Britain. Archaeological discoveries can help us to decide on the truth behind the written records where, according to what you are reading, the Vikings are either vicious heathen seafarers (the official English/Irish history version) or great warriors and heroic explorers (the Viking saga approach). Violent raids, ruthless attacks and the supernatural may make for an exciting story, but little is written about the Vikings when they weren't actively engaged in typical Viking activities. Who were these people, and where did they come from?

CHAPTER 3

THE VIKING HOMELANDS

He said that the land of the Norwegians was very long and very narrow. All that they can graze or plough lies by the sea; and even that is very rocky in some places; and to the east, and alongside the cultivated land, lie wild mountains.

OTHERE'S ACCOUNT TO KING ALFRED, TAKEN FROM *ANGLO-SAXON PROSE*, ED. MICHAEL SWANTON, J.M. DENT, LONDON (1975)

LEFT | *The Gokstad ship was discovered in Norway in 1880. A 23 metre long, oak built warship, this represents the Vikings' ultimate weapon.*

To start on the trail of the real Vikings I had to cross the North Sea, but to which country? Some of the historical documents that I had read referred to 'heathens' or 'pagans' – not much help, but others used the terms 'Northmen' or 'Danes', so should I start in Norway, or Denmark – and what about Sweden where I knew there were runestones referring to raiding in England?

As the first Vikings to reach Britain were almost certainly Norwegians, I decided to start in Norway. There is a possibility that the name Viking came from the term 'Viken' referring to the region around the Oslo fjord. The Anglo-Saxon Chronicle also points to Norway, stating that the ships that reached Portland were from somewhere called Hordaland. Today there is a province of the same name in south-western Norway. Perhaps this is the area the Chronicle is referring to.

So, Norway was the starting point and my aim was to track the Norwegian Vikings back to their homes. One way to do this was to look at the distribution of what are known as 'insular' finds. These are objects that were clearly manufactured in the British Isles, often with a religious significance, such as book decorations or reliquaries. Surely clusters of such objects, 'loot' from raiding religious sites in Britain or Ireland, should pinpoint the Vikings' home bases and effectively catch them red-handed. However, these objects may have been traded on when the marauders

Norwegian dig sites and reconstructions

arrived back in Norway, a useful source of revenue as well as a way of proving your prowess as a raider. So their distribution may end up reflecting more the location of rich chieftains rather than the places from where the raids were mounted. But even with this qualification, it does seem as if the recovered objects point to certain areas as being of great influence. One of these is the Vestfold region around the Oslo fjord, the location of many rich burials, while to the north Trøndelag stands out as a region rich in finds. In both Rogaland and around the Sognefjord on the west coast there are clusters of Irish artefacts that suggest these areas as likely departure points for the Vikings who went to Dublin.

Norway today has a tourist image of fjords and mountains, a sparsely populated country of great natural beauty where everyone is a winter sports fan. Even the medieval map of the world, the Mappa Mundi, in

Hereford Cathedral has a figure skiing across Norway wearing what looks suspiciously like a bobble hat. Flying over the country reinforces the sense of a sparsely populated and largely untamed landscape of waterfalls and lakes, of dark rock meeting dark water.

In the late ninth century a great traveller and writer called Ottar described his homeland in the following terms:

the land of the Norwegians was very long and very narrow. All that they can graze or plough lies by the sea; and even that is very rocky in some places; and to the east, and alongside the cultivated land, lie wild mountains.

Norway provides a huge contrast to the ordered patchwork of neat fields that characterises the agricultural landscape of southern England. In Norway, tiny fields wrap around the base of huge immovable rock outcrops and traces of ancient fields sandwiched between fjord edge and towering cliffs show that Ottar's description of his homeland was a truthful one.

It is also possible, through the results of archaeological excavations, to gain some idea of what life was like at home for the Vikings. Although they travelled the seas, the Vikings were essentially farmers. The iron remains of farming implements have been found in many Viking graves, while excavated settlements often show traces of buildings that can be identified as stables and animal pens. Life on a Viking farm could be quite solitary. Settlements were scattered along the coastal fringes where the only agricultural land lay. The Vikings grew various types of grains, including barley for making beer, and oats and grasses for winter animal feed. Crops varied from region to region, depending on the climate. The west coast was rather cold for growing grains, but there were advantages here: the pastureland was good, and the mountains provided summer grazing and bog-iron ore for making tools and weapons. Cows and sheep were the most common animals, and keeping animals alive throughout the harsh winters was crucial. Beef was the main source of meat, and sheep's wool provided much of the clothing. The extreme winter cold even led the Vikings to invite their animals into their farmhouses, where man and beast would help each other to keep warm.

The evidence for Viking houses comes from the excavation of their remains, often little more than the foundations, within which the distri-

Even today, it is easy to see why Ottar said that the Norwegians could farm only a narrow strip of land between the ocean and the mountains.

bution of finds and changes in the soils indicate the uses to which different parts of the house have been put. On the island of Karmøy a group of archaeologists have turned archaeological data into a three-dimensional reality. There is something wonderful and slightly eerie about disembarking from a modern high-powered boat at a modern jetty and walking through woods, to be confronted by a full-sized Viking house with smoke curling from vents in the roof.

My visit to Karmøy was in December and I have fond memories of exchanging the cold of a Norwegian winter for the warmth of the Viking house. The gently curving walls (perhaps reflecting the shape of an upturned boat?) were of an ingenious cavity-wall construction. The outer skin was of stones, laid without any bonding, the inner of stout, vertical wooden planks, while the gap in between was stuffed with grasses and moss. Gochen Cumber, one of the engineers involved in building the house, admitted that they had not got this quite right; it was the first house of this type that they had built. The outer stone wall stopped short of the elegant overhanging roof of wooden shingles, with the result that water ran down into the cavity. This would eventually rot the inner wooden wall so plans were in place to raise the stone wall and extend the overhang of the roof. To me, this showed clearly the lessons to be learnt from turning two-dimensional archaeological plans into real buildings.

The house was an ideal place to sit and think about what it would have been like to be a Viking over one thousand years earlier. The overwhelming impression was of solidity, of timber everywhere, in the plank walls and the great posts that supported the roof. Despite the cold outside, the house was warm and free from draughts; there were even windows that let in light through transparent sheets of mica. But the focal point was the hearth that lay in the centre of the house floor, raised up on stones and clay above the plank floor. This was the blazing heart of the house where the chief would have sat on his carved chair, surrounded by his family, servants and slaves, while tales of heroism were told.

The Viking house was meeting place, workshop, byre for animals and home. At one end of the replica house was a sleeping compartment with a fine wooden bed and a proper door that could be locked from the inside. It was easy to imagine curling up under a pile of animal skins and being very snug indeed. Getting up on a winter morning to a dead fire and ice on the drinking water did not seem quite so appealing, although the volunteers who had tried it said that it wasn't as bad as I suspected. Perhaps these descendants of Vikings are simply tougher than me . . .

But for all the power of the house, which is a magnificent achievement and one that will continue to teach and inspire for many years to come, it was something far smaller that really gripped my imagination on that visit. I was surprised not to find any pottery in the house; household utensils that I would have expected to have been made of clay were either

This reconstructed farmhouse is heated by an open fire. The Vikings would have shared their homes with their livestock to stave off the bitter winter cold.

of wood or of stone. Bowls and baking plates were made from kleberstein, a versatile stone that we know as soapstone or steatite, robust, yet easily carved and heat-proof. Some of the light in the house was provided by lamps carved from this stone, greasy marks on the floor indicating the places where the fish-oil fuel had dripped. It did not take long to identify the places to avoid lingering or leaving coats and hats. But it was not the lack of pottery that most intrigued me, or the lamps themselves. It was the wicks. I had noticed bundles of what appeared to be a sort of marsh grass inside the house and watched as one of the volunteers peeled the green outer casing from a stalk, leaving the white pith looking and feeling for all the world like a polystyrene worm. This was *lyssiv* ('light straw') and the pith makes a perfect wick. Who first discovered the use to which this grass could be put? How many generations of Viking children sat by the fire as tales were told and peeled the grass so that they could have light throughout the long dark winter?

Farmers they may have been but, living by the coast, the Norwegians did not ignore the secure food supply which the sea provided. For part of the year the men fished and hunted sea mammals, while the women tended the farm. Evidence of how seriously the fishing was taken can be seen in the excavated remains of small buildings which make up separate fishing outposts. Some lie close to farms but others are located in remote coastal areas where fish were plentiful. When excavated, the buildings contain a range of implements including knives, line sinkers and hooks, as well as the bones of many types of fish. Egil's Saga reports that he sent his men out to such an outpost to catch cod, an important fish as it could be dried or salted to provide a source of food in the winter months.

Hunting was also an important part of the Viking economy, and considerable effort was put into the digging of large pit traps in areas where moose and reindeer were known to pass frequently. The reward was both meat for food and a number of valuable by-products. Skins were used for clothing while antlers could be fashioned into a wide range of small items such as knife handles and combs. The fur of other smaller animals was also desirable. It is thought that the Vikings trapped ermine, fox, marten and even squirrel for their pelts, although, unlike the deer pits, no archaeological evidence for this trapping remains. Sea-birds were valued for their eggs, feathers and flesh. The methods used to catch these birds seem hair-raising, but persisted until the last century. Birds were seized by hand from their precarious nests, or were caught with snares on long poles. It was dangerous but the feathers and down that were the reward were not only functional for quilts and coats, but could easily be traded.

For the inhabitants of Scandinavia, whether farmers, fishers or hunters, the most obvious way to travel was by water. Land travel was difficult, with mountains, forests and bogs creating natural barriers, and much of the ground could be frozen hard in winter. Norway, and the rest of Scandinavia, is well provided with fjords, sheltered coastal water, and rivers. Thanks to the Atlantic Gulf Stream, the sea along the Norwegian coast remains ice-free, even in the coldest winter. Well before the Viking Age, Scandinavians had realised that the best way of getting around was by boat.

In a culture so water-based it is not surprising that the design of ships became so sophisticated and that the ships themselves became such highly regarded possessions, something that in special circumstances the Vikings would take to the grave. Over the past two hundred years many boat graves have been unearthed, the burial of this large and precious object alongside its owner expressing great wealth and raising the prestige of the surviving relatives as well as that of the deceased. Most boat graves reveal

Because of the large number of waterways, the Norwegians usually travelled by boat, even before the Viking Age.

only the ghostly outline of the vessel and a few iron rivets. But the boats discovered at Oseberg and Gokstad in Norway were buried in clay soils that preserved much of the original wood, providing an invaluable insight into boat technology.

Today these magnificent ships are preserved and displayed in a wonderful museum on the outskirts of Oslo, close to other museums that celebrate Norway's rich maritime heritage, from arctic exploration to Thor Heyerdal's *Kon-Tiki*. The interior of the Viking Ship Museum is like a vast white cathedral, celebrating the craftsmanship and ingenuity of the Viking shipbuilders. Inside this cool, domed space the sheer size of the vessels is staggering, as is the extraordinary fact that these are real Viking ships, not replicas. Today they are still and quiet, fragile after a thousand years underground, but once sails flapped, oars creaked and the shouts and curses of Viking sailors rang out on the decks. Staying on in the museum after the last visitors had departed, I stood by the prow of the Gokstad ship and tried to imagine how I would have felt as an Anglo-Saxon peasant or an eighth-century monk if I saw a ship like this nosing its way towards the shore where I lived. And imagine if there was not just one ship, but a whole flotilla, all hung with shields and crewed by Vikings. There was only one emotion that came to mind – blind terror.

The Gokstad ship represents the ultimate Viking weapon, a vessel capable of crossing open sea and landing on shallow shelving beaches. In

The Oseberg textile was part of the rich boat burial unearthed near Oslo in 1904. It appears to depict some sort of religious procession.

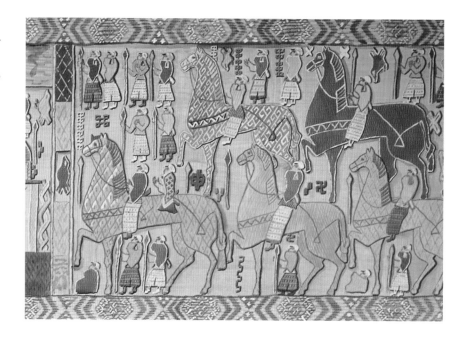

contrast, the Oseberg ship, discovered in 1904, appears not to be a sea-going vessel but one intended for short voyages in sheltered waters. When the huge mound within which it lay was excavated, the ship was found to contain the largest collection of Viking Age artefacts ever found, all in an extraordinary state of preservation. Highly decorated carved wooden sledges, a wagon, furniture, including beds and chests, carved tent poles, kitchenware, sewing equipment and even rich textiles including silks all show that the grave was of a person of very high status. Tradition identifies this as the final resting place of the Viking Queen Asa, the mother of the Norwegian King Harald Fairhair. Unfortunately, the archaeological facts do not fit with tradition. Recent dating suggests the burial is too early to be that of Queen Asa, and the boat contained not one woman's body, but two. One was about fifty or sixty years old when she died, and the other much younger, between twenty or thirty. Both were buried in beds hung with silk and fine wool tapestries. It is tempting to think of them as mistress, perhaps a queen of some sort, and servant. But which was which, and was the servant sacrificed on the death of her mistress?

Viking culture is always seen as being very male dominated, so it may seem strange that the richest boat burial yet discovered should belong to a woman. Not all women could expect such lavish treatment at their funeral but graves like these show that women were clearly able to hold positions of importance within Viking society. In Scandinavia and in Viking settlements outside their homelands, women probably enjoyed a higher status than many of their European contemporaries. The culture of raiding meant that many men had to leave their farms, at which point women would take control of finances, harvests and livestock. In view of such equality it is hardly surprising that women could inherit goods and property, although their male siblings were likely to receive a greater share. Male children inherited on the death of their father but, in the event that any of them were killed, the money would pass to his wife. Even some of the Icelandic sagas reflect the powerful role of women, celebrating the achievements of leading characters like Gudrun and the most famous female Icelander of the Viking Age, Aud the Deep-Minded.

Burials provide the best way to find out about people's lives in the early Viking Age. At this time the Vikings were pagans, and while their beliefs did not endear them to their Christian neighbours, these same beliefs resulted in a wonderfully rich archaeological record.

A Viking funeral was an elaborate affair. In the early Viking Age the dead were often cremated, burned on a pyre dressed in their finest clothes and surrounded by some of their most treasured possessions. These were needed by the dead to allow them to live well in the afterlife.

One of the most enduring images of the Vikings, along with the ubiquitous horned helmet, is the funeral. In the film *The Viking* Kirk Douglas (or was it Tony Curtis?) says in ringing tones, 'Prepare me a funeral for a Viking!' and you know immediately that this will involve a burning boat cast adrift on a fjord. Only last year in the Dorset town of Wareham, close to where I live, a Viking event culminated in a replica boat being burned: flaming arrows shot from Viking bows igniting the sail and eventually engulfing the admittedly flimsy 'boat'. Yet, romantic as it appears, there appears to be no archaeological evidence for this practice.

Fortunately for today's archaeologists, by the ninth century inhumation, burial rather than burning, was becoming much more common, and the Vikings continued to ensure that the dead would take their valuable goods with them.

One of the reasons that the Vikings took such care with their funeral ceremonies was due to their belief that the dead could return to haunt the living, and would do so if not treated with sufficient respect. Objects were chosen to reflect who the person had been in life. A warrior might be entombed with his shield and sword, sometimes bent out of shape to ensure that it too had been 'killed'. A smith might be buried with his hammer, and a seamstress with her spindle-whorls and bone needles.

Unlike Christianity, the pagan religion of the Vikings had no official doctrine and many gods. These varied in power and were headed by Odin, the high god responsible for kings, warriors and poets, and Thor, god of thunder and lightning. The Vikings created a mythology around their gods, the most famous of them being Ragnarok. This was the Norse equivalent of the end of the world, heralded by three years of treachery and evil in the human world, and a spell of continuous winter, when even the gods would fall from power. Then the final battle between Odin and the people of the fire realm would begin.

Odin's warriors in this final battle would come from Valhalla, a region of the afterworld populated by human warriors who had died valiantly on the battlefield. Personally selected by Odin, they were collected from the site of the battle by Valkyries, fearless female warriors. But Valhalla was no warriors' paradise. Each day its inhabitants went out to do battle in preparation for the final stand at Ragnarok and in return enjoyed feasting and mead each night at Odin's table. For the rest of the Viking population, the prospects after death were varied. Unmarried girls were looked after by the goddess Freya, while righteous men had a hall to themselves. But the old and infirm ended up in Niflheim, the icy world of the dead.

Wherever they might find themselves after death, the Vikings knew they would need precious objects to keep them going in an afterlife that resembled the temporal world. While graves like Oseberg are exceptional in their richness, this universal belief meant that most people were buried with at least some of their possessions. But as well as telling us quite a lot about their owners, at times these artefacts can lead us to question some of our most strongly held archaeological ideas.

One of the richest and most exciting burials discovered in recent years was found on a farm in the Trøndelag region in the north of Norway. So this was where I headed next, excited to be returning to Trondheim which I had last visited as an archaeology student over twenty-five years before. Then I had travelled up from Oslo by train, but at least in 1975 I had arrived at the same time as my luggage! This time I flew to Trondheim, and, once reunited with my warm clothes, I met up with Lars Stenvik, the archaeologist who had excavated this new grave and who, as it turned out, had also worked as a digger on the Kjopmansgate site in the centre of town.

Lars took me to see the grave field at Skei, a bleak hilltop covered with mounds and standing stones, and known since the eighteenth century as a place of great archaeological importance. Lars thinks Skei was probably a power base for a local chieftain, possibly linked to a central settlement that may lie close by. The grave field certainly seems large enough to have been inhabited by a substantial population. It was clear that some of the minor country lanes that circled the hilltop must have flattened smaller mounds, perhaps centuries ago, and the most recent find had appeared when the improvement of one of these lanes had clipped the corner of a burial chamber. Inside the chamber was the skeleton of a woman who had been buried in a wooden coffin with a rich selection of metal objects that, together, tell a story of very early contact with both the Anglo-Saxon and Celtic worlds.

Some of the objects seemed far from feminine. There was a triangular sheet-bronze bowl, its interior divided by a pierced strainer that bridged one corner. Decorated with three delicately cast bronze birds it is a very unusual object of which Lars knew only two other examples, both from Ireland. Somehow this bowl had found its way across the North Sea.

The grave also contained a small wooden bucket, capable of holding about three or four pints of liquid. It may not sound a very rich or exciting find but this bucket, constructed of thin staves of yew wood, was bound with beautifully engraved bronze bands and had a bronze handle. The style of decoration, animals chasing each other's tails and complex geometric patterns, occurs on both ornaments and manuscripts found in one specific area of the British Isles. It is thought that this bucket, perhaps used as a measure for selling wine, beer, or honey, was made in Northumbria in the eighth century.

This woman's grave is particularly interesting. The objects that she was buried with show that she must have been very rich and influential, but how did she end up with these Irish and Anglo-Saxon goods? It is a difficult question to answer, especially given the very early date that some of the objects were made. They may all have been stolen, perhaps on an expedition during which the local chieftain made his name. But there is no reason to rule out peaceful contact. Viking travellers may have traded furs

This bucket and ladle were discovered in a grave at Skei, in Norway. The decoration on the bucket suggests it was made in Northumbria.

and ivory for the bronze goods or there might even have been closer contact than this. What if the woman in the grave was not a Norwegian, receiving gifts from foreign lands, but an Anglo-Saxon herself? She might be the daughter of a wealthy British aristocrat, who brought with her prized possessions to remind her of home when she married a Norwegian chief.

There is also the question of the date of the burial. A circular argument runs like this: the first recorded raid on the British Isles took place in 793, so this was the earliest date that 'insular' objects could come back to Scandinavia. So if a grave is found that contains insular objects then it must date to 793 or later, even if the objects themselves can be dated earlier than 793. Of course the objects themselves could have been old when they were buried but this seems unlikely in all cases. Lars considers that this thinking, often referred to as the Shetelig axiom, should be challenged. What if unrecorded raids took place before 793? What if peaceful trading had been going on for decades, even centuries, before raiding started? It seemed perfectly fair to me to challenge the tyranny of 793, the assumption that there can have been no meaningful contact before this date just because the Anglo-Saxon Chronicle didn't mention it.

Along with the written evidence for the raids in the British Isles and Ireland, there are finds in Norwegian graves that support the idea that the Vikings were carrying off valuable goods from overseas monasteries. Some of these British and Irish artefacts are ambiguous: bowls, buckets and even a water sprinkler that could have had a domestic function, but could equally well have come from a monastery.

However, there is better evidence that the Vikings were bringing back monastic goods. A brooch decorated with three-dimensional mythical animals and a gilt-bronze pendant reveal themselves to be more than just small pieces of jewellery. The pendant is covered with Anglo-Saxon designs, while the brooch is decorated in a Celtic style. But they were not designed as pieces of jewellery. Both started life as decorative mounts, and were most probably prised from the covers of holy books.

These artefacts suggest that raiding voyages were just as much a part of Viking culture as running farms. But what was the purpose of the looting in Britain and elsewhere? In the Viking Age, Scandinavia was a warrior society, as were many other areas of Europe. Divided and controlled by local chieftains, different factions would sometimes clash in violent arguments. Part of becoming a respected member of this society

This reliquary was designed to contain sacred relics. The decoration is typical of Irish artwork, but it was found in a grave in the North Trøndelag region of Norway. It probably belonged to a Viking, stolen when raiding in Ireland.

This book clasp was probably stolen from a monastic book by Vikings, who then made it into a brooch. It was found in Kaupang, where archaeologists have discovered the remains of a Viking trading centre.

seems to have been to go to a faraway land and return with spoils. Having proved himself, a Viking could settle down on his own farm, pledging loyalty to a local chieftain, or perhaps become a chief himself. This idea is easily recognised in the sagas, where young warriors go out to earn their fortunes, returning to set up their own estates. And turning their stolen treasures into ornaments which they could show off also fits with this idea.

Christian valuables in a pagan society seem to be pretty firm evidence that what the 'victim' reported really did happen. But seafaring ability and an adventurous nature could easily be put to other profitable uses by the Vikings who, by this time, I was beginning to regard as a highly adaptable, if not entirely likeable, bunch. So where was the evidence of the Vikings as traders rather than raiders? Back down in the south of Norway was the answer, where archaeologist Dagfinn Skre has been excavating what he thinks could be the first Viking town. The coastal site at Kaupang lies in a small inlet, hidden from the sea by two small islands. Today the water is little more than a pond, but a thousand years ago the sea level was about three metres higher, making a safe, sheltered harbour. The layout of the channels to the open sea meant that ships could sail in from both north and south, and could sail back out in whatever direction the prevailing wind came from; it was the perfect spot for ships from across Scandinavia to gather and exchange goods.

Standing on a rocky outcrop looking over the site, it was not difficult to imagine the sea teeming with trading ships.

Although the site has been known for many years, Dagfinn's excavations have revealed its true extent and layout. The recent programme of research started by courtesy of a large pipeline that was inserted parallel to the modern road and which provided a long narrow slice through the site. This showed that traces of occupation stretched over a distance of 600 metres, a far bigger area than had been previously thought. There was undoubtedly an extensive settlement here and Dagfinn is now trying to find out what sort of habitation it was. Larger areas are being opened to see if Kaupang became a permanent town, with people living there all year round, even if the market only really came into its own during the summer. The key to answering this question is to find substantial buildings that could have been permanently inhabited rather than flimsier structures that could be the dwellings of itinerant summer traders. To

Excavations at Kaupang have revealed a Viking trading site – the earliest town ever discovered in Norway.

me, the answer lay in the well-built hearths, substantial post holes and traces of stone foundations that Dagfinn showed me. These are clear evidence for proper buildings capable of withstanding a Norwegian winter; and the arrangement of the buildings, in rows along the shore, seems to point to the sort of organisation that would be found only in a permanent settlement. But it was perhaps only the core of the settlement that consisted of these more substantial buildings. In the summer months, when trading was at its height, tents may have been erected all around by visiting salesmen.

Dagfinn's team, as well as having the best on-site office that I have ever seen, complete with showers and what can only be described as a sundeck, had an astonishing system for sieving soil. Rows of sieves, power hoses and an efficient method of flushing away the mud meant that they could rapidly process very large quantities of the excavated soil. The benefits of this meticulous approach could be seen in the range of finds that had been recovered and in the minute size of some of them that would have surely been overlooked even by the most careful digger.

The finds show clearly the trade connections enjoyed by the merchants of Kaupang. Glass and pottery from the Rhineland and beads from the Orient have all been unearthed at the site, suggesting that the Vikings travelled far and wide in their search for valuable goods. These goods were not just bought and sold: craftsmen in many materials seem to have been hard at work turning the riches brought into Kaupang into decorative objects. Glass beads appear to have been manufactured and there is evidence of metalworking, both in bronze and in more precious metals. It seems as if there was a resident jeweller at Kaupang. Sitting outside their site offices (of which I was still very jealous) Dagfinn showed me a mould for casting a brooch. The puzzle was that the brooch that would have come out of the mould was in an Irish style. Had the brooch itself been found in Norway, then it would have been regarded as a traded or looted object. But here was evidence that jewellery manufactured in Viking Norway was being influenced by Irish styles. Dagfinn also showed me a small pottery crucible, its crusted and blackened exterior indicating that it had seen much use, and explained that they were not yet certain what metal had been smelted in it. As I turned it in the sunlight, both of us suddenly saw the glint of something bright, tiny flecks of gold, and with the aid of a light we could see more of these deep inside. This was the first time the crucible had been looked at in sunlight since it had been dug up, and what an exciting discovery! Despite this evidence of precious metal, the majority of the jewellery found at Kaupang would not have been reserved for the highest levels of society. It was being produced for a mass market and could well have ended up adorning farmers' wives all across Norway.

Despite the overwhelming emphasis on trade that has emerged from the excavations at Kaupang, there is still the possibility that its inhabitants augmented their more peaceful earnings with a spot of raiding. Among the beads and pottery and the objects that were obviously manufactured on site, there are the inevitable mountings from books and other metal objects that Dagfinn does not think the Vikings would have bought legitimately.

So Kaupang could well have developed as a port for traders from all over Northern Europe, a place where Vikings from across Scandinavia could meet to exchange the spoils from their voyages. But such a honeypot would require protection. Its success would depend on it being seen as a place where trading could be carried out in safety. The benefits to any local chieftain who was strong enough to provide such guarantees would perhaps be a slice of the profits and whatever could be earned by providing lodging and food for visiting traders.

Such an arrangement, with the status of a local chieftain linked inextricably to the success of the trading establishment, would have worked well until competition emerged. Rival chieftains, enviously viewing the rich pickings, might have tried to muscle in on the act and the fall of the protector might well have spelled the end for the port. At a distance from the actual trading centre of Kaupang, Dagfinn thinks he has found the chieftain's house. At first the low hillock next to a farm looks just like a natural landscape feature. But, as Dagfinn pointed out to me, natural hillocks do not have perfectly flat tops. His excavations revealed a stone-built platform on which the traces of substantial foundations marked out the plan of a huge building. At some time it had burned down, perhaps accidentally, perhaps in an act of violence as part of an attempt to take over the running of Kaupang. If this is what really happened, then, in the long term, it failed. Kaupang was eventually abandoned and its traders and craftsmen drifted away.

This mould, found at Kaupang, was used to make brooches decorated in an Irish style.

It was nearly dark when Dagfinn and I stood inside the chieftain's house, walking from room to room until we stopped by what I was told was a doorway. This was the door into the great chamber, where the chief would have received important guests. From his pocket Dagfinn produced a large iron key which had been found between the stone flooring blocks next to the doorway. Could this really be the key to the chief's chamber? This was one of those finds that seemed to have such a wonderful story locked inside it. Who had seen that key a thousand years ago? What had it seen? And then I realised that if this was the door key, there was one historical figure that must have seen it: Ottar, the great ninth-century traveller and writer, a lone Scandinavian voice from the Viking Age. We know from his writings that Ottar visited Kaupang and, as an important visitor, he would almost certainly have been entertained at the chief's house.

His words come down to us through a ninth-century book, a history of the world written at the court of King Alfred. Ottar was a Norwegian seaman who visited the king's court. The scribe called him Othere, an Anglo-Saxon interpretation of his Norwegian name, and his account of life in Norway was considered important enough to be added to the historical book. What remains for us to read today appears to be a verbatim copy of his story.

Othere is described as a rich man owning a lot of animals, including something called reindeer, with which the scribe who recorded his tale is not familiar. Othere has some cattle and sheep, but he does not need to rely on ploughing the land and farming because he has another very fruitful source of income. To the east lie a range of wild mountains and in these mountains live the Lapps.

The Lapps gave tribute to the Norwegians, paying according to their rank. The most noble Lapps paid 'fifteen marten skins, and five whales, and one bear skin, and ten ambers of feathers, and a bear- or otter-skin coat, and two ship's ropes . . . one to be made of whale's hide, the other of seal's'. Othere probably brought a selection of these goods with him for sale in England.

One day Othere decided to sail northwards from his farm, already in the far north of Norway, to see what he could find. He began his adventure by travelling north for three days, passing the farthest point the whale hunters ever reached. He carried on for three more days, until the land turned due east, reaching the Arctic Circle. Sailing close to the coast until the land turned south, he saw no signs of life, but after five more days of sailing south he came across a great river. The land bordering the river was inhabited, and well cultivated by a people he called the Permians who spoke a language almost the same as the Lapps, and captured walruses. Othere bought some of their precious tusks as a gift for King Alfred. The Permians also hunted a type of whale that Othere had not seen before, smaller than those that were found off the coast of Norway. But Othere is certain that the Norwegian whales are the best, and even claims to have been part of a six-man team that killed sixty of them in just two days.

The Norwegians' intimate knowledge of geography, so evident in Othere's descriptions, was probably passed down from father to son, especially the directions needed for sea voyages. The directions for a journey to Denmark are included in Othere's tales, naming the lands in the south of this country as the region where the Angles lived before they reached England. Divisions between the Scandinavian countries are also made clear. The Swedes occupy the land on the other side of the Norwegian

The Vikings may have hunted whales. The Viking Age Norwegian traveller Ottar claimed to have killed sixty in two days.

mountains, and the Finns live in the land to the far north of Norway. From here, Othere describes how they carry their small and light boats overland to the lakes in the north of Norway and make war on the Norwegians.

Othere's description and the archaeological finds from Norway suggest a mixture of raiding and trading and, in the grave from Skei, there are hints of earlier contact with Anglo-Saxon England than has previously been accepted. But the Vikings may not have been the first Scandinavians to start trading with, or even marrying, people from the British Isles. The famous ship burial from Sutton Hoo in East Anglia suggests strong links with Scandinavia as far back as the early seventh century.

Although the Sutton Hoo ship burial contained no body, it is thought to have been constructed to commemorate an East Anglian king. The impression left in the soil after the timber rotted away indicated a massive ship over twenty-four metres long. A wealth of other goods was also found, including some forty-one items of solid gold. Even though the burial dates to the early seventh century, well before the Vikings reached British shores, it does suggest contact between the East Anglian kingdom and the rest of Europe. There is a Byzantine silver dish, spoons inscribed in Greek and a bronze bowl from the Near East. But most interesting is a possible Swedish connection.

The practice of burying ships was common in an area of Sweden around Vendel and Valsgarde and some of the grave goods from Sutton Hoo bear a remarkable similarity to objects found in burials in this part of Sweden. Maybe the relationship between Scandinavia and Britain and Ireland involved a lot more than just raiding. Perhaps chieftains throughout Northern Europe were already making diplomatic contact before the Vikings even existed.

If it is possible for an Anglo-Saxon chieftain's daughter to end up in Norway, then Vikings could just as easily have ended up being buried in Britain. The Scandinavian sagas point to widespread settlement, particularly in the Northern Isles of Orkney and Shetland, and the Western Isles of Hebrides. If the Vikings settled and stayed, then the evidence should be there in the archaeology, in language and place-names, and even in the genetics of the people themselves.

CHAPTER 4

PIONEERS

He preferred to go west across the sea to Scotland because he thought it was good living there. He knew the country well, for he had raided there extensively.

FROM *LAXDŒLA SAGA*

LEFT | *Picture stones on the island of Gotland show the development of sailing ships in Scandinavia. It was their well-designed ships which allowed the Vikings to reach the British Isles.*

Orkney was a place that I had always meant to visit, lured by reports of wonderfully preserved prehistoric tombs and settlements but, until making the second series of Meet the Ancestors in 1997, I had never made the long trip from Dorset. My first impression, having endured the sea crossing from Scrabster in a gale, was that I would not like to live on the islands if I had to make that trip very frequently. I was also immediately struck by how barren the landscape appeared until I realised why it seemed so bleak. There were simply no trees to be seen. But even on this first visit I noted that, despite the lack of trees, and the heather and bracken that covered the interior of the islands, each of them was fringed with broad sweeps of fertile arable land and good pasture. Having seen Norway with its thin strips of cultivable land, I could suddenly see why Orkney had seemed so appealing to the Vikings.

In Laxdæla Saga, a thirteenth-century Icelandic text, the mighty chieftain Ketil decides to leave Norway because his relationship with King Harald Finehair has deteriorated. He calls a family council and announces:

I have true news of King Harald's enmity towards us, and to me it seems that we may abide no trust from that quarter. It seems to me that there are two choices left us, either to fly the land or to be slaughtered each in his own seat.

A unanimous decision is taken to leave the country, and Ketil's sons hope to go to Iceland. But Ketil is unconvinced by their tales of seas full of whales and rivers stocked with salmon. He decided that in his old age he does not want to go to this land of fishing, but instead to try his luck in Scotland. As the saga records.

. . . he preferred to go west across the sea to Scotland because, he said, he thought it was good living there. He knew the country well, for he had raided there extensively.

Ketil's reference to having raided extensively in Scotland is intriguing. Just where was he referring to? If he lived in King Harald's time, then he would have been too late for the famous Viking raids on Iona. But the Vikings are recorded not only raiding in northern Scotland, but also using this region as a base from which to raid Ireland. Perhaps Ketil had been on one of these trips. The raiders must also have noticed the promising farmland during their voyages, and it is not surprising that they eventually decided to claim some for themselves.

The history books record much Viking settlement in the Northern Isles of Scotland, where it is often referred to as Norse settlement. The word Norse applies to those Vikings who came from Norway but, much like the word Viking, is ambiguous in nature. It is usually applied to settlements that outlasted the period of Viking raids. On Shetland and Orkney they certainly did, with history books recording Norse influence well into the fifteenth century.

Whether they came to raid or to stay, the Vikings only made it across the North Sea because of their expertise in sailing and navigation. They had no compasses or navigational charts; instead they relied on word of mouth. When Ottar described his voyage around Norway he relied on descriptions of the coast, and the number of days to sail in each direction. This is probably the way the Vikings tended to sail, using coastal landmarks and signs of bird or marine life for guidance. A later copy of the *Landmanabok*, the Icelandic Book of Settlements, recording details of the first settlers in Iceland, gives these directions for arriving at Greenland:

From Hernar in Norway one should keep sailing west to reach Hvarf in Greenland and then you are sailing north of Shetland, so that it can only be seen if visibility is very good; but south of the Faeroes, so that the sea appears half-way up their mountain slopes; but so far south of Iceland that one only becomes aware of birds and whales from it.

Viking age sites in Shetland and Orkney.

Although Iceland is invisible to those following these directions, the sight of birds and whales would suggest that it was close and an imminent landfall on Shetland or Orkney would be signalled by sea-birds. You could also take along your own guidance system. Flóki Vilgerðarson, the discoverer of Iceland, is said to have taken three ravens with him on his journey. When the first was released, it flew straight back over the stern of the ship towards Norway. The second remained near the ship. But the third flew off in the direction of Iceland, pointing Flóki in the right direction.

If, as the sagas tell us, Viking settlers reached the Northern and Western Isles of Scotland, then we should expect to find traces of them. And we do, in the form of boat burials, although not of such magnificent proportions as those at Oseberg or Gokstad. As far back as 1882 a site in Kiloran Bay on Colonsay in the Western Isles revealed a man buried with his boat and his horse. In the 1960s, a cemetery in Westness on the island of Rousay, Orkney, included two Viking warrior boat graves, complete with weapons and tools.

The most recent boat burial discovered in Orkney was excavated in 1991 at Scar on the island of Sanday. Many years earlier a farmer, John Dearness, had been walking on the beach in the aftermath of a storm

Boat burials are found in the Northern Isles as well as in Scandinavia. This one was excavated at Westness, on the island of Rousay, Orkney.

when he noticed some bones sticking out of a low sand cliff. He thought they looked human, and assumed that they must have belonged to a sailor who had died at sea and been buried on the shore.

In the sand in front of these bones was a small dark object, the size of a pound coin and apparently made of lead. John took it home as a souvenir and held on to it despite a neighbour telling him that it was nothing more than part of a car battery terminal. It was still with his possessions, tucked away in a drawer of special things, when John died a few years later.

A rumour of bones on the beach finally reached the Orkney archae-

This Celtic-style ring-pin was found in the pagan burial of a woman at Westness in Orkney.

ologist Julie Gibson, so she went to Sanday to investigate. The report, made by a visiting archaeologist, had hinted at an Iron Age burial and, not having seen many of these, Julie thought she ought to go and have a look. The first thing she noticed was the apparent outline of a boat in the sand and, like John Dearness, she too found metal objects. To Julie's trained eyes, the rusty lumps of iron were immediately recognisable as rivets, the sort that come from Viking boats.

Julie decided to take up the trail and went to see John Dearness's widow who showed her John's original souvenir from the beach. As soon as she saw it, Julie recognised the 'car battery terminal' as a Viking lead weight. It was made of lead, covered in bronze as a sort of security device. If anyone tried to file a bit off the weight, to deceive other traders into believing they were receiving more goods than they really were, the bronze coating would be removed, revealing the attempted fraud.

Julie realised that all these clues pointed to there being a Viking boat burial on the beach at Scar, but excitement was tempered with anxiety. The sea had exposed the site and another storm could destroy the fragile remains before they could be recorded. Funds were raised and a team of archaeologists from Historic Scotland were called in, but by the time excavation leaders Olwyn Owen and Magnar Dalland arrived on Sanday it was already November. In Orkney the light fades fast, and the archaeologists had to bring generators and lights to this remote site, to enable them to work beyond the few hours of natural daylight available.

It was a race against both time and the elements. As Julie pointed out to me, the site lies on the north side of Sanday and, heading out to sea from that point, the nearest landfall is somewhere near the North Pole. The excavation team worked with the waves sometimes washing around their ankles, using sandbags to try to keep the spray from the boat and its precious contents. Conditions grew steadily worse as the Christmas deadline drew closer.

The team completed the excavation the day before Christmas Eve and headed back to their families. Just after Christmas a particularly stormy high tide washed over the entire site, making it clear just how lucky the team were to have recovered the artefacts they did.

The results of the excavation revealed that Julie's hunch had been correct. This was a Viking boat burial. Three skeletons were found with the boat: those of a man, a woman and a child. It is tempting to see these

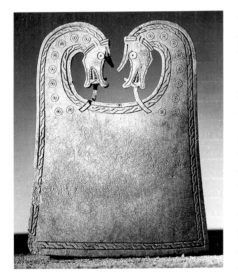

This whalebone plaque was found in the boat burial at Scar. It was probably used as a kind of ironing board by the Viking woman it was buried alongside.

three individuals, who were clearly buried at the same time, as perhaps members of the same family. The objects that were buried with the two adults were obviously precious to them and must show how they saw themselves. The man was buried with his sword, a quiver of arrows, a comb, a lead scale-weight and twenty-two whalebone gaming pieces. On the basis of these, the man seems to have been a typical Viking, warrior and trader with a love of life and willing to take a chance. In contrast, the woman's objects represent more peaceful domestic activities: a brooch and a maplewood box together with tools for weaving, stone spindle-whorls, shears and a needlecase. The final and most beautiful of her possessions was a whalebone plaque, carved with horses' heads in a very Scandinavian style. This would probably have been used for smoothing pleats and polishing linen caps, so was effectively her ironing board.

These objects can also provide vital clues about the origins of the people buried in the Scar boat. The style of the woman's plaque and brooch suggest that she was of Scandinavian origin and that they date from the ninth century. This is the period when many Norwegians are thought to have set out for the Northern Isles, so maybe she arrived with her family as one of the first Viking settlers on Orkney.

There is more evidence of a direct link with the Viking homeland. Although the wood of the boat had decayed completely, the iron rivets survived and their pattern showed that the boat was clinker-built, in Viking style. It is possible, of course, that the boat was built in Orkney but in traditional Viking style. But there was one tiny clue that contradicted this idea. Despite the appalling conditions during the excavation, the diggers noticed some unusual grains of sand lying in the hollow of the decayed boat. These sand grains were probably trapped in the gaps between the planks of wood and released as it rotted away. There is nothing like them to be found anywhere in Orkney or in other parts of northern Scotland. As this was a Viking burial, the obvious place to look for similar grains of sand is Scandinavia. Although a comprehensive analysis of Scandinavian sand types is not available, the research team have found some similarities. It seems the Scar boat contains Scandinavian sand. So this could well be the very boat that brought these early settlers across the North Sea.

The Scar boat burial is a wonderful time capsule of Viking life in Orkney but its discovery and excavation is little short of a miracle. What if John Dearness had not taken that walk on the beach and taken home his little souvenir? What if Julie Gibson had not followed up the rumour of bones on the beach? What if the storms that had first exposed the site had swept the whole thing away before any excavation could be mounted? If chance had not worked in archaeology's favour we would have lost this boat and its occupants with their tantalising glimpses of their Norwegian homeland.

Boats had existed in Scandinavia well before the Viking Age, but in a region so easily traversed by water it would have been strange if they had not. In the Bronze Age, thousands of years earlier, boats were as slim and light as the Viking longships, but they relied on manpower. These early boats were designed to be rowed in sheltered waters and even the Vikings did not brave the waters of the open sea until they had invented sails.

In Gotland, Sweden, we can see the development of this crucial bit of technology. Carved on runic picture stones are the original long rowing boats, but around the beginning of the seventh century a change starts to take place. The boats become broader with deeper hulls, a change in construction that would have enabled sails to be used for the first time. The Oseberg ship, dating to the early ninth century, is the earliest sailing ship yet discovered, but it could also have been rowed. On each side of the vessel are fifteen oarports that could be closed when it was under sail.

Ships like the one engraved on the Hejnum Stone in Gotland would have been eminently suitable for the Viking raids in the ninth century, and for trading throughout the Baltic Sea. The date at which sails were first used is controversial: perhaps as early as the fifth century, as a letter exists suggesting that the Saxons living just to the south of Denmark were using sailing ships at this time. Despite this, it is generally accepted that the Gotland picture stones, which date from the seventh and eighth centuries, provide the first positive evidence of this advance.

Once in possession of sails, it would be relatively straightforward to make the journey across to the Northern Isles and Scotland, as well as to Iceland and the Faeroes. Many people have since made the same journey in reconstructed Viking sailing ships. The exact shape of Viking sails is unknown, as only fragments have ever been recovered, but they are thought to have been square. We can be more certain of the material that they were made from, though, as small fragments of woollen Viking sails were uncovered with the boat burials at both Oseberg and Gokstad. Although to us this may seem a strange material to choose for a sail, conjuring up images of Viking grannies furiously knitting sails, there are references to woollen sail-making in Shetland, the Faeroes and Iceland. There is also a living tradition of wool-working throughout the North Atlantic region settled by the Vikings.

Weaving was an important part of Viking life. The evidence can be seen in the many tools associated with this task that have been found in graves across Scandinavia and the British Isles. The process first involves untangling the wool, using a comb. The wool is then spun on a drop spindle for which the whorls, small circular pierced weights of clay, antler, bone, glass and amber, have been found. The resulting threads can then be woven on an upright loom on which heavier weights are used to keep the vertical thread taut. These objects, combs, spindle-whorls and loom-weights, together with shears and needles, are always found in female graves, suggesting that women took responsibility for this important task. This may also have included sail making and it is even possible that each Viking expeditionary force included a talented seamstress to carry out running repairs to frayed or damaged sails. What is obvious is that women at all levels of Viking society were involved in weaving. The Oseberg ship burial contains an extensive collection of weaving equipment, suggesting that even a queen might have been involved.

As an experiment, a team at the Viking Ship Museum in Roskilde decided to recreate a handspun and hand-woven square woollen sail using entirely traditional methods. The first stage was to gather the wool, by pulling rather than shearing, from primitive Norwegian sheep. This is a very hardy breed that lives off the land, surviving on a diet of mainly heather and seaweed with little human interference.

Exactly the same kind of sheep-rearing techniques can be seen in Shetland where the sheep are famous for the quality of their wool. In the Viking Age they would have been providing the raw material not just for clothing but for a wider range of important goods. Shetland sheep produce two different types of wool: an outer fleece that is coarse and very tough, ideal for rugs, and inner layers that are extremely soft. This delicate wool would have made underwear and other clothing, while the tough outer coat could even be used to make fishing lines.

We know there were sheep on the Northern Isles before the arrival of the Vikings, as sheep bones have been found on Iron Age sites, but the similarity between primitive Shetland sheep and primitive Norwegian sheep suggests that early Norse settlers may have brought their own sheep with them. As these animals provided so much of their clothing and sailing equipment, a couple of sheep might have been a wise addition to a Viking settler's boat.

If Norwegian sheep did arrive with the new settlers they might well have interbred with local sheep and become the dominant strain. A similar story has been suggested for the small mammals in the Northern Isles.

In 1979 an investigation was conducted in an attempt to differentiate the types of rodent found on the Scottish islands, the Scottish mainland and Norway. The conclusion was that the mice from Shetland were closest to those in Norway. They must have accidentally arrived on these faraway islands after sneaking on board ship in a cargo of grain or fodder.

So there seems to be evidence that certain species of Norwegian animals have made a home on the islands. If it is possible for animals to yield up their ancestry, can we then expect the same from the human population? The preliminary finds from the UCL genetic survey suggest that we can.

Primitive Shetland sheep bear a remarkable resemblance to those found in Norway. Unlike many modern sheep breeds, they survive well in the harsh climate of the Northern Isles.

One member of David Goldstein's team had a particular interest in finding out just how much Norse influence remained in the DNA of present-day Orcadians. Jim Wilson, who is from Orkney and familiar with the history of the Northern Isles, decided to find out if Norse connections would show up in the genes of his fellow Orcadians. The history of the islands suggested to Jim that he should find at least some remnants of Norwegian DNA in modern-day residents. The thirteenth-century *Orkneyinga Saga* is no more the complete historical truth than any other saga, but it does make it clear that both Shetland and Orkney not only came under Norwegian control, but were settled by Norwegians.

There were several preliminary stages to go through before Jim could begin his genetic study in earnest. He first needed to identify what other types of DNA were likely to be present. In the fifteenth century, when the Orkney islands became part of the kingdom of Scotland, there was a large influx of Scots. So, if the history books are reporting the truth, Jim's results should show a mixture of Scottish and Norwegian DNA.

The next stage was to try to identify DNA signatures indicating Scottish and Norwegian ancestry. To find Norwegian Y chromosomes representative of the ancient Vikings, Jim first tested men whose paternal great-grandfathers were Norwegian. From the majority of these modern Norwegian men Jim was able to identify two DNA signatures. These became his 'Viking' markers.

Next Jim examined samples gathered in both Ireland and Wales. In the far north of Wales, Jim took samples in Anglesey, and in Ireland he selected only those with Irish Gaelic surnames. What he discovered was that the Irish and Welsh samples were almost indistinguishable. Nearly all the samples from both regions were from a particular group of Y chromosomes which Jim could then use as a 'Celtic' DNA signature. Because this was found in both the Irish and Welsh samples Jim suggested that it might be what the Y chromosomes of all early Britons looked like. So it seemed safe to assume this is also what ancient Scottish DNA might have looked like.

Jim uncovered a strange relationship between the 'Celtic' Y chromosomes and those of another group of European people. The Basques, from northern Spain, are thought to be descended from the very early Palaeolithic inhabitants of Europe. The DNA of the Basque men seems to be strikingly similar to that of men tested in Ireland and Wales. In all three populations Jim found the 'Celtic' marker on 89–90 per cent of the Y chromosomes.

Because of the similarity of their Y chromosomes, all these different groups of people must trace their paternal heritage back to the same group of ancestors thousands of years ago. This genetic link might mean that all the ancient inhabitants of Europe carried a similar Y chromosome. But Jim suspects there is a more specific connection. It is possible that the paternal ancestors of the Welsh and Irish migrated up into Britain from Iberia thousands of years ago. So the Celtic-speaking populations of Britain and Ireland might be descended from the people who made this journey.

Now that Jim knew what 'Viking' and 'Celtic' DNA should look like, he could return to Holm, the parish where he grew up, and start to collect samples of Orcadian DNA. He was careful to sample only those whose great-grandfathers had also come from the islands and whose surnames were found on Orkney before 1700. Although this only takes into account ancestry over three centuries, it is very likely that these families had lived on Orkney for many generations.

In the Pierowall, a pub on the island of Westray, after a supper of their 'celebrated' fish and chips, Jim and I met up with some locals to collect DNA samples – mouth swabs, fortunately, rather than blood. It struck me as we sat and chatted that some of my companions were probably the descendants of the Vikings who had come to the islands in the ninth century and that eleven hundred years ago I probably wouldn't have been quite so relaxed about our meeting.

Understanding an event as complex as Viking colonisation is inevitably difficult, trying to balance recorded historical events with archaeological evidence, hoping for confirmation rather than contradiction. Now, it seemed, we would be able to bring in a third strand of evidence to see if the Vikings really did set up a permanent base on the Northern Isles.

But how did the Norse settlers manage to gain control of islands that had been inhabited for thousands of years by the time that they arrived? Despite the archaeological evidence, the sagas mention no native inhabitants at all, not even in a minor supporting role. The *Historia Norwegiae*, a Latin chronicle of Norwegian history written in the thirteenth century, refers to only two types of people the Vikings had to deal with: the Peti and the Pap. The Pap are described as people who dressed in white cloaks and were probably clerics of some sort, whether native to the islands or from nearby Scotland. The Peti, who are definitely the native inhabitants of the Northern Isles, are described as a pygmy-like race with peculiar habits and are more commonly known as the Picts.

The Picts are a very mysterious group of people who lived in the far north of Scotland and were first mentioned by a Roman writer who talked about Picts and Scots attacking Hadrian's Wall. It was the Romans who named them 'Picti' from the Latin word meaning painted, perhaps a reference to the paint or tattoos with which they decorated their bodies. In fact, very little is known about the Picts. They have left some archaeological remains, in the form of settlements such as Jarlshof in Shetland, some wonderful engraved stones and a series of Ogham inscriptions. Ogham is a script consisting mainly of single strokes that was developed in Ireland some time before AD 400. By the seventh century it had been adopted by the Picts.

Although the name is an invention of the nineteenth-century novelist Sir Walter Scott, there are remains of a genuine Viking Age farming settlement at Jarlshof in Shetland.

Enigmatic, and apparently under-represented in the archaeological record, we cannot be sure who the Pictish people really were. Very little trace remains of them on Orkney today, prompting one of the main areas of debate about the Viking settlement of the Northern Isles. Did the Vikings settle down nicely with the local Pictish population and live in comparative harmony or, as many historians have suggested, did they wipe them out and then set about aggressively destroying the Pictish culture?

Pictish combs and pins turned up in a Norse settlement excavated at Buckquoy, in Orkney, suggesting the two cultures may have lived side by side.

In the early 1970s the Scottish archaeologist Anna Ritchie believed she had found evidence to support the harmonious faction. To her surprise, the Norse settlement she was excavating at Buckqouy on mainland Orkney started to turn up Pictish artefacts, including bone pins and combs decorated in a highly distinctive style. This was the first archaeological evidence that the Scandinavian settlers might not have arrived in an aggressive frame of mind, as had previously been assumed.

Anna estimates that the site was a Norse settlement for the majority of the ninth century and that during this time the Viking newcomers seemed to be obtaining domestic equipment from the Picts. If the Picts and Vikings were exchanging goods, this implies that they must have had some sort of working relationship. But Anna does not think the Vikings would have treated the Picts as equals. The relationship probably resembled that between the Vikings and the native Lapps in northern Norway. Ottar described how the Lapps paid tribute to the Norwegians in furs and animal pelts; perhaps the Picts also had to pay for their guaranteed safety.

Still in Orkney, archaeologist Olwyn Owen is absolutely convinced that the Vikings were peaceful towards the Picts and uses the evidence from a cemetery on the island of Rousay to back up her argument. The cemetery began as a Pictish burial ground and was then taken over by Viking settlers as a suitable place to bury their dead. However they do not seem to have disturbed a single Pictish grave, and to Olwyn this shows that the Vikings had a good relationship with the natives and respected Pictish culture. Other, more recent excavations appear to back up this idea of integration, including a site on Shetland being investigated by Steve Dockrill, an archaeologist at Bradford University.

The site he has been excavating at Old Scatness spans a huge time-scale, from the second century BC to the seventeenth century AD, two thousand years of intermittent use testifying to its prime location. Within its complex archaeological record is evidence for a well-developed Viking settlement where Pictish artefacts are found mixed in with some that are more distinctly Norse. Among these are objects made of steatite or soapstone, similar to the material that I had seen used for making lamps back in Norway.

Steatite is a soft stone, easily carved and very resistant to heat. It is not commonly found in Britain, but there are deposits in Shetland and at Catpund, while close to the Norse settlement at Jarlshof, the face of a quarry still shows the outlines of bowls carved from the solid rock.

In their homeland, with access to abundant sources of steatite, the Vikings did not bother to make pottery. But at Old Scatness, alongside the steatite vessels, there is evidence for pots being made and used. They are made in the Pictish style, barrel-shaped pots with thin walls, suggesting that native potting skills survived into the period of Norse settlement. Steve Dockrill sees this as strong evidence that the Vikings coexisted with

The Vikings were not skilled potters. Instead they made cooking bowls like these from soapstone – a soft but tough mineral found in Norway and the Shetland Islands.

the locals, but probably in a position of dominance. He feels that if the takeover of Orkney by the Vikings had been violent, then evidence of battles would have been discovered. Instead we find evidence of Pictish skills surviving and being utilised, native pottery found alongside the steatite bowls that represent Norse culture. Steve thinks this mix of cooking equipment from two cultures could even be due to the Norse incomers taking wives from among the Pictish population.

However, the Vikings were now firmly in control and, although there is no evidence of the Pictish population being killed off, their authority appears to have been usurped. Environmental studies at Old Scatness suggest that the Vikings soon took over the better-quality farming land and on the island of Westray a recent excavation has shown an even more dramatic change in the economy that coincides with the arrival of the Vikings.

Archaeologists like rubbish. Stuff that people have thrown away often says a great deal about their diet, their relative prosperity, even their beliefs. So York University archaeologist James Barrett is a happy man because he is digging a midden, a rubbish dump. The site he is excavating lies close to the shore on Westray and was first spotted when a thick layer of white bone and seashells was seen eroding out of the nearby low cliff face. Coastal erosion is a fact of life on Orkney and new sites are exposed after each winter of gales and high seas.

James's excavation took place on a farmstead called Quoygrew, but an ancient map revealed that it was originally called Nether Trenabie. In

On the island of Westray in Orkney, large quantities of fishbones, discarded during the Norse period, suggest that the Vikings changed the diet of the Northern Isles.

Orkney, there are a group of place-names, called 'bu' names, which are of Norwegian descent and signify high-status farmsteads, the estate centres of local magnates. Nether Trenabie is one of them. Here James has found deep deposits taking him back to before Viking times.

Before the arrival of the Vikings, the inhabitants of Westray appear to have been farmers, throwing away the bones of cattle, sheep and pigs. A Pictish site only about a kilometre from Quoygrew is full of bones from these farm animals. But some time in the ninth or tenth century there is an abrupt change. Suddenly, at sites like James's, the animal bones are joined by huge quantities of seashells and fishbones.

It is possible that this dramatic change in diet was a result of disease spreading through the animal population of the islands. But James thinks this is unlikely. To him, it is a sign that the Vikings have arrived on the islands, bringing with them their fishing skills and immediately starting to exploit the rich seas that now surrounded them. It might also be the case that the increase in the island's population, caused by an influx of Vikings, meant that the inhabitants had to expand their range of food to survive. But there is evidence that this change in economy had a much wider purpose than just survival.

James's excavation of the midden at Quoygrew has shown fishbones being produced in the later stages of Viking occupation in such quantities that the fishermen were catching more fish than could possibly be eaten by their immediate families. The bones themselves show that cod and saithe were a major part of the catch and that the fish were being cut up in a very specific way. It seems likely that the Vikings were developing a thriving trade in 'stockfish' ('stockfisk' in Norwegian), drying and salting the fish to preserve it. In this form it could be traded not only within the islands but further afield. In the twelfth-century there are records of 'stockfish' being shipped to Grimsby and then on to Bergen. So the Orcadian Vikings could have been supplying their Norwegian homeland from their rich new fishing grounds.

On Westray, archaeology has provided yet more evidence of a Viking takeover, a dramatic change in economy and presumably in the lives of those who lived in the islands. The evidence of this change can also be seen in the bones of those who lived at this time. Analysis of carbon within the bones of Pictish and Viking inhabitants of the islands shows a distinct change in diet, suggesting that the Picts obtained the majority of their protein from land-based foods while the Vikings' diet was mainly based on marine protein. So the Orcadian Vikings' were eating the fish, not just exporting it. But the question still remains: even if their presence was comparable to a migration of peasant fishermen, was it a complete takeover or simply integration?

In the Outer Hebrides, Cardiff University archaeologist Niall Sharples has uncovered evidence that suggests integration and assimilation, but at a slightly later date. His excavations on the island of South Uist show an exchange of skills between the Vikings and the native inhabitants. But whereas at Old Scatness in Orkney the Vikings appear to have been either trading pottery with the locals, marrying locals who make it, or simply allowing the natives to continue making it for themselves, on South Uist the Norse settlers appear to be actually learning how to make pottery.

In comparison to their other practical and artistic achievements, the results of the Vikings' first attempts at pottery are very crude. Niall thinks these early pieces are the result of the Vikings trying their hands at this new skill. It seems strange that they had not already developed potting skills themselves since most cultures tend to develop pottery before, or at the same time as, metalworking skills. Both require the ability to raise, maintain and control high temperatures and the Vikings' skills in doing this can be seen in the beautiful objects of bronze, gold and silver which they made. Good clay is hard to find in Norway though, and as the Vikings had already learnt to exploit steatite for cooking utensils they obviously felt no need to experiment with it. Perhaps the sturdy steatite vessels were seen as more appropriate for the roving life, less likely to get broken on a sea voyage.

I had known Niall from the days when we were both excavating prehistoric sites on the Wessex chalk, so it was quite a surprise to find him in Uist, several hundred miles further north and about four thousand years later! He had first been drawn to the site by a collection of low mounds on the machair, the sandy plain close to the coastline of the island. Here he had found evidence of ancient cultivation and of settlement dating from the Iron Age through to the fourteenth century AD. When I visited him, Niall was investigating one of the larger mounds and had found that it contained a Viking building, one of perhaps twenty or so of various types that made up what is effectively a village. This is unusually large for a settlement of this date, but there is a natural harbour nearby, making it a very attractive place for the Viking settlers. The buildings varied in size, from what may have been small workshops to large constructions, and it was within the large house that was currently being investigated that Niall had found the evidence for pottery manufacture.

The excavation appeared to be staffed by Bedouins. Everyone had their heads shrouded in scarves and wore protective goggles. As soon as the wind began to blow I realised why. It was like being sandblasted and the excavation was a constant battle to keep the drifting sand from refilling the trench and obscuring the levels that were being worked on. It was not the most popular site with our film crew – one grain of sand in the works of the camera could mean a trip home.

Within the trench cut into the centre of the sand dune, low walls marked out the plan of the house. The outer walls curved, just like the replica I had visited in Norway. And instead of a blazing fire in the centre there was a patch of reddened sand. This was the archaeological evidence on which these ideas are founded and it was fascinating to wander around inside a real Viking house and see the clues emerging from the sand about how the house had been built and used.

It had obviously been extended at some stage of its life and then subdivided at a later date, although no matter what changes were made, the hearth remained as a constant feature. The house was a living entity, each generation using and modifying it according to their needs and to changes in their economy. Visiting the old barn where Niall's team worked on the finds from the site gave me some idea of what the Viking village may have looked like. The yard was filled with boats rather than tractors, sheep wandered in and out through open doors; lobster pots and nets lay ready for use in the yard. This was, and still is, an island of farmers and fishers; there are even whalebones from the site, and the evidence for both these activities lay in the trays of shells and bones sieved from the excavated layers of sand.

Niall's Viking settlement shows the range of crafts which these integrated Vikings were involved in. As well as pottery, there is evidence of iron-working, possibly involving recycled boat nails, while offcuts of bone hint at a comb-making industry. And underlying all of these craft skills (except perhaps in the case of the decidedly crude pottery) is the Vikings' sense of artistry, never more apparent than in a beautiful engraved bone found within the house.

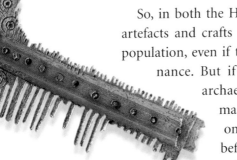

Bone combs are a classic Viking artefact, found at many locations in the British Isles and Ireland. Their detailed decorations show that the Scandinavians were skilled craftsmen. Bone was a favourite material, used for pins, board-game pieces, and even ice skates.

So, in both the Hebrides and Orkney, the archaeological evidence of artefacts and crafts suggests that the Vikings integrated with the local population, even if they, the Vikings, were in a position of some dominance. But if this is the relationship that developed, and the archaeological evidence certainly does not hint at any massacres of the native Pictish population, there is still one puzzle. If Pictish society carried on very much as before, even without its aristocracy, then what happened to the Pictish culture and language?

The Vikings who settled in northern France soon adopted French traditions and language. The Scandinavians who settled in Ireland and Britain left their mark on the local society, but they merely added to the local culture rather than destroying it. So why do we find virtually no trace of the Picts surviving after the Vikings arrived in the Northern and Western Isles? Archivist Brian Smith thinks this is conclusive evidence that the Vikings were not just trying to exert control over the locals, but were bent on wiping them out.

The argument for this type of aggression essentially boils down to language. On Orkney and Shetland there are a huge number of place-names of Scandinavian origin and some that are not. But of the non-Scandinavian names there are none that can be conclusively proved to have Pictish origins. This lack of a surviving Pictish language could be because the Viking settlers soon occupied all the positions of power, in which case the remainder of the population would have been compelled to adopt Norse as the 'official' language. If the Norsemen had little communication with the natives, and a low regard for their culture, they might not have adopted any Pictish words into their vocabulary, whereas Norse survives to this day in the form of place-names.

Most Norse place-names are concerned with geography and topography, describing the lie of the land or distinctive local landscape features. Sanday literally means 'sand island' and accurately describes the miles of sandy beaches to be found there. The name Westray comes from the Old Norse Vestrey, meaning the west island. The Orcadian capital, Kirkwall, also has Norse roots. Originally pronounced Kirkwaa, it comes from Kirkjuvagr meaning the Church Bay. But Scottish settlers associated the Orcadian '-waa' with the Scottish pronunciation of wall, and turned Kirkwaa into Kirkwall.

Another remnant of Viking language can be found in the Neolithic tomb of Maeshowe, four thousand years old when the Vikings arrived and one of the few sites where a story told in the *Orkneyinga Saga* can be supported by archaeological evidence. In the middle of the twelfth century, the Earl of Orkney was forced to cede half the islands to another warrior. But he decides to go back and raid, in an attempt to win back the land. On the way he and his men need to shelter from a snowstorm, and find cover in a place called Orkahaugr, where two of them are said to have gone insane. To guess that the Stone Age tomb of Maeshowe is Orkahaugr is not unreasonable. A 'haugr' is a mound, and Maeshowe is not only in the right geographical area but would have been big enough to provide space for all the Vikings who are meant to have sheltered here. What really confirms the theory is archaeological evidence.

When Maeshowe was excavated in the late nineteenth century, the archaeologists discovered that someone had broken in before them and that there were Viking runes carved all over the walls. One of them says: 'Jerusalem-farers broke open Orkahaugr.' It is possible that whoever carved this inscription was referring to somewhere else, but another inscription reads: 'Jerusalem-men broke open this mound.' So it seems fairly clear that Maeshowe really is Orkahaugr and what we can see here is Viking graffiti. The 'Jerusalem men' are likely to be Crusaders, visiting Norwegians rather than those resident on the islands, who gathered in Orkney in the winter of 1150, before setting out for the Holy Land. Bored, trying to pass the time during the long cold winter, they broke into the ancient burial mound and left their boastful messages carved into the stones.

Maeshowe is a magical place. To crawl down the low-roofed passage and finally stand upright in the great stone-built burial chamber is a wonderful experience. The Neolithic architecture is best appreciated when fully lit, but to see the delicately carved Viking runes it is best to turn off the lights and just use a small torch to shine across the stones. Then you can see why the Earl of Orkney's men went insane there overnight.

The Norse language of the Viking settlers was gradually transformed into the Norn dialect, still spoken in Shetland and Orkney as late as the eighteenth century. It eventually died out as the Scots took over, but some traces still remain in the local Shetland dialect. Norn words for types of animals, plants, food, weather, and tools are still used. Even these remnants of Scandinavian language will one day disappear, leaving just the place-

Vikings carved these runes after breaking into a prehistoric tomb at Maeshowe, Orkney.

names as clues to this Viking linguistic legacy, but there is no doubting the massive impact which the Norse language had on the Northern Isles.

This huge presence of Norwegian roots in the language is in stark contrast to the lack of Pictish evidence in either language or place-names. But some scholars argue that because we do not know what language the Picts spoke, it is impossible to know what to look for. They suggest that there are Pictish names in use on Shetland and Orkney, but we cannot identify them. This is not a view accepted by Brian Smith, however; he does not believe that there are any hidden remains of a Pictish language in the Norse place-names. He is also unconvinced by the argument that the Norse looked down on the natives so much that they employed none of their language or names.

According to Brian, we cannot simply say that the Vikings overwhelmed the native population; to him, the linguistic evidence points to their extermination by the Vikings. The best support for this theory comes from takeovers we associate with relatively recent empire-building. The indigenous populations of the Americas and Australia were treated with little respect by modern settlers and in both these situations the incomers soon became dominant. The cultures of Native Americans and Australian aborigines were dramatically affected by the foreign settlers, but in both cases huge numbers of modern place-names stem from the languages of these native people. If there was any sort of integration between the Scandinavian settlers and the Picts in Shetland and Orkney we should surely expect to see a similar number of Pictish place-names there. But there seem to be virtually none.

Brian Smith has found only one modern example of a country where the native language has completely disappeared. In Tasmania, very few linguistic links to the original inhabitants remain and this is a place where the entire native population was killed off, partly by violence, partly by disease. Brian believes that a similar fate for the Picts is the only explanation for the lack of Pictish place-names in Shetland and Orkney. The

Picts essentially ceased to exist when the Scandinavians arrived in the Northern Isles.

However, Norse language expert Michael Barnes thinks the situation would not have been quite so drastic. There are two names, he says, that cannot be easily explained as having Scandinavian roots. They belong to the Shetland islands of Unst and Fetlar, both possibly derived from Pictish names but recorded in the way that Scandinavian ears might interpret Pictish sounds.

The linguistic argument rages on, the Pictish voice drowned out by the overwhelming tide of Norse. But there is one artefact that hints at what the language in Orkney and Shetland was like before the Vikings' arrival. The Bressay Stone, which was found on the island of Bressay in the 1850s, is engraved with two words, probably of Pictish origin, and also the word DATTRR. This is Norse for daughter and the inscription uses dots to separate the words, a common practice on Norse rune stones. This stone, with its few words, has been taken as evidence that there was some sort of intermingling of Norse and Pictish cultures.

The dating of the Bressay Stone is not conclusive, but Michael Barnes believes it shows an indigenous language being used a hundred years or more after the Scandinavians began to settle. His view is that the Picts must therefore have survived the conquest by the Vikings. But he concedes that there is no recognisable adoption of foreign words into the Norn language that developed in the Northern Isles. The Vikings took little or no notice of whatever words and place-names these native inhabitants were using.

Perhaps the Norse settlers did not communicate with the natives in any way, or held them in such low regard that none of the natives' words survived. The possible use of violence by the Viking settlers is an ongoing debate. Those from the violence camp do not believe that simply 'holding the natives in low regard' explains anything. They would argue that colonisers are notoriously lazy, easily adapting to native place-names even when their language is quite alien. This is what happened in Australia, although the aboriginal tongue is completely dissimilar to English. But how, then, to explain the apparent archaeological evidence for co-operation? Both the Picts and the Vikings left us little in the way of direct evidence, so the discussion continues. It may be some time before we can say for sure just why the Pictish culture seems to have

The Bressay Stone. Inscriptions running down the side (right) *of this stone contain what appears to be the Norse word for daughter, alongside carving suspected to be Pictish.*

vanished after the Vikings arrived on the Northern Isles.

I was thoroughly confused by this time. I could not believe that the Vikings had totally wiped out the Picts; the archaeological evidence that I had seen simply did not support this idea and yet I found it hard to see why the Pictish culture, and almost all trace of its language, had so totally disappeared. I was relying on Jim Wilson's DNA results from Orkney to help me to step down from the fence where I found myself rather uneasily perched.

The results of the tests were just as Jim had expected. The percentage of Celtic signatures was less than in Wales and Ireland but higher than in Norway. Similarly the percentage of Viking signatures was lower than in Norway, but much higher than in either Wales or Ireland. The Orcadian Y chromosomes did seem to be a mixture of Norwegian and Celtic, supporting the idea that modern Orcadians have a mixture of genes from both Vikings and Scots. The people of both Orkney and Shetland are well aware of their Norse heritage, apparent not only in the place-names and ancient dialects but in people's surnames. In Orkney these can be divided into two categories, some indigenous to the islands, others that were introduced by Scottish settlers.

Jim Wilson also examined these two groups of people in his DNA study of Orkney. The group with Scottish surnames was indistinguishable from the Welsh and Irish and could be assumed to have Celtic ancestry. The people with indigenous surnames proved to be slightly more problematic. Jim had uncovered two different Norwegian DNA signatures in the sample of Y chromosomes from Norway. One signature showed up in a sample taken from West Friesland in the Netherlands and might also be present in Anglo-Saxons, as they came from what is now northern Germany. Orcadians with this type of Y chromosome might therefore have Norwegian ancestry, but there was also the possibility that they could have inherited this signature from an Anglo-Saxon ancestor.

The other Norwegian DNA signature which Jim examined is far more conclusive. This is common in the Norwegian population, but is rare in the Netherlands. So, of the Orcadians with an indigenous surname that were sampled, the 32 per cent who had this Y-chromosome signature almost certainly had Viking paternal ancestors.

I was very impressed and a little envious. Could genetics provide some hard answers to questions which archaeologists and historians had been arguing over for decades? There is certainly a strong Scandinavian genetic presence in Orkney. For Jim, there must have been an additional fascination in reaching far back into the ancestry of his fellow Orcadians, sharing with them the excitement of newly discovered roots.

But for me there was still an unanswered question. There was clear evidence for Norwegian genes in Orkney, probably brought across by the Vikings and settlers throughout the Norse period in the Northern Isles. But the Orcadians also have Celtic genes. Were these brought to the islands solely by later Scottish settlers, or might some be traces of the Picts themselves? It seems that we cannot be sure. This study may have provided us with some answers, but, as in archaeology, these always brought a new set of questions.

As the genetic results show, the Vikings firmly established themselves in the Northern Isles. History tells us that they remained here as a strong presence until far later than anywhere else in the British Isles. In fact, both Orkney and Shetland were part of the Norwegian kingdom until the fifteenth century, even though the Vikings here and in the Hebrides saw themselves as separate from Norway. What these islands provided for the Earls of Orkney, men like Sigurd the Mighty and Sigurd the Stout, was a convenient base from which they could raid in the Irish Sea. The early Viking colonisations seem to have been accomplished with little resistance, but Ireland would not prove quite so easy.

CHAPTER 5

THE RAIDING OF IRELAND

In a word, although there were an hundred hard-steeled iron heads on one neck, and an hundred sharp, ready, never-rusting brazen tongues in every head, and an hundred garrulous, loud, unceasing voices from every tongue, they could not recount or narrate or enumerate or tell what all the people of Ireland suffered in common, both men and women, laymen and priests, old and young, noble and ignoble, of hardship and injury and oppression in every house from these ruthless, wrathful, foreign, purely pagan people.'

FROM *THE WAR OF THE IRISH WITH THE FOREIGNERS* (COGADH GÁEDHEL RE GALLAIBH) TAKEN FROM *VIKING EXPANSION WESTWARDS* BY MAGNUS MAGNUSSON (BODLEY HEAD, 1973)

LEFT | *Monasteries across Ireland were raided by Vikings. They are recorded to have burned down a round tower like this one at Clonmacnoise, with Irish monks inside.*

A quick glance at a map plotting all the Viking raids on monasteries in Ireland shows that the Irish had a particularly bad time of it. Could it be the descriptions of hardship, injury and oppression at Viking hands recorded in the twelfth-century Cogadh Gáedhel re Gallaibh are true? Might the Vikings have been as violent as it suggests?

When they first set out across the North Sea, the Vikings could not have known what they would find. But from their bases in the Northern Isles they saw in Ireland a country rich in monasteries, and with more opportunities for raiding. What they did not know was that their relationship with the people of Ireland would be rather different to that enjoyed with the people of the Northern Isles, or of England. The locals would certainly put up a fierce resistance, but as a warlike and quarrelsome people themselves they would also exploit the sailing and fighting skills of the Viking invaders. Very soon the Scandinavians would find themselves acting as mercenaries in a number of internal Irish battles.

By the time of the Viking raids, politics in Ireland were complicated

RECHRU
(RATHLIN ISLAND)

ULAID

NORTHERN

UÍ NÉILL

ARMAGH

CONNACHTA

KELLS

BREGA

SOUTHERN
UÍ NÉILL

CLONMACNOISE

DÁL

OSRAIGE

CAIS

EOGANACHT

and the country was split among several kingdoms. As Ireland had been Christian for several centuries, the monasteries were very powerful and the Church should have exerted a unifying authority. But each king was more than happy to fight to maintain his control, and skirmishes between different clans and monasteries were common. The unwelcome appearance of the Vikings was just another destabilising factor, a threat to both Church and state.

Ireland had become a Christian society some time in the fifth century, when St Patrick arrived as a missionary. Two hundred years later his biographers claimed that he had converted the entire country, but in reality this process is likely to have taken a little longer. St Patrick was, however, remarkably successful in the north and west of the country, and by the sixth century the Irish were enthusiastically embracing the new religion.

Over the next few centuries Irish missionaries were sent to convert the pagans in the north of England and Scotland, and some set out for a harsh and simple existence on the uninhabited islands off the Atlantic coast of Ireland. St Columba is probably the most famous of these Irish monks, founding a monastery on Iona, an island off the west coast of Scotland. It was monks from here who would later establish the monastery at Lindisfarne, and eventually convert the kingdom of Northumbria to Christianity.

The Viking Age in England had begun with the attack of 793 on that same monastery of Lindisfarne. Two years later the Vikings raided the monastery on Iona, and in the same year there was an attack on the Irish monastery of Rechru. The Annals of Ulster report: 'The burning of Rechru by the heathens, and Skye was overwhelmed and laid waste.'

Rechru is thought to be Rathlin Island, off the north-east coast of Ireland and just across the water from Iona. The proximity of the two raids on monasteries carried out in the same year, 795, suggests that it may have been the same Viking crew that was responsible for both. Rechru was certainly a rich establishment so maybe one lucky band of Vikings took loot from both religious houses back to their homelands that winter.

This is the first reported raid on Ireland, However, a year earlier the Ulster Annals had recorded the 'devastation of all the islands of Britain by heathens', which suggests that the Viking threat was readily apparent well before the attack on Rechru. The author is probably guilty of exaggeration.

LEFT | *Sites of Viking raids in Ireland. Many other attacks were not recorded.*

But while his comment may not be entirely accurate, the annalist has not gone quite as far as the Anglo-Saxon Chronicle in demonising the Vikings. He sticks to a far more straightforward description, leaving out any mention of lightning or fiery dragons in the sky.

Although the Anglo-Saxons are more dramatic in their tales of Viking attacks, Ireland probably suffered more severely from Viking violence during these early raiding years. The annals record raids on Ireland over a period of two centuries and examination of monastic artefacts found in Viking graves in Scandinavia suggests that many are Celtic rather than Anglo-Saxon in style. These finds are the spoils from extensive raiding in Ireland.

Raids by heathens rapidly became a permanent fixture in the Irish record books. In 798 Vikings burned a church on St Patrick's Island, off the east coast, smashing up shrines, and during this year they are said to have made inroads into much of Ireland. By 807 the Viking raiders had reached the west coast, attacking as far south as Galway Bay. But it is also about this time that the Irish began to fight back. In 811 the Vikings were defeated by the Irish from the Ulaid kingdom, and Irish kings would claim victory over these foreign invaders twice more, in 812. These victories were short-lived, however. The Vikings were not going to give up the fight and in 813 they slaughtered the Irish and killed the local king.

After these initial raids and skirmishes there was a brief period of respite. Perhaps the Vikings were sizing up the new enemy that had proved tougher than any they had previously encountered. But then wholesale war broke out between the Vikings and the Irish. Attacks around the Irish Sea intensified in 821, and in 822 monasteries like that at Cork on the south coast felt the full effect of Viking ferocity. In north-east Ireland, Bangor was particularly badly hit in 824 when its monastery was attacked, the relics of St Comgall flung from their shrine, and the bishops killed.

The Vikings now began to take people as well as valuable objects. When they attacked the monastery at Skellig, they abducted the superior to hold him for ransom. Skellig is a tiny island off the south-west coast of Ireland, and cannot have contained many riches for the Vikings to take. Perhaps their frustration at finding little in the way of material goods led them to try their chances at kidnapping. Sadly for the unfortunate superior,

This reliquary from a Scottish monastery was probably looted by Vikings. A runic inscription on the bottom states: 'Ranvaig owns this casket'.

Clonmacnoise monastery was the victim of several Viking attacks. But it was also attacked by rival Irish groups, well before the Vikings even arrived.

the Vikings would never claim their ransom; he was subjected to such ill-treatment that he died in their hands.

While the written records are full of tales of Viking raiding, the archaeological evidence for these early raids is very similar to that from England: almost non-existent. One of the few Irish monastic sites to undergo large-scale excavations is Nendrum Abbey, County Down, raided, according to the annals, in 974. Here evidence was found that some of the buildings were destroyed by fire but although it has been suggested that the blaze was the handiwork of the Vikings, it could just as easily have been an unfortunate accident.

The most obvious evidence for raiding is the insular metalwork found in Norwegian graves, although some would argue that these ecclesiastical objects could have been acquired by peaceful means, such as trading. However, it does not seem credible that monks would have handed over precious religious items to these same Vikings whose raids they described in their annals. Although they could have been traded once they reached Scandinavia, it is more likely that they were initially obtained in a less legitimate manner.

We can be certain that the Vikings acquired Irish goods, and the written evidence at least suggests this was from raiding. But did they make an effort to settle in Ireland? Until the 830s the Vikings attacked only coastal sites or those by rivers, timing their raids for the summer months when sailing conditions were favourable. In the winter they returned to their permanent bases. Then tactics changed: the Vikings began to move inland. This meant that they needed bases and, more importantly, it meant that from these bases they could raid throughout the year.

These early settlements are known as *longphorts*, the *long* part of the name being a reference to ships. So they are often thought to have been fortified bases for ships, but the annals mention some in places where ships could never have landed. The conclusion must be that there was no standard *longphort*. In some cases it could have been a temporary encampment – the Vikings were said to have established one of these for only two days – but in other cases it might have been a relatively permanent base. Add to this the possibility that the Vikings may have taken over existing buildings or structures, even monasteries, and the *longphort* becomes one of the most confusing and elusive sites in the archaeological record.

In Ireland early Viking raiding parties built fortified settlements known as longphorts.

The first of them is recorded on Lough Neagh in 839, and by 841 the Vikings were overwintering at Dublin. But despite these references to specific locations, no archaeological remains of *longphorts* had been confirmed until a couple of years ago. This was when Ned Kelly from the National Museum of Ireland in Dublin visited a site in County Clare to follow up the reported discovery of some Viking period metalwork. Ned took me to have a look at what he had found on that visit, a collection of low banks and shallow ditches close to a bend in the River Shannon. The site's name is a corruption of the Irish Athlongphort, meaning the ford, or river crossing, of the *longphort*. But while the name itself is a promising clue, what convinced me were the earthworks in the pasture field. Three sides of an enclosure were formed by two ditches, shallow now after over a thousand years of silting and erosion, while the fourth side was formed by the river. Inside this enclosed area was a low rectangular mound that Ned explained could mark the strongest and most defensible part of the whole *longphort*. The layout of the site made perfect sense. Ships could be drawn up on the river bank where people and goods could be offloaded into the enclosed stronghold. The landward side was protected by water-filled ditches, each most likely with a parallel bank and palisade. Beyond this was marsh land, not the ideal terrain over which to mount an attack, especially in winter.

On our way to the site Ned told me that he had encountered a certain amount of scepticism concerning his identification of the site as a *longphort*. I could not understand this. There were the finds, the place-name and the earthworks in the field, all of which seemed to point in the same direction. Just because no examples of this sort of site have been found previously does not mean that one cannot turn up. I was convinced, and I would not be surprised if a lot more *longphorts* are discovered quite soon.

The Vikings who set up these camps would almost certainly have encountered local resistance and would have had to fight to maintain their position. Their new tactics worked, though, and they managed to successfully remain in Ireland over the winters, rather than simply raiding in the summer and then returning to Norway. According to the written records, they had set up camp in Dublin by 841 and while there is ample evidence for the town which the Scandinavians would later establish, the remains of this early settlement have yet to be discovered.

Although no formal archaeological excavations were carried out in Dublin until the 1960s, objects that suggested it might have an ancient past had been coming to light throughout the eighteenth and nineteenth centuries. There are records from the 1850s of a Thomas Ray buying up artefacts that had been uncovered while foundations were being laid for houses and roads.

In 1840 a skeleton, complete with weapons, was discovered by labourers working on the railway line in the Kilmainham area of Dublin. This was the first hint of the Viking burials that, over the next twenty years, would produce many more objects, including weapons and tools, shears and jewellery. The finds, the property of the railway company and the nearby Royal Hospital, were donated to the Royal Irish Academy.

In the 1930s archaeologists returned to the site and excavated more burials, including one with spears and axes found by workmen during the construction of the War Memorial Park. In 1934 another grave was uncovered and excavated by a team from the National Museum of Ireland. From the first records of discoveries in 1785 to the excavations of the 1930s thirty-four Viking burials were unearthed at the Kilmainham site, making this the largest Viking cemetery ever found outside of Scandinavia.

Archaeology itself went through enormous changes during the nineteenth century. In the 1840s there were no professional archaeologists and the recovery of finds and recording of sites was left to interested antiquarians, often members of the clergy, doctors or members of the professional classes. Today, when the value of recording on site is taken for granted and when the smallest changes in the soil are drawn, photographed and described, the records from the past often seem woefully inadequate. But these early field archaeologists were recording what they thought would help us to understand the past. To them, there was little point in collecting bones; it was the objects that were important.

In the 1930s, excavations revealed a number of Viking graves in Dublin.

By the late nineteenth century the Royal Irish Academy possessed a huge collection of objects from the Kilmainham and Islandbridge areas of Dublin. Along with all the other antiquities owned by the Academy, these finds appear in a catalogue produced by Sir William Wilde. Despite his enthusiasm for antiquities, Sir William Wilde was not himself an archaeologist, he was a doctor. He was also the father of Oscar Wilde and Sir William's interest in all things archaeological may have been what led Oscar to apply for an archaeological position in Athens after his time at university. But he was rejected and went on to become the poet, playwright and wit we remember him as today.

The catalogue of these artefacts, which Sir William was involved in compiling, is still used today by staff at the National Museum of Ireland. There are inevitably problems associated with a record of this age and so a massive project is now under way to re-examine and analyse all the objects found in the Islandbridge and Kilmainham area. Researchers in the past have tended to rearrange records by artefact type, compiling lists, for example, of all swords or all brooches. This often reflects the specialist interest of an individual researcher but can have unfortunate consequences if the original records are muddled in the process. Information about which objects were found together, and in which grave, can be confused or simply lost, making estimates of date, gender and status very difficult. If a grave has one easily datable object, a brooch for example, and another that is less easy to date, then one can be used to help date the other. Create separate lists, and omit to record that these two objects were found in the same grave, and that potential may be lost for ever.

Stephen Harrison has the daunting task of making sense of the records and objects held at the Royal Irish Academy, determining who made each discovery, when each find was made, and from where. Stephen's task has been made a lot easier by a collection of watercolour illustrations of many of the finds from the 1840s. These are so detailed that not only can the individual objects be recognised but it has even been possible to reunite fragments of the same object that have become separated over the last hundred years. But the greatest clarification has come from the discovery of Sir William Wilde's original draft of the catalogue. Here, in neatly written columns, are far more detailed descriptions of the objects than were transferred to the final version. Sir William records not only measurements and descriptions but also the names of those who discovered the objects and the payments made to them. So, if two objects were brought in on the same date and bought from the same person, there is a possibility that they came not only from the same site but also from the same grave. By patient detective work Stephen is gradually making sense of Dublin's Viking graves.

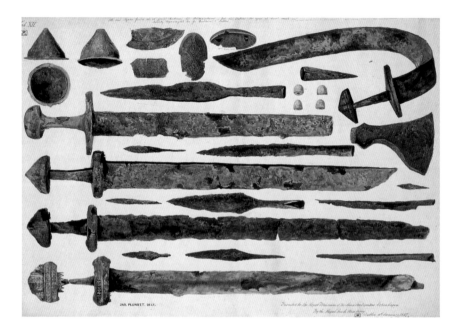

This water-colour was painted in the nineteenth century, after these swords and other weapons were excavated in Viking Dublin.

In the 1890s artefacts from the sites at both Kilmainham and Islandbridge were combined, as the prevailing belief was that one cemetery extended across both sites. It seems ironic that despite all the records of Viking activity in Ireland in the ninth century, these finds and the burials that they are recorded as coming from are the best evidence for a Viking presence. This may simply be due to the recognisable nature of the burials: the combination of a human skeleton and large, easily identifiable objects like swords. If the Vikings in Ireland at this time had cremated their dead we would presumably still be searching for them.

Although the sort of detail that would have been recorded using modern archaeological techniques is lost for ever, we now have a much greater understanding of Viking burials from Dublin. A previous study by Elizabeth O'Brien found two separate cemeteries in the Kilmainham and Islandbridge area and Stephen Harrison's work confirms this. The first, at Kilmainham, contains twenty-nine men, four women, and one uncertain burial, unearthed between 1785 and 1861. At Islandbridge, Stephen has determined that between 1866 and 1934 ten men and two women were discovered.

Both sites revealed rows of graves containing a wide range of weapons, ornaments and personal possessions. As no skeletons survive for study, the identification of men's and women's graves has had to be on the basis of distinctively 'male' and 'female' objects. These assumptions can obviously be questioned but burials with swords, spears and shields are assumed to be of men. Some, very similar to warrior burials at Kaupang in Norway, may perhaps be regarded as among the first Norwegian settlers in Dublin. The women most commonly had brooches, some of which were made in an Irish style and may well have been converted from monastic book mounts. Other objects, assumed to be female in character, include a needlecase and a linen smoother.

As well as these obviously pagan graves, each cemetery also appears to contain several burials with no grave goods. These may be the graves of Christians. The cemetery at Kilmainham was probably established in connection with the early Christian monastery at Cell Maignenn where the Viking settlers may have taken over the existing buildings, adding their dead to those already buried by the Irish. At Islandbridge the burials without grave goods also imply a native cemetery, although the site probably does not have the religious significance of that at Kilmainham.

The disturbance of so much archaeology in the nineteenth century has made it difficult to interpret other finds in the Dublin area. A single female grave is thought to have been found in Phoenix Park, but early records of the discovery mention 'several skeletons . . . [which are] supposed to be Danish'. Another single grave in Parnell Square could also have been one of many, as a contemporary account says swords, spears and human bones were found throughout the area. So, apart from Islandbridge and Kilmainham, which together account for only forty-six burials, hardly the entire population of Viking Dublin, other cemeteries might well have been scattered across Dublin and some no doubt still await discovery.

The settlement in which these people lived has never been found. The location of the burial sites suggests that the Vikings were keen to establish themselves in the Liffey estuary where the monastery at Kilmainham may well have provided a useful stopping point. There may also have been other individual settlements, destroyed as Dublin expanded during the seventeenth and eighteenth centuries.

From these sites the Vikings attacked many regions of Ireland but, contrary to popular belief, they did not bring raiding and violence to this country. It was home to many kings whose relationships were often hostile, particularly as some laid claim to the whole of Ireland. Territorial rights were loudly claimed and rigorously defended.

The Church also had a powerful presence in Ireland. The Irish kings accepted a Christian influence, and being anointed was a major advantage in the competition to inherit a throne. Kings and monasteries often combined resources, with members of aristocratic families becoming abbots and abbesses, while abbots sometimes ruled as kings.

The relationship between Church and state was not always harmonious, though, and long before the Vikings arrived, monasteries and kings had often found themselves drawn into battle. The monasteries were wealthy, with widespread property holdings, and conflicts easily arose. In 807 the Ulster Annals report 'innumerable slaughter of the ecclesiastical men and superiors of Cork', as the monastic dynasty of Cork battled with that of Clonfert. In fact there were at least twenty-seven violent incidents involving monasteries in the eighth century, some battles involving important kings, others squabbles over land.

While in Ireland I felt that I had to visit the site of one of the Viking raids, and so, on a glorious sunny January day, I went to the monastery of Clonmacnoise, County Offaly. The ruinous state of the monastic buildings that can be seen today cannot be blamed on the Vikings; almost without exception they date from centuries later. What surprised me was to find out that the Vikings were not the only ones to raid here, or the first. Clonmacnoise actually produced its own set of annals, which makes it one of the better-documented places in early Ireland.

The first recorded Viking raid was in 842, but as early as the 720s the monastery is reported as being burned. Whether these fires were accidental or deliberate, and who was responsible, is not clear. But by the 760s there are unmistakable reports of religious violence. In 764 a large-scale battle with a neighbouring church settlement involved a number of the local nobility and resulted in two hundred of these rival locals being killed.

By the time the Vikings began to attack in the 840s, the Irish at

Clonmacnoise had witnessed their fair share of bloodshed. It was probably the Vikings' mobility and the speed of their attack that led to their success, as the monks must have been quite used to defending their settlement. And even though the Vikings are held responsible for these monastic raids, there were over ten incidents of native violence against Clonmacnoise during the main Viking period, compared to only six by Vikings.

Overall Clonmacnoise had a rather turbulent history; finally, after all those raids by heathens and Christians, the monastery was destroyed by the English in 1552. I felt that the Vikings were still regarded as the villains, though. In the churchyard stands a cross, and carved on its shaft were some figures that I recognised. Small helmeted figures, they looked almost exactly the same as those on the stone at Lindisfarne. Was this another appearance by the Vikings as instruments of divine retribution?

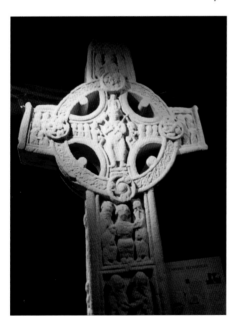

The head of the great carved cross from Clonmacnoise monastery. The picture opposite shows a detail of the 'Viking' figures on the cross's base.

With this aggressive heritage, it was not surprising that the locals fought back when faced with this new threat from raiding Vikings. In 831 the Vikings raided north Louth, and seized the local king for ransom. The monks of Armagh sent troops to defend their property in this region, but were defeated and many were taken captive. They probably regretted their prompt defensive manoeuvres as the Vikings, now aware of the wealth of the monastery at Armagh, raided it three times during one month in 832.

Despite the obvious threat, the monasteries continued to function, and even to prosper, sometimes within Viking-controlled areas. The Church's connections with the Irish aristocracy, and the practice of passing on high Church offices to family members, must have contributed to its resilience.

There is also the pragmatism of the Vikings to consider. Raid a monastery once and destroy it, or damage it so badly that it ceases to function, and that source of loot and captives is exhausted. Allow it to survive, and even prosper, and it can be raided again in the future; a sensible policy from the Vikings' point of view, nerve-racking for the monks.

As the Vikings developed more permanent bases in Ireland, giving them the chance to move their raids further inland, the Irish kings began to

treat them as a very serious threat. Kings across Ireland began to defend their territory and to score victories over the Vikings. Niall Caille, King of Tara, defeated them in 845, and his successor, Mael Sechnaill, killed seven hundred Vikings in a battle near Skreen. The defence mounted against the Vikings seems to have been far more successful in Ireland than elsewhere in the British Isles. The kings may have bickered among themselves, but they were also united by important cultural links and a shared historical myth. Irish scribes initially found it difficult to place the Vikings within the context of this myth. The semi-historical figures of the Irish heroes generally had to deal with strange mythical creatures, whereas the Vikings were decidedly real.

However, the Vikings were eventually given a place in the Irish myths, as an evil foreign enemy of the *fianna*, ancient Irish heroes. The fact that the *fianna* existed during the third century AD, centuries before the Viking Age, did not seem to worry the authors.

Despite the stories which the Irish would concoct centuries later, to the people of the time the Vikings became just another part of Irish politics. When the annalist who had recorded the Vikings overwintering at Dublin in 841 realises they are still there the following year, he expresses mild surprise and merely comments: 'Pagans still in Dublin.' However, they soon had bases on the River Shannon, on the north coast of Ireland and at Cork, Waterford and Limerick. In the 840s, as they began to fight back against the Viking invasion, the Irish kings realised that these fearsome warriors could also be put to good use.

The first reference to Viking co-operation with the Irish is in 842, when an abbot was killed by a group of Vikings and Irish. The idea stuck. These alliances served the Irish well, but the Vikings were not always loyal allies. In 855 they attacked a monastery in the heart of Meath, despite entering into a pact with the Church authorities. Following this raid, the Vikings promptly transferred their allegiance to another Irish kingdom, presumably having been offered a better deal by its leader.

The Vikings probably acted as mercenaries for many Irish kings, such alliances marking the start of the assimilation of the Scandinavians into Irish culture. They may have married the daughters of local chiefs, and adopted Irish customs in a process of intermarriage and cultural blending. In Ireland today there are still remnants of Scandinavian culture, the use of names like Ivar, Ragnall and Sitriuc hinting at the legacy of Old Norse.

The first settlers in Ireland are thought to have come from Norway but other Viking groups soon realised the potential for loot in Ireland. In 851–2 the Vikings already in Ireland had to fend off a group of Danes keen to have their share of the spoils. By this time there must have been some sort of Danish settlement in Dublin, because in 853 the Viking leader Olaf (Amlaib in Irish) is said to have recaptured Dublin from the Danes.

After defeating the Danes, Olaf became the first king of Dublin. He was probably of Norwegian descent, but was most likely to have reached Ireland after ruling one of the Scottish Viking kingdoms, perhaps the Hebrides. Olaf and his brother Ivar (Imar in Irish) prospered in early Dublin, particularly as a result of Irish internal conflicts. They allied with the minor Irish kingdom of Osraige against the powerful Southern Uí Néill king, and Olaf even went so far as to marry one of the daughters of the King of Osraige. But when these two Irish kingdoms eventually made peace Olaf found himself out of work.

Olaf and his followers headed for Scotland, which he successfully ravaged in 866. They made sure no one in Ireland had forgotten their power by returning to attack Armagh in 869; plundering, burning, and killing or taking prisoner over one thousand people. Then they set out on another raiding voyage across the Irish Sea. An attack at the mouth of the Clyde led to such a crushing defeat of the Strathclyde Britons that it is even mentioned in the Welsh Annals. They returned to Dublin with two hundred ships and a large number of captives. Despite their successes, Olaf soon left Dublin for good, perhaps to help his father back in his home kingdom. But Ivar remained to rule the kingdom of Dublin and when he died in 873, the Annals of Ulster described him as 'the king of the Norsemen of all Ireland and Britain'.

At Ivar's death Dublin was left in political turmoil, with at least three different Viking families claiming the kingdom. During the power struggle, one of Olaf's sons, two of Ivar's sons, his grandson, and two other unknown individuals entered into the dispute. Olaf's son was murdered by the Danes in 875, after which Barid, recorded in the annals as a 'great Viking tyrant', became powerful for a time. In 881 he too was killed and, after his death, a Viking called Ottar Jernknaeson tried to assert control by making an alliance with the king of Meath.

The sons of Ivar then returned from the south coast where they had been waiting for an appropriate opportunity to regain control. They ousted

The Vikings arrived off the coasts of Ireland in the early ninth century, but at the beginning of the tenth the Irish managed to chase them out of the country.

Ottar and immediately swapped sides, allying with the Northern Uí Néill. Raids into the heartland of Ireland were still commonplace, however, and the Uí Néill king can have been none too pleased when Armagh was attacked. There seems to have been some degree of co-operation between the rival Viking groups in this raid during which 710 prisoners were taken.

The coalition was not to last, however. In 896 fellow Vikings killed one of Ivar's sons, and the Irish his brother. Warriors again left Dublin to set up camps all over Ireland. By this time Viking Dublin was fading fast and when a united force from Brega and Leinster attacked in 902, there was no fight left.

The pagans were driven from Ireland . . . and they abandoned a good number of their ships, and escaped half-dead after they had been wounded and broken.

The eventual result of all this infighting between various Viking factions seems to have been their defeat. The leadership problems that faced Dublin at the end of the ninth century may have been worsened by the difficulty in persuading warriors to stay. There was also increasing resistance by the Irish that must have led many Vikings to opt for the easier pickings available from raiding in England and Francia.

Although the Irish managed to kick out the Viking leaders in 902, there is evidence that ordinary Vikings remained in Dublin, living much as they had until this point. Their powerful leaders would not return for another fifteen years but having been expelled from Ireland, these Vikings do not simply disappear. Raids are still taking place in Francia and England. But Olaf and Ivar had shown that there was an even quicker road to riches. All that was required was a short voyage across the Irish Sea.

CHAPTER 6

CONQUERING THE IRISH SEA

*A great raiding ship-army came over here from the south from Brittany . . .
and then went around west until they got into the mouth of the Severn,
and raided in Wales everywhere along the banks where it suited them.*

ANGLO-SAXON CHRONICLE 914

LEFT | *Several Viking Age
burials have been found in the
cemetery on St Patrick's Isle,
Isle of Man.*

Vikings had appeared in the Welsh Annals as early as 852, their first
recorded raid in this country. History suggests that repercussions
from the Vikings' expulsion from Ireland were felt all around the Irish
Sea, including Wales where, in the early tenth century, a second wave of
raiding was the result. But the Vikings, referred to by the Welsh as
Llychlynwyr, or 'people of the fjords', have always been a rather shadowy
presence in Wales. As in England, they are represented by some place-
names, a selection of potentially unreliable historical references and a few
distinctive finds. This did not deter archaeologist Mark Redknap, from
the National Museum of Wales, in his search for Vikings in Wales.

Finds of Viking-period artefacts are not common in Wales but many
were discovered long ago and there may be little information about the
precise location where they were found. In cases like this the finds, though
interesting, can often provide no more than an indication of a Viking
presence in a broad area. But if the precise find spot is known, and the
circumstances of discovery are recorded, then a simple object may provide
a valuable clue to a site or an event and may eventually shed light on this
enigmatic time in the history of Wales. In Anglesey, Mark thinks that he
has found evidence for a Viking raid. It all started in 1992 when someone
brought a collection of tiny objects to his museum for identification.

The finds included some coins and weights that had been discovered
by metal-detector users in a field at Llanbedrgoch close to Red Wharf
Bay. The coins all dated to the ninth century and Mark recognised the

lead weights as a type used by Viking merchants. There was already some evidence of a Viking presence in this part of Wales. There are Scandinavian place-names on Anglesey; in fact the name of the island, *Onguls-ey*, is thought to incorporate that of a Viking leader. A hoard of five beautifully decorated silver arm rings, buried very early in the tenth century, comes from Red Wharf Bay and one of only four possible Viking burials in the whole of Wales was discovered at Benlleth in the 1940s.

A visit to the new find spot was clearly essential but Mark's first impression, of a gently-sloping, south-facing field beside a small stream, was that there were no obvious signs of settlement. However, a geophysical survey revealed a buried ditch enclosing a large U-shaped area running down to the stream and when the first exploratory trenches were dug, the ditch proved to be about 2 metres wide and 1 metre deep. Since then, over several seasons of excavation, the history of the site has been revealed. The enclosure is large, nearly 100 metres long and 90 metres wide, and extends beyond the stream that would have provided a source of water for both people and livestock. It started life as a seventh-century native settlement, but later its character changes.

At several points where the ditch has been excavated Mark has found the remains of a substantial wall, in part built of massive stone blocks and about 2 metres wide at its base. The wall, which appears to have replaced an earth embankment, may originally have been as high as it is wide, and, together with the ditch, would have made an impressive defensive blockade. It may even have had room for a walkway on top and could have been crowned with wooden spikes.

Radiocarbon dates place the construction of the wall in the ninth century, but why, at this time, did the inhabitants of this settlement find it necessary to refortify their camp with a massive limestone wall? There must have been some real threat that led the inhabitants to carry out this major task. There may be a clue in the Welsh Annals where there are reports of raiding from the second half of the ninth century and into the tenth. The date that the wall was built fits well with the records of Viking attacks on Anglesey, attacks that include one on the monastery at Penmon, just twenty miles from the site of Mark's excavation. The combination of archaeological evidence and historical records convinced Mark that it was a Viking threat that led to the construction of the wall.

By this time excavations within the enclosure had shed more light on the nature of this now fortified settlement. Traces of stone buildings were recovered, arranged in an organised manner, alongside signs of industry, including metalworking. There were more finds of Viking metalwork too, some made by the metal detectorists who had located the site and had come back to help with the excavation. These included pieces of 'hacksilver' cut from decorated armlets and used as currency. But typically, as the project to investigate the site continued, more questions were raised. Was it a Viking settlement, or a native settlement taken over by Vikings? Who were the defences built against, and were they ever needed?

The answer to the last question started to emerge during the 1998 excavation season when an unexpected discovery was made. Two skeletons were found lying north-south along the axis of the enclosure ditch. In ninth-century Christian Wales, the normal practice would have been to bury the dead in an east-west grave, and in a recognised cemetery, not under a pile of stones in such an unusual place. The skeletons were found to be of a young woman aged about twenty lying on her back, with a child of about ten crouched beside her. They raised the possibility that here Mark had found the first evidence of people who had maybe not simply witnessed a Viking raid, but had been among its victims. There were hints from the ditch that these were not the only skeletons buried there. Over the winter of 1998 tiny samples of bone were taken from the skeletons and sent off for radiocarbon dating. The answer that came back suggested that the woman and the child had most probably died some time around the end of the ninth century, the time of the Viking raids.

Mark contacted me as soon as the results of the 1998 excavation were known, and I arranged that we would visit the site during his next summer excavation. In the meantime I would learn how to pronounce Llanbedrgoch correctly. By the time I arrived, Mark's team had uncovered another group of three skeletons, again lying in the ditch, again roughly covered with stones. There was an adult man and another child but it was the third skeleton that provoked the most discussion on site that summer. It was of a young man who, as his bones were gradually uncovered, seemed to be lying in a strangely contorted position.

There was something very unnatural about the way this young man lay in the ditch. I had never seen a skeleton like this, with both hands so

This young man's skeleton was uncovered during the excavation on Anglesey. His wrists are so close together that his hands must have been tied behind his back. He had been thrown into a ditch, along with four others, probably the victim of a Viking raid.

close together in such a position. Both Mark and I agreed that there seemed to be only one plausible explanation: his hands must have been tied behind his back.

The skeletons provided Mark with a unique opportunity. Here were a group of people, a mixture of men, women and children, buried without ceremony in a place that they may have inhabited. This is in marked contrast to normal practice where people were buried according to local rituals, in a formal place away from where they had died. All these factors may help to remove clues about how people died but, in this case, Mark believes he has enough evidence to suggest that these people died violently.

There is, of course, the possibility that the people buried here died of disease or other natural causes. However, Mark considers that the way they were buried makes this an unlikely explanation. They were left together in the ditch, all at one level, and were covered with stones before the ditch was filled in. While this shows that they were deliberately buried, it does not seem to have been done with the respect one would normally see if relatives or friends had been responsible. If their deaths had been natural, it is likely that other surviving members of the community would have ensured they had a proper burial. So Mark began to look for alternative explanations.

An examination of the skeletons themselves showed no markings that could indicate violence, but this does not mean that these people could not have been killed. There are plenty of ways to carry out a murderous attack that damage only the soft tissue of the skin and flesh, slicing through veins and arteries but leaving the skeletons completely unmarked. This is what Mark suggests may have happened at this peaceful rural site. To him, the evidence lies in the remains of his five people in the ditch and in their contorted bones.

The fortifications, rebuilt as a massive wall around the time of the Viking raids, suggest that the people who lived here might well have been under threat from Scandinavians in the Irish Sea. Smarting from their expulsion from Ireland, these Vikings may have set sail with the intention of finding settlements which they could take over, ready-made bases from which they could continue their raiding. Or maybe, like most Vikings, they had not taken many provisions with them and were simply searching for food and other supplies when they came across the settlement at Llanbedrogoch. It seems that some Viking invaders may have seen the well-fortified settlement and simply decided to take it for their own.

Mark feels that it is very unlikely that the skeletons in the ditch are those of Vikings. If they had been members of a Viking party then, whether they were killed in battle or died a more natural death, they would surely have been buried in a more appropriate setting and with some ceremony. Like the grave at Benllech, a site overlooking the Irish Sea would have been a more suitable burial place for a Viking. So that leaves the explanation that the skeletons in the ditch must be Welsh victims of violence, perhaps by Vikings.

But if they were killed, why did their killers bother to bury the bodies at all? Although little respect seems to have been involved, the Vikings would probably have wanted to dispose of the bodies in order to prevent them from being eaten by animals. So they piled them into the ditch and covered them with stones. It seems a very violent story to uncover in such a peaceful part of rural Wales. If this interpretation is correct, it is the first real archaeological evidence of a Viking raid in Wales.

Mark had exposed what could be a rather unsavoury side of the Vikings' contribution to Welsh history, but, in contrast, Anglesey historian Eryl

Rothwell Hughes thinks he has evidence for the Vikings contributing to Welsh culture in Anglesey. Not far from Mark Redknap's dig lie the remains of the monastery of Penmon, said to have been raided by Vikings in 871. Here, in the church of St Seiriol, Eryl has identified what he believes to be Scandinavian artistry, carved into its ancient walls.

The church of St Seiriol was founded in the sixth century. Anglesey was the perfect remote location for a monastery, highly suitable for the ascetic lifestyle which the monks were meant to lead. Seiriol and his friend Cybi chose locations at either end of Anglesey for their religious settlements. St Cybi's monastery is now Holyhead, although its Welsh name, Caergybi, reflects its founder.

St Seiriol's early Celtic church was associated with a holy well, as were many of the early churches. In pre-Christian times the wells were thought to have healing powers and may have been used for pagan rituals. Christianity often simply took over, as it did with many pagan festivals and traditions, adopting the sites and using the water of the wells for baptism. Even today there is still a tiny and picturesque well-building up a winding track from the church where prayers and offerings are left by the faithful.

The original church of St Seiriol was destroyed when Vikings attacked the monastery in 971. It was rebuilt under the reign of Gruffudd ap Cynan and of his son Owain Gwynedd in the twelfth century, and expanded during the rule of Llewelyn the Great in the following century. The monastery was dissolved under Henry VIII in 1537, but the church continued to be used and today, together with the adjacent ruins, represents the most complete monastic site of its age in north-west Wales.

When the church of St Seiriol was rebuilt, a number of carvings were made, including a monster over the church door. It appears to be some kind of a dragon, head bent backwards, and with its tail passing through its back legs and up into its open-jawed mouth. Eryl has found two parallels for this dragon. One, in a Danish style, is on an eleventh-century gravestone in the churchyard of St Paul's Cathedral. The dragons look as if they could be cousins but the St Paul's example, rather than having its tail in its mouth, appears to be fighting a snake.

An even better parallel with the Penmon dragon can be drawn with a brooch which, although from Kilkenny in Ireland, could well be of Viking manufacture. The dragon on the brooch also has its head turned back-

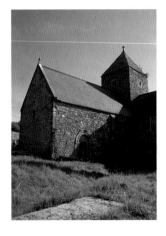

St Seiriol's Church was built in the eleventh century on Anglesey. It is now thought that this church may be one of the many renovated by the Welsh leader Gruffudd ap Cynan, whose mother was a Dublin Viking.

This carving, over a doorway at St Seiriol's Church, portrays a dragon with its tail curved round towards its mouth. Similar creatures can be identified in both Celtic and Scandinavian art.

Eryl Rothwell Hughes believes this dragon on an Irish brooch bears a remarkable resemblance to the dragon at St Seiriol's Church.

wards and its tail in its mouth. This link with Ireland appears to be further supported by historical evidence.

The Welsh king at the time the church was rebuilt was either Gruffudd ap Cynan, or his son Owain Gwynedd. Gruffudd ap Cynan was King of Gwynedd in north Wales from 1075 to 1135. The son of a Welshman, he spent his childhood in Dublin with his mother, the daughter of the Viking Sihtric Silkbeard. But when the English King Henry I took over Wales, Gruffudd decided to reclaim his homeland.

His early attempts were successful, and he recovered Anglesey. So, despite internal power struggles that soon forced him back into exile, he would not be discouraged. He made a second trip to Wales, was captured and jailed in Chester, but managed to escape and once more returned to Ireland.

Finally, on his third attempt, Gruffudd met with further success. He first regained Anglesey and then, with a combined army of Norse and Irish followers, as well as men from Anglesey, he took back the kingdom of Gwynedd. In achieving this he was aided by the Norwegian king, Magnus Barelegs.

In another reversal of fortune, Gruffudd was forced to submit to Henry I in 1114 after the king had attacked Gwynedd. However, Gruffudd managed to retain some control and became a celebrated leader of the Welsh. He is also said to have restored many churches throughout Anglesey during his reign, his biographer writing that 'he rebuilt the Christian churches in stone and they glowed in the darkness'. So this might be the explanation for the carvings in St Seiriol's Church; they may be the result of Gruffudd respecting his Irish-Scandinavian roots and insisting that some Viking artwork be included.

As well as the potentially Scandinavian dragon, inside the church at Penmon is another carving that almost certainly has Scandinavian roots. This figure was reset during the Victorian era, but was probably initially installed just underneath the roof of the original church. It is of a small bearded man, with either a hammer or an axe in his hand.

The only parallel to this figure which Eryl has been able to find comes not from Scandinavian Dublin, or England, but from Sweden. In a church in Gotland there is a similar bearded figure, holding in one hand a hammer and in the other smith's tools. This is Völundr, the Norse dwarf god of smiths to whom the figure in Penmon church bears a remarkable resemblance. He may represent the Welsh god of smiths, Gofannon, but the figure seems to have a Scandinavian connection. Although Eryl does not suggest that there is a direct link between St Seiriol's Church to Sweden, it may well be that somehow this image of the god of smiths found its way to Wales, along with the Scandinavians who travelled the Irish Sea.

The church at St Seiriol had both suffered and benefited from the attention of Vikings. In the tenth century it had been destroyed by pagan Vikings, only to be rebuilt by a Christian Viking two centuries later. The tranquillity of the present church seemed more in tune with Gruffudd's beneficial attentions but Eryl could provide solid evidence of the earlier, more destructive Vikings. Inside the church are two stone crosses, one heavily worn, its designs almost indecipherable, the other far fresher-looking with crisp carving but lacking one of the horizontal arms of its cross-head. Eryl explained that the worn one was probably the replacement for a cross, recorded as having been desecrated during the Viking raid of 971. Its current appearance is due to it having stood outside for nearly a thousand years before being moved inside the church. Less seems to be known about the newer-looking cross, except that it was found being used as a lintel in one of the medieval monastic buildings. The missing cross-arm was presumably removed to make it a better shape for its new role. This puzzled me. Why would a Christian community take a perfectly good cross, deface it and use it as building stone? And then a thought struck me. What if this was the original one, the cross that was defaced by the Viking raiders? What if the defacing was not physical but was considered so awful that the cross could no longer function as a sacred symbol and had to be replaced with one that was not tainted? What if the old, defaced cross was then tucked away in a wall, serving a useful but non-spiritual purpose? There were a lot of 'what ifs' in this train of thought but to me it seemed to explain why St Seiriol had two crosses, one worn, one fresh, one that had stood as a Christian symbol for a thousand years, one that had been hidden away for almost as long. I wondered what the hidden cross had witnessed to have been banished for so long.

It was not just Wales that suffered as the Vikings swarmed all over the

The church of St Seiriol in Anglesey boasts two crosses, one of which looks far more worn than the other. The fresher one had been used as a lintel in a medieval monastic building.

Irish Sea; the Isle of Man was also open to attack from all sides. Perhaps because of this, the Viking exiles from Ireland who chose to settle here built homesteads on coastal promontories, unlike those found anywhere else at the time. The fort at Cronk ny Merriu overlooks the entrance to Port Greenaugh and was first constructed in the Iron Age. Just as they had done in Anglesey, Norse settlers took over the site, and used the massive rampart as ready-made protection around a small, almost rectangular building with a central fireplace.

A Norse house was discovered at Cronk ny Merriu, on a site which had previously been used as an Iron Age fort.

A farm from this period was also uncovered at Doarlish Cashen on the Isle of Man. Here, three buildings, at least two of which are thought to be Norse in date, cluster together in the middle of empty fields. One was a small house, with benches built on either side of a hearth, and a corn-drying kiln was also excavated. Although both crops and animals were raised here, the lack of any artefacts at the site suggests this may have been a relatively poor settlement.

In comparison, evidence for more wealthy settlers has been found in the hoards of Viking-Age silver discovered throughout the island. At least twenty of these are known, perhaps the profits from trade centred around Dublin, buried from the mid-tenth century right through to the late eleventh. Burying such riches might have been seen as a way of keeping them out of the hands of passing fortune seekers.

Pagan Viking graves contain the remains of some of these wealthy inhabitants. Several boat burials, mirroring those found on Orkney, have been excavated on the Isle of Man. These early Norse graves contain boats about 5 metres in length and were for men, probably warriors to judge from the spears and swords found in them.

Not just the boat burials, but nearly all of the Viking graves uncovered on the Isle of Man contain male skeletons. This suggests that relatively few Scandinavian women can have been involved in the settlement of Man. It may be that the invading Viking warriors intermarried with Manx women, forming a cross-cultural community. It certainly seems that the local Celtic population did not disappear for there are many Celtic names mixed in with runic inscriptions on the island's stone crosses.

Marriage between Manx and Norse might also help to explain why

Christianity was adopted relatively rapidly by the settlers. The kingdom was converted in the tenth century, while most Scandinavian countries would hold out until at least the beginning of the eleventh. There are nearly fifty carved stone crosses from this period, many combining Scandinavian and Celtic Christian symbols. Some show scenes from pagan myths, while other memorial stones, carved in runes, commemorate people with Celtic names.

While many Manx women might have been commemorated by a rune stone, some have been found who almost certainly were not. Several of the male burials also included a female companion and two of them contained evidence that the Vikings practised human sacrifice. The boat burial unearthed at Balladoole contained both male and female skeletons. These might have been a husband and wife buried together, but at different times. However, their grave goods suggest the possibility of a less equitable state of affairs.

The bodies are laid in the boat alongside objects considered to be almost exclusively male and reflecting comparative wealth, including stirrups, spurs, and a bridle. In contrast, the woman is buried with nothing. Perhaps she was considered so unimportant that she needed nothing for the afterlife, prompting the question of whether or not she was a slave. And if she was, did she die a natural death or was she sacrificed on her master's death, just another part of the man's worldly possessions to take with him to Valhalla?

The boat burial at Balladoole leaves some questions unanswered but a grave discovered at Ballateare, also on the Isle of Man, has far stronger evidence for human sacrifice. It contained the body of a man, placed in a small pit, or possibly a coffin. Above this a layer of burnt animal bones was found, perhaps the remains of a funeral feast, and within it lay the skeleton of a young woman. The back of her skull had been sliced off and she had been buried before the pit was finally filled in. Maybe this Viking funeral included not only feasting but a pagan offering.

Not all Manx women in Viking times were of lowly status, or were treated in this apparently casual and brutal way. On St Patrick's Isle, on the west coast of the Isle of Man, seven pagan Viking graves were discovered, some buried with ornaments similar to those excavated in Dublin, and others with belts and elaborate cloaks. But the most impressive of all these graves belongs to a woman, the 'Pagan Lady of Peel'.

This slashed skull was excavated at Ballateare, Isle of Man. It may have belonged to a female slave, sacrificed on the grave of her master.

She was buried in a grave lined with stone slabs, fully clothed and with her head resting on a down-filled pillow. Accompanying her to the next world were shears, a comb, a decorated knife, and needles. A cooking spit, complete with a goose wing and herbs, made sure she would not go hungry on her journey. She wore a belt decorated with amber, and an extraordinarily colourful necklace of seventy-one beads, of glass, amber and jet.

The 'Pagan Lady' must have been someone of great importance to have warranted such a lavish burial and may even have been a wealthy landowner. Most of her possessions came not from Scandinavia itself but from the Irish Sea region, or from that part of England which was under Viking control. Yet she and the other people buried on St Patrick's Isle probably thought of themselves as Norse. It is possible that they arrived on the island in 927, when the English King Æthelstan captured the Scandinavian settlement at York and drove out its Viking inhabitants.

In its heyday, the Isle of Man played a powerful role in the Irish Sea region. In the 1030s silver pennies appear to have been minted on the island, mimicking those struck in prosperous Dublin. These coins are likely to have been minted on St Patrick's Isle, the island's centre of political power at this time of wealth and stability. The links forged between different areas of the Irish Sea region and beyond can be seen clearly in the reign of Godred Crovan, King of Man and the Hebrides from 1079 until 1095 and who also ruled in Dublin for three years.

Godred is the first King of Man to enter the history books but his death in 1095 plunged the kingdom into civil war, making it an easy target for Magnus Barelegs of Norway. Godred's son Olaf recognised Norwegian sovereignty and managed to revive the Kingdom of Man in 1113. But it soon fell into decline, losing the Hebrides to the Scots in 1263. Its last Norse king died in 1264, and Man was ceded to Scotland by Norway the following year.

Because of the long period of Norse rule, the Isle of Man, together with the Northern and Western Isles of Scotland, is perhaps one of the most obvious places to look for evidence of our Viking heritage. But, important though they obviously became, the Vikings did not confine themselves to these smaller outlying regions after their exile from Ireland. In a very short time they were back to stay.

CHAPTER 7

FROM RAIDERS TO TRADERS

'. . . there shall come great tempests, and many fiery lightnings, and thunder, and sulphurous fire which shall burn tribes and nations, and heavy stony hail-storms, and flying serpents, and heathens shall come to you from me,' said god himself, 'a race of pagans who will carry you into bondage from your own lands and will offer you up to their own gods.'

FROM THE OLD IRISH TEXT *EPISTIL ISU* (THE EPISTLE OF JESUS)

LEFT | *The Vikings enjoyed games, and demonstrated their skilled craftsmanship in the creation of the Lewis Chessmen.*

The Irish no doubt congratulated themselves on managing to expel the Norse leadership from Ireland at the beginning of the tenth century, but it would not be long before they returned. The Norwegian Vikings Olaf and Ivar had been successful in setting up the first Viking encampment at Dublin in the mid-ninth century and it was Ivar's grandson, Sihtric Cáech who would reclaim this region for the Vikings.

In 914, a fleet arrived at Waterford determined to re-establish a Viking presence in Ireland. The next year they were joined by even more Scandinavians and once again churches throughout the region suffered as the raids resumed. In 917 Sihtric Cáech and his brother Ragnald appeared on the scene. Whether or not they were connected to the original fleet is uncertain but they soon took over Viking operations in Ireland. Ragnald took control of Waterford, while Sihtric established a camp on the border with Leinster.

Niall Glúndubh, leader of the Northern Uí Néill and king of Tara, travelled south with an army to meet the new Viking invaders. They had kicked the Vikings out of Ireland once, and thought that they could do it again. But despite persuading the Leinstermen to join in the attack on the Viking camp, the Irish were defeated and Sihtric pressed on to Dublin, recapturing the city.

Perhaps due to an element of surprise, or maybe just to the force of this initial invasion, it was two years before the Irish would react. In 919 they attempted to force the Vikings out of Dublin, but again suffered a devastating defeat at the hands of Sihtric's men. Niall Glúndubh was killed, along with many other Uí Néill leaders, and Sihtric held on to Dublin for the Vikings. This was to be the beginning of a true Norse kingdom in Ireland.

Having already experienced one wave of Viking attacks in the ninth century, the Irish throughout the country must have been very wary of this new Viking threat. At the same time that these first attacks took place, ring forts, defended settlements often strategically placed on hilltops, were being constructed, perhaps as a means of defence against marauding Vikings. But even the defences of a ring fort would probably not have provided much protection from determined Vikings and so the Irish developed a cunning means of hiding.

Souterrains are stone-built underground passages, abundant in Ireland and often found within ring forts. The only one that has been effectively dated is a waterlogged one in County Antrim where wooden planks were preserved and dendrochronology indicates that the timbers used to build it were felled in about 822. This fits well with the time of the first Viking invasions.

Souterrains (literally 'undergrounds') often have recesses, small cupboard spaces, shelves or even benches inside. Some may have been used to store valuables, such as one in County Cork where a bell, carefully wrapped in moss for protection, was found hidden under the flagstone floor. Others, entered from a house, would have made a convenient storage space for less precious household goods as well. But some of these underground chambers may have been used to hide people rather than just valuables. Several of the souterrains discovered are part of ring forts and are reached from an entrance passage leading underground from inside the defensive settlements.

Although it is difficult to be certain whether souterrains were built as a hideaway from the Vikings, they do seem to have been invisible from above ground. Perhaps lookouts were placed inside to warn of encroaching Vikings, allowing the Irish inhabitants to drop down underground, out of sight. Their hope would be that the Vikings thought the fort had been deserted.

I was taken to see an example of a souterrain that lay within a ring

John Sheehan introduces me to the joys of life in a souterrain. They may have acted as hiding places for the native Irish during Viking raids.

fort at Leacanabuaile, close to the coast in County Kerry. My guide was John Sheehan, and without his confidence and expert knowledge of the site I would never have squeezed myself into the tiny entrance that led into the souterrain. It looked just like a drain, a rectangular slab-lined recess close to a house wall, and the water that lay on the floor inside would I am sure have convinced any Viking who poked his nose inside that it was simply that: a drain. But if the Viking was still suspicious and followed the passage, through deeper water and round right-angled corners, he would eventually come up against a blank stone wall. This was the really cunning part of the whole design. The roof of this passage was effectively the floor of a large chamber built into the outer wall of the ring fort. Move a slab and there was room for a dozen people to crouch in pitch darkness. Slide the slab back into place and the chamber was effectively invisible. As I crouched in the chamber with John, the walls lit by the lamps on our helmets, I tried to imagine what it would have been like to hide here with marauding Vikings ransacking the houses above: the dread of what you would find when you finally ventured out, the fear that the Vikings might still be lurking nearby, waiting to see where the natives had gone, looking for slaves.

Once again, in the early tenth century, the Irish may have had to rely on their underground hiding places. While Sihtric Cáech was busy reinforcing Dublin, his brother Ragnald was ravaging the coasts of the Irish Sea. But Ragnald had wider ambitions. He first appears in the annals on a raiding trip to Scotland from where he turned his attention to England, briefly holding York in 911 and managing to issue a few coins in his name. Battles ensued with the kings of the Scots and the Northumbrians, as well as the conclusive defeat of a rival Norse leader in the Isle of Man. By this time Ragnald had become a much feared ringleader of violent attacks in the Irish Sea.

Once Sihtric was safely installed in Dublin, Ragnald decided he ought to have a kingdom of his own and, in 919, he retook control of York. On Ragnald's death, Sihtric too left for York, perhaps considering it a more prestigious kingdom than its Irish counterpart.

Sihtric was the first of this new wave of Viking invaders, but his other brother Guthfrith is remembered as far more violent. In 921 he was left in control of Dublin and immediately began to attack Irish sites, raiding and taking prisoners. His reign began with a perfectly timed raid on the monastery at Armagh. He struck on St Martin's Eve, when it was packed with pilgrims who had gathered for the saint's festival, a ready source of captives. Interestingly, he spared the churches and the hospital but not through any feelings of compassion or charity. It was a calculated move. Like some of the earlier Viking raiders, Guthfrith realised that allowing the monastery to continue to function would ensure that there was sufficient booty still being produced to make further raids lucrative.

It is easy to see why the Vikings were so feared. Faced with a vicious, pragmatic and, to the Irish, godless enemy who would time attacks to coincide with religious festivals, fear was the only natural reaction. It must have placed the devout in a terrible dilemma. Stay away from church and risk divine retribution or follow the path of the faithful and risk ending up a captive of the Vikings.

During this period of renewed activity there may have been as many as two hundred ships raiding in the north of Ireland. Many would have been under Guthfrith's direct control, although some would have been individuals trying their luck in the region. But Guthfrith's violent onslaught eventually failed due to the fierce resistance of the king of the Northern Uí Néill. Muirchertach was the son and successor of Niall Glúndubh, who had fallen during the battles with Sihtric Cáech only a few years before. Not only would Muirchertach expel the Vikings from Armagh, but in 925 he beheaded two hundred Viking prisoners captured in a battle at Carlingford.

In another example of Viking adaptability Guthfrith, having had little success against the Irish, turned his attention to a rival Viking encampment at Limerick. Unlike the Waterford Vikings who were under the control of his son, those at Limerick were operating completely independently. But his attempt to force them into submission failed, and a large number of his army were slain by their Scandinavian rivals.

In 927 Guthfrith was diverted from his Irish struggles by the death of his brother Sihtric and immediately left Dublin to claim York. But this too was not a wise move. He was soundly defeated, and, to add insult to injury, when he returned to Dublin he found that Tomar mac Ailche, the leader of his old adversaries the Limerick Vikings, had taken over the town. Guthfrith did manage to drive him out, but the Limerick fleets remained in the region, posing a permanent threat to the Dublin kingdom.

During a reign in which he seems to have had as many setbacks as victories, Guthfrith had a reputation for extreme violence. On his death he was described as 'a most cruel king of the Norsemen'. But was this description justified? Just north of Kilkenny is a cave that contains possible evidence for his brutality. Dunmore Cave is said in legend to be one of the darkest places in Ireland. Its ancient name is Dearc Fearna, or the Cave of the Alders.

Over the years, a lot of human bones have been found in Dunmore Cave. Some, discovered many years ago, have vanished into private collections, but when the remaining bones were analysed it became clear that the cave contained parts of at least forty-four skeletons. Of these, only nineteen were adults, mostly females. Of the twenty-five children, thirteen were under six years of age. None of the bones bore any marks to show how these people had died.

None of them were buried with any possessions and the cave contains no evidence of habitation. But the annals kept in Ireland during this period may provide a clue to explain this bizarre discovery.

In 930 the Annals of Ulster report the following incident:

Guthfrith, grandson of Ímar, with the foreigners of Áth Cliath, razed Derc Ferna – something unheard of from ancient times.

Ath Cliath is Dublin and the foreigners described here are, of course, Vikings. It seems highly unlikely that the Vikings intended to plunder and

Dunmore Cave was the site of a bloody Viking raid in the tenth century.

demolish the cave itself. But two Irish ring forts have been discovered close to the cave and it may have been these settlements that attracted the attention of Guthfrith and his Viking compatriots. The Limerick Vikings had been establishing relations with the Irish in this area and neither the Dublin nor the Waterford Vikings would have taken kindly to that.

Perhaps Guthfrith took an army down to Dearc Ferna to punish the native Irish. The Irish would have seen him approaching and known just what to expect. As the menfolk prepared themselves for battle, the women, children and elderly men would have run for the cave, hoping to evade capture. Hiding in its depths, they would have heard the sounds of a bloody battle, hoping and praying that if their kinfolk could not defeat these Vikings, they at least would remain safe, concealed in the blackness of the cave.

Unfortunately these Vikings were thorough. Having defeated the men at the ring forts they turned their attention to those hiding in the cave. For whatever reason, these people would not be taken off as captives. They may have been shut in and smothered, but it is more likely that the bloodthirsty Guthfrith simply ordered the slaughter of all the remaining inhabitants, leaving their corpses behind in the cave.

This gruesome story demonstrates just how violent life in the Viking Age could be. Yet despite Guthfrith's brutality, he failed to defeat any of the other bands of Vikings in Ireland and managed to lose York after the death of his brother Sihtric. But if he effectively failed, then his son and later descendants succeeded, going on to rule both York and Dublin, two towns that became closely associated under Viking rule.

A connection between these two settlements had existed long before the Viking Age. Similar styles of Bronze Age metalwork reveal tentative links between northern England and Ireland and according to Irish traditional tales many heroes led expeditions into northern Britain. Christianity was also brought to the people of Northumbria by Irish missionaries.

The Vikings, arriving at York in the early tenth century, would have noticed that it was quite different to the encampment they controlled in Dublin. York was a thriving merchant centre that had grown from the roots of a Roman fortress abandoned in the fifth century. In fact, York was something that no other settlement in Ireland could justify calling itself. York was a town.

The Scandinavians came from a land of farms and homesteads, a land which, with the exception of the embryonic Kaupang, had no real towns. The settlements developed by Viking pioneers on Shetland and Orkney reflect this Norwegian heritage. Prior to the tenth century, the native Irish had not developed the idea of towns either, but by the end of this century Dublin could justifiably be regarded as Ireland's first example. It is thought that the Vikings adopted the idea of a town from York but in Dublin, because they effectively had a clean sheet on which to start, we may be seeing the Scandinavian settlers' ideal town.

The second settlement at Dublin appears to have made no use of the existing *longphort*. The Vikings chose a new space on high ground between the River Liffey and its tributary, the River Poddle. This site could easily be defended against attacks from the native Irish and was initially surrounded by a low earth bank, replaced in 950 by a wooden wall topped with staves. These defences would remain largely unchanged until the Normans invaded Ireland in the twelfth century.

Within this second Viking settlement, excavations that began in 1962 and continued over the following decades have revealed much of the extent and layout of the Viking town as well as shedding light on its dwellings, its trades and crafts.

To the north, the town was bounded by the River Liffey, now much narrower than in Viking times due to a remarkable series of nine waterfronts which gradually pushed the south bank further out into the river between 900 and 1300. Among the streets of modern Dublin that excavation has shown to mirror their Viking predecessors is the peculiarly sinuous Fishamble Street. Here Pat Wallace, the director of the National Museum of Ireland and the excavator of much of Viking Dublin, explained to me that the buildings of the most recent redevelopment follow a road line laid out over a thousand years ago.

The town initially appears to have consisted of just a few buildings, but soon the settlers began to plan its expansion. Wattle fences marked out roughly rectangular plots within which houses were built, sometimes occupying almost the whole plot. Large-scale investigations, most notably on the Wood Quay site excavated between 1974 and 1981, have revealed the foundation plans of about two hundred buildings of tenth- and eleventh-century date. Like the plots they lay within, the houses are almost all rectangular, but with rounded corners and doors that allowed access at either end. Their walls were made of posts and woven wattle while much of the weight of the thatched or turfed roof was borne on stout interior wooden posts.

The excavation of so many buildings has led to the identification of a typical, almost standardised Dublin house. This has a central fireplace within a wide central aisle, flanked on either side by raised platforms that probably functioned as both beds and seats. The floors were usually built up from a combination of wood shavings, gravel and paving stones, rarely of wood.

Judging by the size of houses, the wealthier inhabitants of Viking Dublin seem to have made their homes further from the river, away from the risk of flooding. Closer to the river lay the houses of the more humble but, while these would never be very desirable during the Viking Age, their damp location has been a boon for today's archaeologists. Waterlogged ground conditions combined with a build-up of deposits over many years has resulted in the exceptional preservation of organic remains such as wood, plants, leather and textiles that can provide a rare insight into the everyday life of a Dublin Viking. In some cases the interiors of the houses were even found to contain the remains of bedding material. Thanks to the water, some of these bits of grass and other vegetation were still green when exposed by the excavators one thousand years after they had last been used.

Excavating waterlogged sites can be a very mixed experience. It is wonderful to come across objects that do not usually survive; somehow an axe is so much more of a real object when the iron head is still attached to its wooden handle. But there is also the realisation that the excavation itself is going to take much longer than that of a 'dry' site, that tools need to be used that will not damage the surface of delicate preserved artefacts, and that almost everything that is removed from the ground will require special treatment. Wood that has lain buried in waterlogged ground for a thousand years will start to deteriorate as soon as it is exposed to the air and will dry and crumble in days if not kept damp. Metal and other materials can behave in an unpredictable manner when exposed. The problems are immense, but so are the rewards.

Inside the houses excavated in Dublin were clues to many aspects of Viking life. Fragments of garments discovered during the excavation showed that clothing was usually made of wool. The men wore simple trousers, tunics over a shirt, and woollen cloaks. The better-off would splash out on furs and hides and one edging of imported silk embroidered with gold thread was also found. Shoes were flat and low, unlike the boots uncovered in other Viking towns. Heels were deemed unnecessary and the laces were thongs of leather.

Women usually wore a shift, made of wool or linen, over which a dress was draped and held in place with brooches at the shoulder. The archaeologists also found many silk caps and neckerchiefs that would have helped to stop the coarse fabrics used in the clothes from chafing the neck. For warmth, the outfit could be topped off with a cloak, also fastened with a brooch. It is likely that both sexes, at least from the wealthy classes, wore underwear but, as it was probably of linen, a material that rarely survives burial, this is one aspect of Viking dress that will have to remain a mystery.

As well as the houses that were lived in by the Viking inhabitants of Dublin, the excavations revealed many of their workshops. In these, a wide range of crafts and industries could be identified from both tools of trade and discarded waste products. There must have been many more workers, though, whose products have not survived: bakers and brewers, and those who made the nets, ropes and sails so vital for a seafaring economy. Wood too was vital to the Vikings, for houses and boats, planks and barrels as well as for smaller everyday items, and waterlogged Dublin has provided abundant evidence of the Vikings' skill with wood. Within this group of craftsmen there is evidence of specialisation, the coopers making barrels, buckets and churns, the turners fashioning bowls and cups, spoons and ladles.

Dublin was also home to many metalworkers, from the numerous blacksmiths who forged weapons, tools and the nails that were such a crucial element of shipbuilding, to those who worked in more precious metals. Bronze, silver and gold were all used in the manufacture of personal ornaments such as pins, buckles, brooches and rings. The workshops where these items were made can be recognised from tell-tale finds of moulds, crucibles, and metal ingots as well as scraps and droplets of metal and traces of slag. Perhaps these were the workshops where loot from raided monasteries was melted down or where book clasps ripped from holy books were turned into brooches for fashionable Viking women.

Beads were popular as decoration, the more brightly coloured the better. The raw glass was sometimes imported, but often fragments of broken glass utensils were fused together to create intricate patterns in the beads. Amber was often used in pendants and other jewellery and one of the most convincing workshops discovered during the excavation was of an amber craftsman of Fishamble Street. Although no tools were found, the workshop was littered with hundreds of chips and unworked lumps of solid amber.

Apart from these comparatively exotic materials, there were substantial industries based on animal by-products. The waste from shoe manufacture provides evidence of leatherworking that would have required the skills of the tanner before reaching this stage. Spindles and whorls, weaving equipment and needles of bronze and bone are the tools that produced the fragments of textiles found in the waterlogged excavation sites of Dublin. Large numbers of carved bone pieces, used to give examples of available

The excavations of Viking Dublin revealed many artefacts, including these bone needles.

styles, were found in the metal workshops while both bone and antler were used to make combs and comb cases, pins, needles, spoons and even whistles.

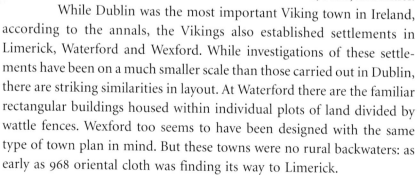

Music was popular and as well as whistles made from the leg bones of birds, harps and pipes might be used to accompany stories and poetry recitals around a roaring fire in the depths of winter. Bone provides more evidence for the Vikings at play as the leg bones of horses were used to make the blades of ice skates. The Vikings also appear to have had a fondness for board games, and bone was used to make pieces for games like *hnefatafl* in which the object is to surround your opponent's king piece.

The artefacts discovered in the houses show that Dublin was undoubtedly a thriving trading town. As well as being ideally situated for defence, it was the perfect location from which to conduct commerce throughout the Irish Sea and beyond. But Dublin could not exist without supplies from the Irish countryside that surrounded it. Farms provided bread, meat and a plentiful supply of wool. Few millstones were found within the Dublin excavations, so it seems likely that flour rather than grain was brought into the town. As well as essential food, the countryside could also provide the townspeople with raw materials such as wood, bone, and antler.

Viking Dublin was a busy trading centre. These scales would have been used to weigh out silver for payment.

While Dublin was the most important Viking town in Ireland, according to the annals, the Vikings also established settlements in Limerick, Waterford and Wexford. While investigations of these settlements have been on a much smaller scale than those carried out in Dublin, there are striking similarities in layout. At Waterford there are the familiar rectangular buildings housed within individual plots of land divided by wattle fences. Wexford too seems to have been designed with the same type of town plan in mind. But these towns were no rural backwaters: as early as 968 oriental cloth was finding its way to Limerick.

Although the various Viking settlements in Ireland may have conducted their own internal trade, there are finds from Dublin that must have originated from much farther afield. Exotic objects, such as silver and a silk hairnet, suggest Viking trade networks to the Near East,

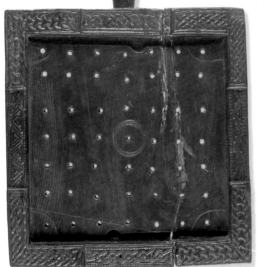

The Viking game of hnefatafl was played on this board found at Balinderry, Ireland.

soapstone was imported from Scotland, walrus ivory from the far north, while the amber that was so popular for jewellery came from as far away as the Baltic Sea.

Soon Dublin became the richest port on the Irish Sea and was reckoned by some to be one of the richest in Western Europe. By this time the Vikings were a force to be reckoned with on an international scale. The kings of Francia had been defending themselves against raiding Vikings since as early as 885 when a Viking fleet arrived on the River Seine. Their leader, Rollo, eventually made peace with the Frankish King Charles the Simple, accepted his authority and converted to Christianity. In exchange Rollo was made the count of Rouen, becoming the first leader of Normandy.

Even before the raids around the North Sea region, Viking warriors, mostly from Sweden, had headed east where they were given the name Rus by the local population. This is the origin of Russia, a country that was named after these early Scandinavian pioneers. As early as the seventh century, Scandinavians were in the Baltic Sea area and by the early ninth century they had developed trading relationships with the Arabs along the Volga and with the Byzantines of Constantinople. They were probably trading furs in return for Arab silver, large quantities of which have since been found in Sweden.

With contacts in so many places, it is not surprising that Viking commerce thrived. Dublin reflects the cosmopolitan nature of Viking society, where goods from many regions were exchanged. It also brought commercial trading to Ireland. Many Scandinavian words concerned with commerce and ships were adopted by the Irish, such as market (*margad*), pedlar (*mangiare*), tax (*mal*), ship (*cnarr*), anchor (*acaire*), and rudder (*stiúir*). All these can be traced back to Old Norse roots.

Trading links with England were also strong. The Vikings were importing weapons from London, tin from Cornwall, salt from Cheshire, and pottery from both Chester and Norwich. Coins found during the Dublin excavations came from mints in York, Oxford, London, Exeter, Norwich, Chester and Canterbury.

The Dublin Vikings also produced Ireland's first local coinage in 997.

But these coins, together with various imports, would not have been used in quite the same way as modern currency. Instead, it was the weight of silver that was used to decide prices, hence the many weights and balances that are found both in Dublin and other Viking sites. In the Viking Age, a merchant could not begin to trade until he had his own weights and scales, as all commerce relied on the exchange of precise amounts of silver. More often than not a Viking trader would use as currency small pieces chopped off an armband or necklace he happened to be wearing. These small pieces of what is known as 'hacksilver' are found throughout the Viking world, where coins too might be chopped up to ensure that just the right weight of silver was exchanged.

It seems a strange idea, wearing your money in the form of jewellery and hacking bits off when you need to make a purchase. It is fascinating to look at the cut marks on a fragment of decorated armband and think about the haggling that probably went on. How many times was the knife blade positioned and repositioned over the silver before the price was finally agreed, and what was the purchase?

Sets of scales, together with their lead weights, have been found in graves across the Viking world. The weights discovered during the Dublin excavations were found to conform to a standard equal to 26.6 grams. The original element was actually taken from the Latin word *aureus*, meaning 'of gold'. This was the *eyrir*, which started its life as a gold standard of about 26.4 grams, although it was reduced to about 24.5 grams by the end of the Viking Age.

The first silver standard was the *ertog*. Its weight of about 8 grams was probably taken from a late-fourth-century Roman coin. The Frankish denier and the Arabic half-*dirhem* both weighed about the same as the Anglo-Saxon *penning*. The Vikings took this weight for their *penningar*; these were the equivalent of pennies and 240 of them were the equivalent of one ertog.

Because it was the weight of the silver that was of paramount importance, coins needed to be weighed just like any other piece of silver. Coins themselves were sometimes used as weights, but only when their own purity and value had been confirmed.

The Vikings brought a large quantity of silver into Ireland, both as coins and jewellery, and would often bury their valuables in the ground for safety. But for whatever reason, some were never recovered by their original owners and over 130 silver hoards have been found in Ireland. Some comprised only silver ingots, others contained arm rings and ornaments, while a few also contained coins.

A large number of the hoards without coins are thought to have been buried between 850 and 905. This is well before the establishment of the trading town of Dublin and suggests that the early Scandinavian settlers had already accumulated significant wealth. It may be that the early *longphort*, as well as a raiding base, was also the focus of lucrative trade with the local population.

The hoards which included coins seem to have been buried mainly during the tenth century and it is interesting to note just where they were discovered. About three-quarters of them were buried in northern Leinster, a region which encompasses parts of three Irish kingdoms. Most importantly, these areas remained under Irish control for nearly all of the early Viking Age so it seems that these hoards cannot have been buried solely by Viking hands. The Irish must have been obtaining large quantities of silver as well.

There is further evidence to support this idea in the development of metalworking traditions in Ireland. Silver brooches become a much more common product of Irish craftsmen in the second half of the ninth century. This is probably due to the fact that there was more silver available during this period, and the most likely source of this silver is the Scandinavian settlers.

Quite how the Irish managed to get their hands on so much Viking silver is not entirely clear but it may have been due to a combination of factors. Both the Irish and the Vikings probably collected, and paid, tribute to reinforce political alliances. An exchange of gifts might help to form a lasting bond between a Viking leader and an Irish king, while a tribute might enlist the help of another kingdom in battle. Although many hoards have been found in Irish-controlled areas, these are usually the same areas that had frequent contact with Scandinavian settlers, such as the kingdom of Leinster, and the region around Limerick.

The Irish may have obtained some of their wealth through trade with the Vikings although, with the exception of food, they had little of any great value to trade. The amber, jet and other precious stones which the Vikings collected on their travels were not found in Ireland, nor could the Irish offer the furs and other goods given by the Lapps and Slavs to the Vikings as tribute. In fact, the most valuable commodity the Irish could barter with was people. Much of the silver found in Irish hoards may well have been the profits of the slave trade.

At this time slaves existed throughout medieval Europe, although they were not as economically important to society as those of ancient Rome, or the plantations in the Americas. And not all of the slaves in medieval Europe would have been slaves in the modern sense of the word. Groups within society who could be said not to be free included serfs as well as slaves.

In Viking Age Scandinavia, the word *thrall* was often used to describe someone we would today label a slave. There are no substantial written records from this period, but the law codes from the twelfth to the four-teenth centuries give many different categories of subservient people. Some were merely servants, while others inherited their slave status from their parents. Debt slavery may also have existed, although those caught in this trap would not have been true slaves. Their slavery was not for life but for a fixed term and would expire when their debt was paid.

In Norway, the law codes make clear distinctions between native-born slaves and foreign slaves, with captives from foreign parts more likely to be pressed into service back in the Viking homelands. Capture of adults may have been the preferred method of obtaining slaves, avoiding the extra cost of supporting a slave child from birth. It has even been suggested, although it cannot be confirmed, that the children of slaves in Iceland were regularly left outside to die of exposure. A practice like this would certainly require a constant supply of adult slaves from elsewhere.

Many of these slaves may have come from Ireland although the Vikings probably did not approach this land with the aim of slave trading. As in England, the first attacks were on monasteries and other wealthy targets, in search of silver and gold. However, the raiders did not always discover quite as many riches as they might have liked and so hostage-taking seems to have started. The Irish Annals record many such incidents by both Vikings and the Irish. Bishops were taken in 824 and 845 and in both cases it is likely that the Vikings demanded ransom payment for the return of these high-ranking individuals. It was only when the Vikings had a permanent base in Ireland that they could begin taking captives on a larger scale. While hit-and-run raiding enabled the Vikings to walk off with portable church treasures, it was less easy to sail away quickly with large numbers of prisoners. But once Olaf had made a secure base for himself at the early Dublin *longphort*, slave raiding could begin in earnest. The Irish were beginning to threaten the Vikings during the second half of the ninth century, so it was also an ideal time for Olaf to demonstrate his strength. He did not restrict his attentions to the Irish, though. At this time no one was safe from Olaf who, during his period of raiding in Scotland in 870, took English, Welsh and Pictish prisoners back to Dublin as slaves.

Other Viking leaders also started abducting the natives. Between 821 and 1032 there are twenty-three entries in the annals describing the taking of prisoners *en masse*. As it would not be feasible to ransom so many people, they most probably found themselves traded as slaves. Mass abduction may well have begun as a means of intimidation. What better way to demonstrate your power than to walk off with a large number of your opponent's subjects?

Slave raiding was also popular with the Viking settlers of tenth-century Dublin. Olaf Godfredson had taken control of the Dublin Vikings, but soon found himself under attack by the Irish and needed some spectacular victories in order to regain control. In 939 Olaf captured and ransomed one of the attacking Irish kings for an undisclosed but no doubt enormous sum. Later in the year the Irish were drawn into the slave-taking raids when the Waterford Norse joined forces with an Irish leader to attack another Irish king at Meath. Included among the captives were two abbots, presumably captured for ransom. One of these captives ended up in Dublin, perhaps sold to the Vikings there when ransom money was not forthcoming. The unfortunate abbot was kept prisoner on Dalkey Island, but drowned when trying to escape.

Slavery was not introduced into Ireland by the Vikings, even though it is only in the Viking Age that the annals record the taking of large numbers of captives. And raiding was not always a simple matter of Viking raiding Irish. Norse settlers were abducted by the Irish, possibly in retaliation for Viking raids, and the Irish were quite capable of turning on their own people, as witnessed by the attack on Meath.

There are many stories describing the journeys of people who were abducted as slaves. One Irishman who found himself in the clutches of the slave traders was the monk Findan. His story is told in a Latin work completed in Germany towards the end of the ninth century: the *Vita*

Findani. Findan's tale begins with the abduction of his sister, and many other women, from their Irish home by the 'foreigners who are called Northmen'. When Findan attempts to ransom his sister, he too is kidnapped, but manages to persuade his captors to release him.

Not long afterwards he attends a banquet organised by a Leinster chieftain – perhaps a little naïve of our monk as this chief had previously killed Findan's father and brother. Not surprisingly he is captured once more, this time by Vikings working in collaboration with the Irish chief, and is taken away to the Orkney Islands. During a battle at sea Findan has his shackles removed, and seizes this moment to escape. He decides 'to endure the frenzy of the sea rather than to fall into the hands of men who surpassed the beasts in all their savagery'. In a moment of rare good luck Findan meets with a bishop who was educated in Ireland, finishes his monastic training and ends his days in piety.

Another Irishman even found his abduction translated into a satirical poem. Moriuht was an Irish poet who, together with his wife, was captured by Vikings. The couple are separated and Moriuht ends up in a Northumbrian nunnery where his behaviour is less than acceptable. Having seduced one too many nuns he is expelled but captured again, and this time sold to a widow in Saxony. Needless to say, this woman also succumbs to Moriuht's powers of seduction. Eventually, after a long journey, and several more adventures, he is reunited with his family in Ireland.

Despite the many written records, both in the annals and in story form, it is difficult to find any archaeological evidence for the Irish slave trade. In the National Museum of Ireland in Dublin there is an evocative display of iron chains and shackles found together with a skull showing clear signs of sword cuts. To some archaeologists these are positive evidence, of both captivity and brutal treatment, and I could think of no other explanation for the shackles but to restrain captives. But until recently there was little else to support the historical records.

Two years ago I was invited by archaeologist Michael Connolly to become involved in the excavation of Cloghermore Cave near Tralee in County Kerry. Some human bones had been found in the cave and the initial suggestion was that they dated from the Neolithic period, about 3000 BC. At first the only way to reach the part of the cave where the bones had

These shackles might have been used on captured slaves.

been found, two chambers nicknamed 'the grave-yard' and 'the two star temple', was to crawl through from one side of a limestone hill to the other. But shortly after I joined Michael's team the original cave entrance was located and cleared, making access much easier. The entrance was built up with drystone walls and had been finally capped with a large stone slab, all of which looked exactly like the entrances to Neolithic stone-built tombs.

The interior of the cave was extraordinarily beautiful. The stalactites and stalagmites, the result of thousands of years of dripping water, make the rock look more like a living creature than something cold and dead. It seemed a very appropriate place to bury the dead, deep in the rock, and there were bones everywhere we looked. It was difficult to recognise whole skeletons, though; the most that could be identified were the odd limb or section of backbone. It appeared that the bones had been dispersed and another immediate impression was that there were too few fragments of skull. Quite simply, there were not enough heads to go round. But all this fitted with the initial interpretation, that Cloghermore Cave was some sort of Neolithic burial site.

It took a while for this idea to be questioned. The bones had obviously been underground for a very long time; some were fused to the walls and floor of the cave by flowstone, which takes centuries to accumulate. But there were lots of lumps of charcoal among the bones and, more disturbingly, an iron object was found close to the blocked entrance. At least this had prepared Michael for the first radiocarbon date from the cave. It was not 3000 BC but some time in the ninth century AD. Michael's response to this news was unprintable but the date raised some fascinating questions. What were these burials doing in a cave at a time when Ireland was Christian? Why weren't these people in a churchyard somewhere, laid out east to west and still with their heads?

The explanation was still being sought in terms of residual pagan beliefs when a small hoard of silver was found in a corner of the cave. The hoard contained tiny silver ingots and pieces of hacksilver, suggesting that the Vikings had appeared on the scene. Suddenly the bodies in the cave were perhaps victims of the Vikings who were recorded as raiding in the area in the late ninth and early tenth centuries. What Michael had discovered at Cloghermore Cave seemed very similar to the finds at Dearc Ferna, Dunmore Cave, with its story of Viking massacre.

But there was still no full explanation of why these bodies should be in a cave, together with lots of charcoal, some animal bones and now a hoard of Viking silver. The answer emerged towards the end of the excavation when a skeleton, complete except for its head, was found buried close to the cave entrance. Within the shallow grave was a fine bronze pin of a type only worn by Vikings and most probably made in Dublin. This man was the last person to be buried in the cave; its entrance was then sealed and remained so for over a thousand years. So what was the story of the Vikings and Cloghermore Cave?

Despite Christianity being the 'official' religion in Ireland at this time, it is possible that the cave was still being used as a place of burial by people who were still effectively pagans. As such, it would be an appropriate place of burial for a Viking who had died far from home. He was obviously buried with appropriate ceremony: the charcoal and animal bones are evidence of a funerary feast and traces of the fire were found close to the cave entrance. But there are two remaining puzzles. What happened to the head of the Viking? There are no traces on the remaining part of the skeleton to show that it was chopped off but maybe it was carefully removed and taken back home by the companions who buried him. And who did the bones that were scattered in the cave belong to? They may just have been local pagans but the Viking connection does raise the possibility that they were captives or slaves and that to them the cave may have been more of a grim prison than a peaceful place of burial.

To the Vikings, slaving was a part of their international interests. In the 860s a Viking raid in the Mediterranean resulted in the capture of a number of Moors, referred to as 'blue men', and Arab records describe how the Rus, Scandinavian settlers in the Baltic, would often have slave girls.

One Arab merchant who was travelling on the River Volga in the tenth century has left us a description of a Viking funeral.

When a chief has died his family asks his slave women and slaves, 'Who will die with him?' Then one of them says, 'I will.' When she has said this there is no backing out . . . most of those who agree are women slaves . . .

These slave women were highly unlucky. Human sacrifice was practised in the Viking world, but it was certainly not expected that a woman would end her life at her husband's death. Women actually enjoyed a relatively large amount of freedom and were clearly able to hold high-status positions within society. The 'Pagan Lady' from the Isle of Man was buried with lavish goods and the Oseberg boat burial is the most impressive grave find from the Viking Age. It too belongs to a woman.

As an important part of Viking society, some Viking women may have found their way to Ireland, although many Vikings probably took Irish wives. In the Viking cemeteries in Dublin there appears to be perhaps one female settler for every ten men. But Scandinavian women most certainly went to Iceland and Greenland, remote uninhabited islands that were settled by whole communities.

The *Landmanabok*, the Icelandic Book of Settlements, lists over four hundred of the pioneers, including their ancestry and descendants. Although most of them are from western Norway, there are many who came from the Norse communities in Ireland and the Northern Isles. However, even though the majority were of Scandinavian descent, some Irish and Scottish names also find their way into the book. These may be slaves who were taken to the new colonies by Norse settlers and were then given farms by their owners.

A recent study into the genetic ancestry of the Icelandic population has added weight to this idea. Agnar Helgason is an Icelander working at Oxford University. He teamed up with deCODE Genetics of Iceland, Ryk Ward and Bryan Sykes of Oxford University, and Dan Bradley of Trinity College Dublin to examine just how the Icelanders' DNA was influenced by these early settlers. Looking at the Y chromosome of men in Iceland, they hoped to determine what percentage of these men had Scandinavian DNA signatures present. The Icelanders' DNA was compared with that in Y chromosomes from Scandinavians, and also with Y chromosomes from Ireland and Scotland. The team identified a 'Gaelic' DNA signature that was found on both Irish and Scottish Y chromosomes. When they looked at the Icelandic DNA they found that most of the men had Norse ancestry but a significant number, somewhere between 20 and 25 per cent, had Gaelic ancestry.

Where did this Gaelic ancestry come from? This study only looked at the male Y chromosome, so the DNA which the researchers were exam-

This was the site of the Norse Thingvellir, in Iceland

ining was only passed down from father to son. The results mean that some of the Icelandic settlers must have been Gaelic men, perhaps the descendants of freed Irish slaves.

Looking at the Y chromosome allowed Agnar to trace the paternal heritage of the Icelanders back to the first male settlers. A second study revealed that their maternal ancestry is even more interesting. This study looked at mitochondial (mt) DNA, passed on to a baby from its mother with no genetic input from the father. So, by examining this particular section of the Icelanders' DNA, their maternal roots could also be traced.

The mtDNA showed that the Icelanders' maternal heritage was different to their paternal ancestry. The results suggested that about half of the Icelanders' female ancestors were Gaelic. So a much larger proportion of the early female settlers came from Ireland or Scotland than did the men. Although some of these women may also have been slaves, the larger number of Gaelic women settling in Iceland might be explained by Norse settlers from Dublin and the Northern Isles bringing along their native wives.

While the Dublin Vikings who found their way to Iceland would have to face a new land and a harsh climate, those left behind in Ireland faced different problems. The battles with the Irish continued and, with the

Vikings' resources perhaps spread too thinly, the Irish gradually regained control.

Sihtric Silkbeard led the Dublin Vikings during their decline. The Irish leader Maél Sechnaill controlled the town, and Sihtric ruled under him. In 997 Brian Boru and Maél Sechnaill divided Ireland between them, with Brian taking control of Dublin. Sihtric attempted to throw off his leadership, but was defeated, agreeing to give tribute to Brian and even marrying one of his daughters. By 1004 Brian was High King of All Ireland, receiving tribute from Irish and Viking leaders alike.

In Irish legend it is Brian Boru who finally freed Ireland from the hands of the Vikings. The Battle of Clontarf in 1014 is said to be the final battle but in reality it was probably just another skirmish in the continuing conflict. By this time Brian was far too old to fight, and was content to let his son lead their followers into battle.

Although the Dublin Vikings would not actually take part in the battle, the conflict had been engineered by Sihtric Silkbeard. He had first allied with Maél Mórda of Leinster in an unsuccessful coalition against the overlordship of Brian Boru. But then, in 1014, he brought together Maél Mórda and Sigurd the Stout, the leader of the Vikings in Orkney. These two decided to take on Brian Boru.

The results of this conflict were bloody. Both Sigurd and Maél Mórda fell in battle and Brian too was cut down by a Viking from the Isle of Man. Sihtric Silkbeard was probably quite pleased at seeing his overlord killed; it may even have been one of his aims in setting up the battle. But his manoeuvring would be in vain as, when Brian's tributary kings began to fight among themselves, it was Maél Sechnaill who would triumph, leaving Dublin once again in Irish hands.

Sihtric would continue to fight for his independence, but the dividing line between Irish and Viking was becoming blurred. By this time Norse settlers had been given the name 'Ostmen' by the Irish, to distinguish them from the true Norse who still lived in the Scandinavian homelands. Most of the Ostmen had now adopted Christianity and Sihtric himself even made a pilgrimage to Rome.

The Ostmen spoke Norse peppered with Gaelic words, and some began to speak only the Irish tongue. Their trading empire had made them wealthy enough for the payment of tribute to whichever Irish leader was in power to be no great hardship. A mercenary Norse fleet was also available to the

Irish for hire, as well as Viking warriors. Gradually any distinction between those of Scandinavian or native Irish ancestry was lost.

Not least due to the powerful Irish mythology, the Irish of today probably would not consider themselves to have Scandinavian links. Yet the Vikings controlled most of the Irish Sea area throughout the ninth and tenth centuries. They brought the idea of a town to Ireland. Their trading empire made the local Irish rich, and left behind many words first introduced by Viking merchants. If the Vikings had never arrived in Ireland, Celtic DNA would probably not today be found as far north as Iceland. Although the obvious Scandinavian nature of the settlers would gradually fade away, the Vikings played a crucial role in the history of Ireland.

CHAPTER 8

THE GREAT ARMY

Here the raiding-army went from East Anglia . . . to York city in Northumbria; . . . they gathered a great army and sought out the raiding-army at York city and broke into the city, and some of them got inside; and an immense slaughter was made of the Northumbrians there, some inside, some outside, and both the kings were killed, and the survivors made peace with the raiding-army.

ANGLO-SAXON CHRONICLE, 867

LEFT | *The Great Army crossed the North Sea from Denmark, arriving in Britain in the ninth century.*

The Vikings had managed to gain a serious foothold in Ireland. They had founded the town of Dublin, controlled Limerick and Waterford and had become a powerful force in the Irish Sea region. We know that the Dublin Vikings had significant interests in the English town of York, but what of the rest of England? How was it faring against the Viking onslaught?

At the end of the eighth century when Viking raids had first started along the English and Irish coasts, both countries were far from united. England consisted of several separate kingdoms, each with its own ruler, and so East Anglia, Mercia, Wessex and Northumbria all faced their own Viking threat alone. As early as 792, the King of Mercia appears to have issued a charter to provide a means for defence against 'pagans' who were threatening his kingdom but, on the whole, the records suggest that the English kingdoms suffered far less at this time than those in Ireland.

Yet it seems that the Scandinavians must eventually have made serious inroads into England. Place-names in the north and east of the country often have Scandinavian roots, both Danish and Norse, while excavations in York have revealed a town that expanded rapidly after the arrival of the Vikings. These excavations uncovered tools used in a wide range of crafts and imported goods from across the whole of Europe. In many ways, Viking York was very similar to Viking Dublin.

York could have been a single strong Viking outpost in England, perhaps run by a few powerful Scandinavians, without many actually settling there. Or the development of the Viking town could have been merely one part of a greater process of mass migration from the Viking homelands. In view of the evidence from place-names the mass migration idea seems more likely, yet archaeological evidence for a Scandinavian presence is generally sparse and physical traces of Scandinavian settlements are virtually non-existent.

Over the past few decades the picture has begun to change as museums across Britain have been inundated with finds of metal objects, about 15,000 new finds every year in Norfolk alone. The majority of these finds are uncovered by members of the public using metal detectors and a good proportion of them are from the Viking period.

As an archaeologist, I have very mixed views on metal detectors. I have worked alongside a detector user on site and the archaeological research benefited from the tiny finds that would almost certainly have been lost if the detector had not been used. I realise that Mark Redknap's fascinating site on Anglesey would not have been found and investigated had it not been for the first finds being reported to his museum. But equally I have seen the damage caused to archaeological sites, seen antiquities on sale that should have been in museums for all to study and enjoy and have suffered the frustration of trying to protect important sites from systematic looting.

Despite my strong reservations, it cannot be denied that the metal objects of Viking date that are found and, more importantly, reported under what is known as the Portable Antiquities Scheme, are starting to change our understanding of patterns of Viking settlement. Among the objects are many brooches in a Scandinavian style that may help us to understand the nature of the contact across the North Sea and to locate the Viking settlements that up to now have remained invisible within the archaeological record.

Finding personal possessions such as weapons or jewellery in a grave can be explained as being part of the Vikings' pagan beliefs. They were there for the dead to use in the afterlife. Similarly, it should not be too surprising to find large quantities of artefacts in excavated towns like York and Dublin since historical records tell us that people were living in these places. But how do we explain the discovery of individual pieces of jewellery, ornaments and pieces of horse harness scattered across the north and east of England?

These objects do not appear to have come from burials, and were most probably lost by their original owners during the course of everyday life. But who *were* the original owners? Only rarely can archaeology tell us the history of a particular item, for example the Alfred Jewel, inscribed with the king's name. But style and ornament can be used to suggest the taste of the owner and can perhaps point a finger at a particular group of people. There is no doubt that many of the metal objects that have been reported have been in a Scandinavian style; so were they therefore lost by Scandinavians? This is a possibility, but not a certainty. They may equally well have belonged to Anglo-Saxons.

Like the native Irish, the Anglo-Saxons are likely to have traded with Scandinavian settlers and may have received these objects as part of a process of exchange, or even as gifts. How we view these objects affects our view of the extent to which Scandinavian settlers spread out around the country. It may not have been the Vikings who reached the place where a piece of jewellery was found. Instead, an Anglo-Saxon trader may have visited York, or even Dublin, and brought the goods back, perhaps as a present for his wife or daughter. And if the jewellery changed hands once, twice, or even three or more times, then the Scandinavian connection may be even more distant.

There is also a third possibility. Many of the brooches that have been found are not of a particularly high quality and are certainly not up to the standards of craftsmanship found in York or Dublin. Perhaps the Anglo-Saxon traders could not afford the better quality goods, or perhaps these brooches were not even made by a Viking craftsman. Maybe the inferior quality of the metalwork was the result of an Anglo-Saxon craftsman trying his hand at a new style or design. It may have been Scandinavian culture that was spreading across Britain rather than Scandinavian people. But separating the movements of people from the movement of culture is a difficult task – perhaps the large number of Scandinavian artefacts really does indicate a significant influx of Scandinavian people.

Despite these difficulties a find is sometimes made that tells an unambiguous story of foreign lands, like the small metal object found by detectorist Kevin Canham in 1999. Unsure of what it might be, he took

This bronze handle would have been attached to a small piece of iron and used as a strike-a-light, the Viking equivalent of a box of matches or a cigarette lighter.

the object to the Norfolk Museums Service where it was identified as part of a bronze handle in the shape of two horses and a rider. It would have been attached to a small piece of iron and used as a strike-a-light, the Viking equivalent of a box of matches or a cigarette lighter. Strike-a-lights were used by Scandinavians in Norway and Finland, but were most popular in Russia. Perhaps this one, the first to be found in Britain, was brought here by a Viking who had also spent time in Russia.

The first step in attempting to disentangle the spread of Scandinavian culture from the movements of the people themselves is to return to the history books. After the initial period of raiding in the late eighth century, the Anglo-Saxon Chronicle reports little Viking activity in the early years of the ninth. But then, in the 830s, the threat returns with various raids reported in England. Hit-and-run affairs, with victories for both the English and the Scandinavians, these attacks are just an extension of what had begun with the raid on Lindisfarne in 793. But by the middle of the ninth century the Vikings were no longer just carrying out isolated raids.

The new threat to England came from Danish Vikings and the conflict escalated in 850 when the Vikings spent their first winter in England, setting up camp on Thanet. Four years later a group over-wintered on Sheppey and in both years the Chronicler noted these more lengthy stays as important events. The Danes were changing their tactics and rather than simply carrying off whatever they could find of value, were probably beginning to consider the possibility of trying to take and hang on to some land of their own.

The size of the Viking forces was on the increase too and although the Chronicler does not always provide specific numbers, the use of the word 'great' is significant. In 865 the first 'Great Army' marks the arrival of more Danes than had previously been seen in England.

And the same year a great heathen raiding-army came to the land of the English and took winter-quarters from the East Anglians, and were provided with horses there, and they made peace with them.

These Danish Vikings had certainly been raiding in Francia, and it seems some had decided to try their luck in England. Their arrival in East Anglia launches a campaign that was to last for decades and the East Angles found themselves the first of many to have to 'make peace with' the Great

Army. The idea was that the Danes would leave them alone on payment of tribute, and in this case it is very significant that the Chronicles specifically mention horses. These were crucial to the Great Army's campaign.

Danish Viking graves often include stirrups, bridle mounts and other horse harness and the Danes would certainly have brought their expertise in horsemanship with them to England. Horses, like those supplied by the East Anglians, were to play a large part in the Great Army's campaigns, providing the same mobility on land as the Vikings' agile ships did on water. Mobility was a vital element in the Vikings' tactics and horses were the quickest and easiest way to move around Britain.

The Danes did not however fight on horseback; they were effectively mounted infantry, using their horses as a means of transport rather than as cavalry. This is clear from contemporary descriptions of battles at which the Vikings arrive on horseback and then dismount to begin the combat. This might seem to be a waste of the tactical advantage that cavalry might have provided, but the Danes would have developed fighting techniques that were appropriate for foot soldiers, and that could not easily be translated to horseback.

Riding a horse into battle is no easy matter. Both rider and horse need to be experienced in mounted warfare and it is not every animal that can stay under control in a noisy and violent battlefield. Horses would have had to be specially trained and, since the Danes often seemed to gather their mounts as they travelled, the chances of finding well-drilled cavalry horses were slim.

In the following year, 866, the raiding-army left for York on their East Anglian horses, arriving to find the kingdom of Northumbria in disarray. One king had been expelled and the people had accepted a seemingly unsuitable replacement, described by one contemporary source as 'an unnatural king', and by another as not actually being a member of the royal family.

In the midst of this internal conflict, the Great Army gathered at the city gate and eventually the people of York took note.

It was late in the year when they turned to making war against the raiding-army, nevertheless they gathered a great army and sought out the raiding-army in York city and broke into the city, and some of them got inside; and an immense slaughter was made of the Northumbrians there, some inside, some outside, and both the

The Vikings may have introduced the English to stirrups. This one was found at Kilverstone, Norfolk.

This twelfth century tapestry portrays a Viking on horseback. They used horses to move quickly around the country, allowing them to mount surprise attacks.

kings were killed, and the survivors made peace with the raiding-army.

With both of their potential leaders now dead, the Northumbrians were forced to put themselves in the hands of the Danes. With their sights set on further conquests in English territories, the Danes left an Anglo-Saxon puppet king in charge. In this manner the city was successfully run for over a decade, providing the Great Army with an essential base from which to conduct the rest of their campaign.

One of the leaders of the Great Army was called Halfdan, but apart from his name, little is known about him. Indeed, the 'Great Army' itself is a bit of a mystery. The only sources we have are the Anglo-Saxon Chronicles, in which the raiding-army plays an important part, and an account of the life of Alfred the Great, who would become involved in the fight against the Danes. Chronicles kept in Francia also refer to raiders at this time, but the Frankish chroniclers very rarely use the word army to describe these raiding bands.

In the Great Army, we may have found an explanation for the metal finds scattered across Norfolk as this area of England certainly fell into Danish hands in the ninth century. There are other finds, though, that could possibly be more closely linked to the Great Army itself.

A ninth-century sword, found in the River Wensum in Norwich, may have been lost by one of its members or may have been deliberately deposited in the river as part of a funeral rite. Swords were highly prized possessions and a Viking warrior would have treasured his most important weapon. On his death, his companions might sacrifice his sword, first bending the blade to 'kill' the weapon, before hurling it into a river.

One aspect of these new invaders which all the record books seem to agree on is that these Vikings came from Denmark. By the ninth century the Danish kingdom included part of northern Germany, and the Danes had a degree of control over local rulers in western and northern Norway. Whether the Great Army was connected with the ruling families of Denmark is not clear, although some of the leaders of raiding bands may have been banished members of the Danish royal family. Having lost their position in society to more forceful rivals, these Danes may have decided to try their luck overseas. But even when engaged in a life of raiding it seems that these Danes may still have been at least partly under the control of the rulers of their homeland. In 838 the Danish king assured the Emperor Louis that the pirates who had plundered in Francia the previous year would be captured and executed.

Other Viking bands were probably led by local chieftains, who, joining with landowners or farmers to create a small flotilla of ships, set out on raiding missions to supplement their income. Some may have returned to their homeland after a single raid, while others might have continued to raid year after year. The Viking forces that became known as the Great Army may have been forced into exile, or might have decided to leave, to try their luck abroad. Whatever their reason for leaving, by the late ninth century they were probably experienced warriors and the Danes who made up the Great Army would have become well armed professional pirates.

This ninth-century sword, found in the River Wensum, Norwich, may have belonged to a warrior in the Danish Great Army.

There were probably a number of different leaders involved in the Danish raiding-army that arrived in Britain in 865. As well as Halfdan, Ivar and Ubba appear in accounts of the early conflicts. Reinforcements, probably under other Danish leaders, are noted as arriving at various stages during the years in which the Great Army is attacking Britain but deciphering the relationship between these various groups is complicated by the shortage of written records.

Even the overall size of the Great Army is a subject for debate. The description 'great army' appears in the Anglo-Saxon Chronicles applied to the forces that arrived in 865, 871 and 892. To have warranted this name, these armies must have been significantly larger than those that had been seen raiding in earlier years, but precise size is impossible to calculate. Smaller fleets, usually engaged in raids or acting as detachments from a larger force, are more likely to have been counted precisely. These fleets usually numbered no more than thirty-five vessels, each of which was probably no longer than 25 metres and would have had a maximum complement of about fifty men. These figures appear to fit well with references in the Anglo-Saxon Chronicle to numbers of casualties when a certain number of ships

are captured and so, on this basis, a small fleet could field an 'army' of 1,750 men.

In 851 the Chronicle records that a fleet of 350 ships arrived at the mouth of the Thames. This does seem an inordinately large number, and may perhaps be taken only as proof that the number of ships was too large to count. But, as calculations show, even a fleet of thirty-five ships, like that said to have won a victory in Somerset in 836, would have carried a substantial number of warriors.

The 'Great Army' that arrived in 865 could well have consisted of two or three thousand men, or even more, the largest force yet to disembark on English soil. Although this number may not seem large in the context of modern warfare, to ninth-century England it could have had a significant effect. Although we have no record of the towns of East Anglia at the time that the Great Army arrived, the Domesday Book gives a unique insight into the population just a few centuries later. In 1086 Norwich, the biggest city in Norfolk at the time, had 5,000 inhabitants. So an army of just a few thousand would have been quite a menace and if further armies were to join this initial force, as they almost certainly did, the combined group of warriors would have been capable of taking on any of the kingdoms of England.

Although the word army carries modern implications of a unified, co-ordinated fighting force, the 'Great Army' was probably something quite different. The variety of Scandinavian leaders that appear in the Anglo-Saxon Chronicles implies a certain disunity and historian Richard Abels suggests that the Great Army was more likely to have resembled the raiding parties active on the Continent during the same period.

LEFT | *Ivar was one of the leaders of the Great Army which arrived in England in 865.*

Here the historical records describing the progress of the Danes into Continental Europe depict many groups of Vikings, under different leaders, occasionally teaming up to attack specific targets. These Danish raiders seem to be professional pirates; more than anything else they are *viking* in the true sense of the word. Deals are often struck with local rulers, but they are not always kept to. These Vikings will not hesitate to put their interests over and above those of anyone else.

Richard Abels turns to the story of a Viking who was active in both Francia and England to illustrate his point. Weland was the leader of a party that raided along the River Somme and into the Frankish Empire where he was not the first Scandinavian to see the potential for riches on these waters. But Weland had been beaten to it as, by this time, another group of Vikings had already built a fortress on the island of Oissel, a base from where they could attack sites throughout Francia.

Weland must have known of his Viking rivals. He struck a deal with the Frankish king, Charles the Bald, promising to attack this other group in order to prevent them causing further damage to Charles's kingdom. In return Weland and his band would receive three thousand pounds of silver. This was a huge sum and so, while Charles set out to persuade the Church and more wealthy members of his kingdom to meet the cost, Weland and his Vikings left with a number of Frankish hostages to ensure that Charles would keep his side of the bargain.

However, their deal with Charles did not stop them from seeing a further opportunity for acquiring wealth. Before turning to their agreed task, Weland's Vikings crossed the Channel to try their luck in England and in 860 they make an appearance in the Anglo-Saxon Chronicle. They attack Winchester but the West Saxons put up a good fight, as the Chronicle describes:

But Alderman Osric, with the command of Hampshire, and Alderman Æthelwulf, with the command of Berkshire, fought against the enemy, and putting them to flight, made themselves masters of the field of battle.

Having perhaps decided that the Franks are an easier target than the West Saxons, the Vikings returned to their deal with Charles the Bald. Weland and his men laid siege to the other group of Vikings, now stationed on an island in the Seine, and eventually they are forced to submit through sheer hunger. Unfortunately for Charles, Weland does not take things quite as far as the Frankish king might have liked. Once the Seine Vikings have paid him 6,000 pounds of gold and silver, he feels he has discharged his duty and, to Charles's undoubted dismay, these two bands of Vikings then join forces.

During the winter, Weland's squad split up into smaller groups and when one of them set fire to a village, King Charles had finally had enough. He raised an army and took his troops to the Seine where Weland and the other leaders agree to release their hostages and leave Francia.

Weland's tale does not end there, however. Despite his duplicity at the expense of the Franks, he is back at Charles's court again that year, after losing control of his fleet. Soon he, his wife and his followers are baptised, and allowed to stay in Francia. But Weland does not last long. One of his own men accuses him of agreeing to baptism 'as a trick' and, in the ensuing fight to the death, Weland is the one to lose his life. The accusations of dishonesty may have had more than a touch of irony to them: it is entirely possible that the episode that ultimately led to Weland's death was engineered by King Charles himself as a means of getting rid of a troublesome presence. After a career in which he seems to have made a habit of double-dealing, Weland may ultimately have died at the hands of another Viking for being untrustworthy.

In England, too, the chroniclers make much of the duplicitous nature of the Danes. In 865, a heathen army arrived in Thanet and made peace with the men of Kent, who

promised money therewith; but under the security of peace, and the promise of money, the army in the night stole up the country, and overran all Kent eastward.

Their behaviour is not dissimilar to that of Weland and his band of Vikings.

The Great Army may have been more of a loose coalition of small forces than a coherent whole, but it still posed a serious threat to the kingdoms in England. Having set up a base at York, the raiding-army began to attack elsewhere. Over the winter of 867–8 the Vikings decided to camp out in Nottingham, to the great displeasure of the King of Mercia. Unwilling to take on the Great Army himself, however, he turned to the southern English kingdom of Wessex for help.

Æthelred, King of Wessex, agreed to his request, and travelled with his brother Alfred to Nottingham where they were thwarted on their arrival.

Since the pagans, protected by the defences of the fortress, refused to give battle, and the Christians could not break the wall, peace was made between the Mercians and the pagans, and the two brothers, Æthelred and Alfred, returned home with their forces.

After briefly returning to York, in 869 the army appeared once again in East Anglia where Edmund, the king in these parts, having paid tribute only four years previously, was obviously not keen to pay up again and decided to resist. The Danes too decided on a change of tactic. Perhaps due to their successes elsewhere, they may have decided that tribute alone was no longer enough. So when King Edmund rode into battle he was brutally killed and this time, rather than simply obtaining the normal tribute, the Vikings overran his lands. This was the Danes' first real conquest on mainland Britain.

An inscription in this gospel book records how it was purchased from Vikings by a pious Anglo-Saxon and given to Christ Church, Canterbury.

The success of the Great Army cannot be attributed solely to its sheer size. Although several bands of Danes may have united as a larger and more intimidating force, the Anglo-Saxons were fighting on home soil, and would also have had access to far greater numbers of fighting men. Nor did the Danes have particularly superior weapons.

For offence, the warriors of the Great Army had spears, axes and swords. Viking swords are about 3 feet (1 metre) in length with a relatively blunt end and are designed for slashing rather than stabbing. Many have been found across Northern Europe, often buried with their owners. For defence, they depended on thick clothing, most probably of leather, and shields but they did not, despite the prevailing Viking image, wear horned helmets. In fact, it is not certain whether Vikings at this time would have worn helmets at all. The famous Coppergate Helmet from York, while of eighth-century date, is in fact Anglian rather than Viking. This leaves the Gjermundbu Helmet, found in a warrior's grave in Norway, as probably the only definite example of a Viking helmet. Warriors depicted on some carvings and coins do seem to be wearing conical helmets much like those on the Bayeux Tapestry, but the majority may well have worn headgear of leather rather than of metal.

Gareth Williams, curator of Anglo-Saxon and medieval coins at the British Museum, has also taken a keen interest in Viking helmets. As well as having a copy of the Gjermundbu Helmet made for an exhibition, Gareth has been investigating what an ordinary Viking warrior might

Virtually no Viking helmets have been discovered, but this figure carved from elk horn suggests that if they were worn they would have been conical, and most certainly did not have horns.

have worn. With the help of a Viking reconstruction group, Gareth has made a leather helmet of his own. He feels this is most likely what a Viking warrior would have been wearing, if indeed he had a helmet at all. Perhaps the conical helmets worn by figures in Viking art were actually made of leather.

Leather might not seem to offer much protection, but if boiled and then allowed to harden in the right shape, headgear could be produced that would certainly deflect at least glancing blows. A metal helmet might not have offered significantly more protection and, if a heavy sword or axe scored a direct hit on either leather or metal, the force would have been likely to break the victim's neck in any case.

The battles between the Great Army and the Anglo-Saxons would have involved similar tactics on both sides. Lines of warriors advanced with shields interlocked for protection, spears would be thrown as the shield walls advanced, and finally the warriors would be close enough to engage in hand-to-hand combat. Considerable space would be needed to employ swords and axes with significant force, making the use of complex or tight battle formations very difficult.

Although both Vikings and Anglo-Saxons used similar weapons and techniques, the Danes did have some advantages. The most important was the speed with which hit-and-run raids could be executed using longships on sea and river and horses on land. It also seems as if the Vikings travelled light, keeping their provisions to a minimum and replenishing their supplies as and when necessary from the areas that they passed through.

Despite their image of uncontrolled ferocity, the Vikings would not march into battle without careful planning and were not over-reckless. If they could raid an undefended town and demand tribute, then that was far preferable to becoming involved in a full-scale battle. But when they did engage in combat they made full use of their mobility to surprise their enemies. Their attack on York was brilliantly timed to coincide with the state of turmoil that followed the Northumbrian civil war, while an attack on Wessex was initiated in midwinter, when the Christian Anglo-Saxons were absorbed in the celebration of Christmas.

The Anglo-Saxon Chronicle reports most of the battles with the Great Army in quite simple terms. One side is said to win the battle, and perhaps overrun the surrounding land, but the details of how success was achieved are left unrecorded. Historian Richard Abels has found one battle, at Ashdown in Berkshire, that gives us a far better description than most and provides some insight into the fighting methods of both Vikings and Anglo-Saxons.

In 871, King Æthelred of Wessex and his brother Alfred went to meet the Vikings who were encamped at Reading. They fought, but the Danes kept possession of the site.

And four days later King Æthelred and Alfred, his brother, fought on Ashdown against the whole raiding-army; and they were in two bands: in the one were Bagsecg and Halfdan, the heathen kings, and in the other were the jarls. And then the king Æthelred fought against the kings' force, and there the king Bagsecg was killed; and Alfred, his brother, against the jarls' force, and there Jarl Sidroc the Old was killed and Jarl Sidroc the Young and Jarl Osbern and Jarl Fræna and Jarl Harald, and both the raiding-armies were put to flight, and there were many thousands killed; and fighting went on till night.

The Danes divided their forces into two units, one led by the kings, and the other by those next in rank, the *jarls*. Æthelred and Alfred followed a similar plan, splitting their men in order to counter the two Danish forces. However, according to the monk Asser, Æthelred spent rather too much time in prayer before approaching the field of battle, leaving Alfred in a position where he either had to attack alone or turn back. In the end he advanced to meet the Danes without the reinforcement of his brother's men.

The Vikings had arrived at the battlefield first, and so secured the better position. Alfred fought valiantly, but could not finally overrun the Danes until Æthelred, who had finally finished praying, suddenly appeared with his men. This threw the Danes into a panic, their shield wall collapsed, and they fled, chased by the English until 'they reached the stronghold from which they had come'. However, despite this resounding victory, the Anglo-Saxons found themselves in battle against the Danes only two weeks later. This time, after a long struggle, their fortunes were reversed and the Danes took control of the field.

It is clear from the large number of Danes who are named individually, as well as those who must have been placed into the general category of *jarls*, that many different bands of Vikings were involved in this battle. Even though the Great Army is traditionally thought of as entirely Danish, it may be only its leaders who came from that country. After all, the Vikings who initially settled in Ireland were mainly from Norway so the Great Army's troops could have been drawn from across the whole of Scandinavia. This may be a good example of the Vikings' pragmatic nature and their willingness to shift allegiances. Relations between Denmark and Norway were not always amicable: Danish kings had fought to control the Vestfold area of Norway, and in other circumstances Scandinavians from these two countries could just as easily find themselves enemies as allies.

This distinction, the separation of Scandinavians into Danes and Norwegians, is also a critical aspect of Professor Goldstein's genetic survey at University College London. One of his team's first tasks was to travel to Denmark (Copenhagen and Southern Denmark) and Norway (Bergen, Trondheim and Oslo) in an effort to find a DNA signature for each of these populations. The DNA evidence will hopefully prove that both Danes and Norwegians found their way to England, but it cannot tell us whether this DNA was left behind by the Great Army, or by later settlers. So can archaeological evidence prove whether or not the stories of the Great Army that appear in the Anglo-Saxon Chronicle have some truth to them?

The recently found brooches that have turned up in such numbers have helped to provide evidence of widespread Scandinavian activity in England and swords of Viking manufacture are an obvious sign of a military presence. But there is another category of find that perhaps hints at a time of uncertainty and fear: hoards, where valuable treasures have been deliberately buried and never retrieved.

In various locations across Britain and Ireland, hoards of Viking Age silver have been discovered. Hoarding has been going on since early prehistoric times when the valuables were fine stone axes and reached a spectacular peak in the Bronze Age with the burial or deposition in rivers and bogs of huge quantities of bronze weapons and tools. There is, however, another peak around the ninth century. Hoarding seems to be particularly common in the Viking Age – it must have been a dangerous time to be alive.

In Yorkshire several coin hoards have been found but unfortunately many were discovered too long ago for records to be considered completely reliable. However, dates on coins that can positively be identified as coming from these hoards suggest that they were buried in the 860s or later. This is the time that the Vikings arrived in York, but it is unlikely that the coins were buried by members of the Great Army. The Danes were concerned about the quality of their silver and many of the coins, minted in Northumbria, are made from such low quality silver that it barely qualifies for the name.

So perhaps the coins belonged to Anglo-Saxons who were driven to bury what little wealth they had in the face of the Viking threat. But the threat may not actually have come from this direction as Northumbria was at this time engaged in what was virtually a civil war. Many Northumbrians may have thought that the best way to safeguard their money in this tempestuous political climate was simply to bury it in the ground.

In fact, the Yorkshire coin hoards turn out to be a bit of a red herring in the search for evidence of the Great Army. At the other end of the country, a far more promising discovery was made in 1862, at Croydon, just outside London. This was a hoard that contained about 250 coins, silver ingots and pieces of hacksilver. Unlike those from Northumbria, the coins were good quality silver, and were not just from the English kingdoms. The very presence of some Frankish coins suggests a possible connection with the Great Army as coins from other lands were not allowed to circulate in Anglo-Saxon England, making these unlikely possessions for a native. The Vikings, in contrast, cared little about the types of coinage they owned, their only concern being that they were of high quality silver that could be melted down, or chopped up for trading purposes.

The silver ingots hint that it was a Scandinavian who buried these valuables and the hacksilver clinches it. As if this evidence were not enough, three of the coins were Arabic and the most likely candidates to own this unusual currency would be the Vikings through their contacts with Arab traders on their voyages down through Russia.

The silver from Croydon looks like a classic Viking treasure hoard, but what is it doing so far from the Great Army's bases in York or East Anglia? The Anglo-Saxon Chronicles provide what may be the answer. At the end of 871 the Great Army move from Reading to London where they spend the winter. In the ninth century, Croydon was part of the Archbishop of

Canterbury's estate and as such would have been well stocked with provisions for the winter, just the sort of place that the Great Army would have looked for to provide winter accommodation. It seems that one of the Viking contingent decided to bury his wealth, to keep it safe from any hostile Anglo-Saxons. Indeed, the owner of this hoard may have been equally worried about keeping his treasure safe from his fellow Vikings; as the individual groups that made up the Great Army had no reason to trust each other. In such a situation and in possession of a considerable amount of high quality silver, one Viking obviously decided that the best place for it was underground.

I had come across the direct evidence for this Viking habit of burying wealth in Ireland, in Wales and now in England, but the scale of wealth that I had seen could not have prepared me for what I saw on the small island of Gotland, just off the south-east coast of Sweden.

Gotland is a small island of about 3,000 square kilometres on which the pattern of farms is still very much as it was in the Viking Age. But these farms were obviously more than just agricultural establishments, they were the headquarters of wealthy traders. The Swedish Vikings were the *Rus* who would give their name to Russia, as they settled around the Baltic Sea and the Volga, and the trading links they forged with the East appear to have been the source of much of their wealth. There is a rune stone on the island that records a journey by five Gotlanders to Russia, but much of their trade is likely to have been conducted on a more local scale.

Each of these wealthy Gotland Viking farms seems to have its hoard, and each of the hoards discovered to date contains large quantities of silver, much in the form of Arabic coins, prized for their purity. But the largest Viking hoard so far was unearthed recently, in 1999, when a farmer found a few pieces of silver in one of his ploughed fields. The find was immediately notified to the island's archaeologists and when the site was excavated not one, but two hoards were found, buried about three metres apart. Between them they contained over 154 pounds (70 kilograms) of silver. This is a staggering quantity but, until I visited the conservation laboratories where the finds are being examined, I had no idea what 154 pounds of silver would actually look like. One entire laboratory bench was covered with silver arm-rings, both separate and twisted together in bundles that each weighed several pounds. There were hundreds of the small silver bar-shaped ingots that I had seen in Ireland and, still in the block of soil within which it had been lifted, was a mass of coins. Jonas Ström and Per Widerström of the Gotland Historical Museum, the excavators of the hoard, explained that in its centre, surrounded by arm-rings, lay the remains of a wooden box that was full of silver coins. The exact number was still unknown as the excavation in the laboratory was unfinished but it was thought to be over 10,000. The coins came from as far away as Italy, Bohemia, and the Byzantine Empire.

The size of this hoard made it unusual, even on the island of Gotland where, due to the extraordinary wealth of Viking archaeology, the use of metal detectors is prohibited. They are used as part of archaeological investigations but only after special permission has been obtained. This approach means that most hoards now end up properly excavated, conserved and in museums, displayed for everyone to see and enjoy.

The Vikings on Gotland were obviously very wealthy, but why did they decide to bury so much of their riches? The reasons are not clear but may be at least partly concerned with security. The island may have been liable to attack by pirates, indeed some of the islanders' silver could have been obtained by attacking ships in the first place. With no safe deposit boxes available, the obvious answer was to hide it well, and the ground is as good a place as any to do this. But if they had buried their silver for protection, were they so rich that they never needed to retrieve it? As so many silver hoards seem to remain in the ground to be discovered by modern-day archaeologists, the Vikings must have had another reason for burying these precious goods.

The two large hoards discovered in 1999 were only about 30 centimetres below the surface of the ground and the archaeological excavation of the area around where they were buried showed that they had lain immediately below the wooden floor of a building. However, it was not even under the floor of a house, which would seem more sensible if security was the requirement, but under an outhouse or shed.

This peculiar place of burial has been noticed for many of the other hoards discovered on Gotland. Some have been in or near to houses, although some have been found in what would have been farmyards. So maybe this practice, of burying the silver close to the house, and never coming back to retrieve it, may not be so much to do with security as some sort of deliberate sacrifice, a religious offering. The Vikings may

Over 70 kilograms of silver was discovered in this hoard on the island of Gotland, Sweden.

have buried their silver for safe-keeping, just before going out on a raid, believing that if they were killed, their buried silver would follow them to the afterlife, just as if it had been buried with them in their grave.

Perhaps a sacrifice of silver served the same purpose as killing an animal to appease the gods. By burying silver on their farms the pagan Vikings may have hoped to ensure a good harvest and successful trading and, if the sacrifice worked, then no doubt their supplies of silver would be quickly replenished.

Or maybe it was just simply showing off, burying so much wealth being the ultimate way to demonstrate to your neighbours that you had silver to spare. After all, if you still lived well after consigning 70 kilograms of silver to the ground, you must be reasonably rich. But there is a very good

As well as the vast quantity of silver found in the Gotland hoards, the island has revealed a number of rock crystal lenses. Some had been made into jewellery.

reason to suspect that there was more of a religious motive, and that the hoards were a pagan offering. The practice ceased just as Christianity was being adopted on Gotland and, as stone churches started to be built, the hoards gradually stopped being buried.

Although much less spectacular than anything found in Gotland, the Croydon hoard does at least seem to support the Chronicles' tales of the Great Army in the London area. But for the most positive evidence of the presence of this great band of Danes I had to return to the Midlands, to Ingleby, not far from the small town of Repton. Here, on a wooded ridge-top overlooking the valley of the River Trent, is a cluster of about sixty mounds, the appearance of which would suggest a prehistoric, probably Bronze Age, date. However, when several were opened in the 1950s, some were found to be empty and some to contain cremation hearths. In among the charcoal and ashes lay the remains of both men and women together with the burnt bones of cattle, sheep, dog and possibly horse and pig. There were also grave goods, or more correctly pyre goods as they too had been through the cremation fires, including swords, buckles, a strap end, nails and wire embroidery. These were Vikings.

Despite all the evidence for Viking invasions, the situation in England is very similar to that in Ireland: there simply are not enough graves. There are less than twenty-five known burial sites of ninth- and tenth-century date, that can be described as Scandinavian in character, in the whole of England and the majority of these have only one or two artefacts buried with them.

Scandinavia at this time was still pagan and although there was no standard burial custom, the dead were generally buried or cremated with their possessions. But in England, apart from a few burials in churchyards, singled out from the Christians that surround them because of their grave goods, Viking burials are extremely rare. Ingleby is unique because it is the only Viking cremation cemetery in the country, a place where Scandinavians were practising the burial rites of their homelands. Even the burnt iron nails, seemingly uninteresting finds, hint at the construction of wooden cremation platforms or biers on which the dead and their possessions for the next life would have been placed.

Given the exciting potential of the site at Ingleby it was not surprising to find that research excavations were planned to investigate more thoroughly a couple of the undisturbed mounds. So, in 1999, I had the strange experience of meeting Julian Richards on site at Ingleby. Julian *D*. Richards is a Viking expert who teaches at York University. We have corresponded over the years, largely due to receiving each other's post, but this was the first time I had seen Julian on site.

The Vikings had certainly chosen a commanding position for their cemetery. The funeral pyres would have been visible for miles around, maybe just another way of announcing that they were here to stay. Julian's team were excavating two mounds and the centre of the larger one showed the signs of a cremation pyre. The soil was burnt to an orange red, flecked with charcoal and here and there were white fragments of cracked and twisted cremated bone. Then, in the last season of excavation, the team found a well-preserved Hiberno-Norse ring-pin on the edge of a small area of cremated human bone. It appeared to have been deliberately placed in the mound.

These Scandinavian artefacts were further evidence that the burial mounds in Ingleby were made by Scandinavians, possibly part of the Great Army.

So who were the Vikings that burnt their dead on this hilltop? There are no signs of where they lived and the burials seem to have taken place over a relatively short time. Perhaps the ring-pin belonged to a Viking member of the Great Army. But then how to explain the presence of the women in the cremated remains? The identity of the Ingleby Vikings remains a mystery but nearby, at Repton itself, there are more Vikings, and here a more positive identification is possible.

Repton today is best known for its public school, elegant buildings and playing fields that cluster on the bank of the River Trent next to a large church with an imposing spire. It may be peaceful today but over the winter of 873–4, the Great Danish Army took up quarters here, as the Anglo-Saxon Chronicle states:

'In this year the army went from Lindsey to Repton and took up winter quarters there, and drove King Burgred [of Mercia] across the sea . . . And they conquered all that land . . . And the same year they gave the kingdom of the Mercians to be held by Coelwulf, a foolish king's thegn; and he swore oaths to them and gave hostages . . .'

When the Vikings arrived in Repton in 873 they found a monastic community for both men and women, ruled by an abbess of high rank. Several kings of Mercia had been buried there, including Æthlbald who died in 757 and Wigstan, murdered in 849 and at whose tomb miracles were said to take place. Repton became a place of pilgrimage and even today it is still possible to experience what a Saxon pilgrim may have felt. The crypt below the church can still be entered down steps worn by generations of feet and although the relics encased in glittering gold and silver have long gone, the sense of drama orchestrated by its pillars and recesses still remains.

The Vikings would have found a monastery in the English countryside when they arrived at Repton in the ninth century.

As well as the reference in the Anglo-Saxon Chronicle there had been archaeological hints of a Viking presence in Repton, including finds of a sword, a bearded axe of Viking type and a hogback stone near the church. These carved gravestones, shaped like Viking long-houses, are found in many places in northern England and although they have no direct parallels in the Viking homelands, the style of the carvings is undoubtedly Scandinavian.

But when excavations, initially an attempt to work out the structural history of the church, began in 1974, no one had any idea of the dramatic and controversial finds that would be made. For Martin and Birthe Biddle the first hint of exciting discoveries to come was the southern half of a ditch about 4 metres (13 feet) deep and 8 metres (26 feet wide) starting at the east end of the church and running eastward towards the River Trent. Remote sensing confirmed its route and also located its continuation to the west of the church. The northern

A small Thor's hammer pendant and a glass bead were found alongside this Viking skull at Repton.

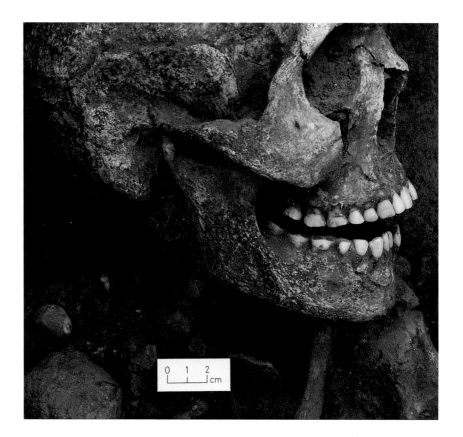

end of this section of ditch, at the point where it met the Trent, was confirmed by excavation. The digging of the ditch could be dated to some time between the Middle Saxon and post-Viking periods by observing which graves it cut through and which were cut through it. All the evidence pointed to a fortification, similar to the Danish *halvkredsvolde*, D-shaped earthworks with water forming their straight sides and at Repton enclosing an area of 1.5 hectares (3.6 acres). The church, stripped of its sacred relics, had been used by the pagan Vikings as the gatehouse of their defensive enclosure.

As the layout of the ditch became clear and the dramatic nature of the discovery was realised, a number of unusual graves were found, the most striking of which lay to the north of the church but inside the earthwork. This was the burial of a tall man, thirty-five to forty-five. He was buried with his weapons and a silver hammer pendant, the sign of the Viking god Thor, around his neck.

The Viking warrior buried at Repton was found with a sword and knife.

This man's burial has given us a glimpse of an individual, a warrior who died a violent death and who perhaps typified the Vikings that roamed the English countryside bringing fear and destruction wherever they appeared. There were more of his kind at Repton.

To the west of the ditched fortification an eighth-century Anglo-Saxon building was re-used by the Vikings for burial. It was first excavated in 1686 and was said to have a floor that was lower than the surrounding ground, suggesting some kind of mausoleum. It was reported to have contained the stone coffin of a 'humane body nine foot long' surrounded by a hundred skeletons 'with their feet pointing to the stone coffin'. Sadly, when the mound was re-excavated exactly three hundred years later in 1986 the nine-foot body was missing, but the remains of at least 249 individuals were found. Of these, about 80 per cent were men but only a very few show any signs of the trauma or injuries which might have been expected from the members of an army. However, a number of Scandinavian objects were found with the mass burial together with coins that suggest a date in the early 870s.

The Biddles consider that the evidence of the grave goods and coins suggests that the people in the mound were placed there by the Vikings. They may have died elsewhere in previous years, and in Repton from epidemics over the winter of 873–4 but they were all finally brought together and reburied around their gigantic 'chieftain'. The Biddles suggest that there is even the possibility that the 'humane body nine foot long' could have been the Viking chieftain Ivar the Boneless.

Ivar is a semi-legendary character who plays a part in twelfth and thirteenth century stories from both Denmark and Iceland. In the stories, his father is Ragnar Lodbrok, a heroic and half-mythical Viking leader whose exploits are included in Saxo Grammaticus's Gesta Danorum. The problem is that he is almost certainly not a real figure, but a composite of several famous Viking leaders. So was Ragnar's son a real Viking or a similarly invented character?

Imhar or Ivar, the leader of the Danish Great Army, is commonly identified with the legendary figure of Ivar the Boneless. Could this giant Viking skeleton have been that of Ivar himself, whose death, together with many of his warriors, may have led to the break-up of the Great Army.

When the Great Army left in 874 monastic life had ceased at Repton

A pendant resembling Thor's hammer was found buried alongside a Viking at Repton.

and the church was in ruins. So Repton provides the most compelling archaeological evidence for the Great Army, evidence that backs up the descriptions in the Anglo-Saxon Chronicle. They tell us that by 870 these bands of raiders had made significant inroads into much of England. York was under their control, the kingdom of East Anglia had fallen into their hands and the Mercians had also been forced to pay tribute to the Danes.

It would seem that only Wessex stood alone against the Vikings. But in 870 the Danes took Reading, leaving Æthelred, the King of the West Saxons, and his brother Alfred to contain the threat. Then, in the next year, Æthelred died, leaving Alfred to face the Vikings who were now reinforced by a second army that had just arrived at Reading. It appeared that Alfred had inherited a kingdom on the verge of being conquered and was destined to go down in history as having a very short reign indeed. So how did Alfred the Doomed (as it must have seemed even to him) survive and prosper to become Alfred the Great?

CHAPTER 9

ALFRED'S ENGLAND

When the next morning dawned he moved his forces and came to a place called Edington, and fighting fiercely with a compact shield-wall against the entire Viking army, he persevered resolutely for a long time; at length he gained the victory through God's Will. He destroyed the Vikings with great slaughter, and pursued those who fled as far as the stronghold, hacking them down.

FROM ASSER'S *LIFE OF KING ALFRED*

LEFT | *Andrew Du Mont's statue of King Alfred stands over the entrance to the school that bears his name in Shaftesbury, Dorset. His shield is inscribed with the words 'Alfred's name shall live as long as mankind shall respect the past'.*

In the same way that a mythology has grown up around the Vikings themselves, Alfred has, through time, become an almost legendary figure: Alfred the Great, the cake burner who first hid from, and then fought off, the Danish army. But Alfred was a very real person and there is a truth behind the myths and folklore.

At the time Alfred took the throne, England was an Anglo-Saxon land, divided into the kingdoms of Northumbria, Mercia, East Anglia, and Wessex. Back in the fifth century the Anglo-Saxons themselves had been the invaders, a mixture of Angles, Saxons and Jutes from northern Germany and Jutland. They came to a land of Britons and Celts who for four centuries had lived as part of the Roman Empire and now found themselves in an abandoned province.

It was early medieval writers on the Continent who began to distinguish these early invaders from the original British inhabitants. They ignored the contribution of the Jutes, coining the term *Angli Saxones*, so, by the time the Vikings began to attack Britain, the descendants of the first Germanic invaders shared a name. This was the beginning of an English identity.

By the time of Alfred's birth, in 849, the descendants of these first pagan invaders had long since converted to Christianity and the monastic communities which were to provide the Vikings with such rich pickings had sprung up across the country. The various English kingdoms were

This map shows the kingdoms of England in the eighth century.

sometimes at war, sometimes allies, as power shifted from one to the other. In the eighth century Mercia was the prominent kingdom, recognised even by Charlemagne, who controlled much of Continental Europe. But this was soon to change.

Alfred was born into the ruling dynasty of Wessex, the fifth son of King Æthelwulf, during whose reign the West Saxons would reach the peak of their power. But power was difficult to maintain and well before the arrival of the Vikings, Alfred's grandfather was fighting for the independence of Wessex against the kingdom of Mercia, made powerful by King Offa.

During his reign Offa effectively took over the independent rulers of Sussex and Kent, as well as exerting a significant influence in Surrey, Essex and East Anglia. Both Wessex and Northumbria managed to avoid the same fate; indeed, the rulers of each of these kingdoms received the hand of one of Offa's daughters in marriage. These were shrewd political alliances and ensured that neither Wessex nor Northumbria would lose their power completely.

After Offa's death King Egbert, Alfred's grandfather, took control of Wessex and embarked on a programme of expansion. First he forced the new ruler of Mercia to submit to him, after which he took control of Kent, Surrey, Sussex, Essex and East Anglia. He then headed further north, conquering the Northumbrians, before turning his attention to the Welsh.

From 825 to 830 Egbert was in a unique position, ruling most of modern-day England, but it proved impossible for him to hold on to all his new lands. The King of Mercia recovered his kingdom in 830, perhaps with Egbert's consent; relations between the two kingdoms seem to have become more friendly at this time. After Egbert's death, the King of Mercia called on his son, Æthelwulf, for help in subduing the Welsh and was also given Æthelwulf's daughter in marriage. The two kingdoms even went so far as to issue coins in similar styles and made by the same moneyer. This was a very practical alliance, providing mutual support during the time when the Vikings began to threaten.

Alfred was Æthelwulf's fifth son, so it is surprising that he eventually became king. He was still a child when the first Vikings set up winter camps in East Anglia and, at the age of four, embarked on a pilgrimage to Rome with his father. Despite the Viking threat, or perhaps because of it, in 856 Æthelwulf returned to Rome with Alfred, stopping on the way at the court of the Frankish king, whose daughter Æthelwulf married.

While Alfred and his father were away, Wessex was ruled by the four elder brothers. Since Egbert's acquisitions of Surrey, Sussex, Essex and Kent, the kingdom had become rather large and unwieldy so Æthelwulf gave control of the eastern provinces to his eldest son. But this son died before the second trip to Rome, so the kingdom was then divided between the two eldest of his remaining sons.

However, the son who had been left in control of Wessex was not loyal to his father and schemed to prevent Æthelwulf's return from pilgrimage. Despite this betrayal, Æthelwulf drew up a document confirming that Wessex would remain under this son's control upon his death. But by 865 both of his eldest sons were dead, leaving the control of the entire kingdom in the hands of Alfred's last surviving elder brother, Æthelred.

It was a dangerous time to succeed to the throne of Wessex. The Great Army had just arrived and by 870 the Vikings had settled at York, forcing the Northumbrians to make peace with them, and had conquered the East Anglians, killing their king. Alfred and Æthelred fought together against the Vikings, travelling to Nottingham in an attempt to aid their Mercian allies. But their journey was in vain and Mercia too was forced to pay tribute to the Vikings.

King Edmund is dragged from church by Viking invaders in this illumination from an eleventh-century English religious manuscript. He refused to submit to the Vikings and was killed.

At the end of 870, the Great Army arrived in Reading and a number of battles ensued, with the Danes and then the Anglo-Saxons each claiming victories. In the midst of these skirmishes Æthelred died and Alfred took control of the kingdom. The new king found himself in a dire position. Another Viking fleet had just arrived and although Alfred continued to resist the Danes as they moved through his kingdom, eventually the West Saxons too were forced to make peace.

The payment of silver, or 'making peace', appeared to work and for the next few years the Danes left Alfred's kingdom alone. They established a winter camp in London and returned to Mercia, where they once again extorted tribute. In 873 they took over the important Mercian political centre of Repton, and this time silver and gold were not enough. The Vikings installed their own choice of king, who agreed to put himself at their service, providing warriors if necessary and returning the kingdom into their hands should they require it.

With East Anglia, Mercia and Northumbria under their control, the Great Army splintered into two groups. Halfdan led a group of Danes up to York where, after a few years of sporadic raiding, they settled and took up farming. Others, led by Guthrum, Oscytel and Anund, moved on to Cambridge but, far from settling peaceably, this group soon returned to raiding in the south of England. In 875 they began attacking Wessex once again, setting up a winter camp in Wareham and forcing Alfred yet again to 'make peace'. The Danes pledged to leave the kingdom, giving Alfred hostages but, in true Viking style, they never fulfilled their promise and simply moved on to Exeter.

Alfred was already showing his determination in the face of the Viking enemy. He chased the Great Army to Exeter, but his men were too late to catch the Vikings before they entered their fortifications and no actual battle took place. The Danes, however, were clearly intimidated by this show of strength and the Anglo-Saxon Chronicle reports that they gave Alfred hostages and swore oaths of allegiance. This hostage-giving shows that Alfred had gained the upper hand and, more importantly, the Chronicles tell us that this time the Danes kept to the terms of the peace.

This appeasement by the Danes does seem slightly incongruous, given their evident power elsewhere. It may in part have been because they lost many of their ships in a storm on the way from Wareham to Exeter, and perhaps felt unable to confront Alfred with reduced numbers. But there may also be another factor at work.

All that we know about the Great Army and their battles with Alfred comes from two documents, the Anglo-Saxon Chronicles and Asser's *Life of King Alfred*. Neither of these was written from a Scandinavian perspective, so it is not surprising that they take the side of the Anglo-Saxons

Alfred was nearly defeated by the Vikings, but managed to rally his troops and defend the kingdom of Wessex in the late ninth century.

rather than that of the Great Army. But even more important is the fact that both of these works are most likely to be biased specifically in favour of King Alfred.

Asser, Alfred's biographer, was a Welsh monk who was summoned to the king's court from the monastery of St David's in Wales. He agreed to spend half of each year with the king, no doubt hoping his local community would in return benefit from King Alfred's protection against neighbouring Welsh kings.

Whatever the reason for his arrival at Alfred's court, Asser became an integral part of it. He helped teach the king to read Latin and travelled with him on many occasions. But his most important contribution was his *Life of King Alfred*. The idea of recording his king's life may have come to Asser from the Continent. Many European scholars visited King Alfred's court and one of the books Asser became familiar with was *Vita Caroli* – a record of the life of Charlemagne. Asser embarked on a similar epic for King Alfred, a book in which he emphasises his admiration for his king. As well as a personal tribute to his ruler, Asser's book appears to have been written with the aim of convincing others of his views. From the detailed descriptions of places that would have been familiar to readers in Wessex, to the inclusion of the Welsh version of some place-names, it seems that he may have had a Welsh audience in mind. The book was probably intended to reassure his recently conquered Welsh subjects that they had a just and wise king, who deserved their loyalty.

The *Life of King Alfred* would never make it into general circulation. Even though Asser outlived Alfred, the work stops abruptly, well before its subject's death, and it may be that what survives today is only an initial incomplete draft. Despite this, it still provides a valuable insight into the battles of the Great Army with the kingdom of Wessex.

It is not surprising that in Asser's book the king comes across as a valiant and noble fighter, defending his kingdom against a heathen enemy. As a member of his court and, if we are to believe his own words, a genuine friend of the king, Asser would wish to portray him in a flattering light. But Asser only joined Alfred's court in 885, and was probably not in direct contact with the king until he taught him to read Latin two years later. So for the initial period of Alfred's reign, Asser relies on the Anglo-Saxon Chronicles, adding his own comments where he sees fit.

These yearly reports of events in the Anglo-Saxon world might be expected to retain a more impartial view on the proceedings than Asser. Granted, the Anglo-Saxon authors would probably have a dislike of the heathen Vikings, but a preference for King Alfred over contemporary leaders is an added dimension.

The reason for this possible prejudice lies in the origin of the Chronicles themselves. During Alfred's reign he encouraged his subjects to learn to read and write, creating a culture in which he hoped books and learning would flourish. Although Alfred himself may not have been involved in their production, it was during his reign that the Chronicles were first 'published'.

The surviving manuscripts of the Chronicles all contain a royal genealogy and a register of the kings of Wessex. They then detail the major incidents in each year until their publication in 893, after which the yearly instalments are continued by different authors. The publication date of the Chronicles coincides with the period when Alfred would have been attempting to promote himself as the leader of all the English kingdoms against the Vikings. It shows Wessex gradually emerging as a leading kingdom, with Alfred the 'King of the Anglo-Saxons'.

Bearing in mind this probable bias, we can return to the events described in the Chronicles, and Asser's *Life of King Alfred*, in 876. Alfred has chased the Danes to Exeter and here they give him hostages and swear oaths. The entry in the Chronicles may of course omit any facts or events that show Alfred in a less favourable light. He may, for example, have had to give the Danes hostages in return, paid them tribute or bargained with them in some other way. But, whatever other deals may have been done, Alfred's efforts seem to have worked. The Vikings returned to Mercia.

Breathing a sigh of relief at their departure, Alfred might have been forgiven for thinking that the worst was now over. The Danes who had returned to Northumbria two years before had settled down and divided the land up between themselves, and Alfred probably hoped that this group would do the same in Mercia. But, although they forced the puppet leader they had installed there to give up some of his land, this group of Vikings were not yet ready to lay down their weapons.

In 878 the Great Army returned to Wessex. The Anglo-Saxon Chronicle tells the tale.

Here the raiding-army stole away in midwinter after Twelfth Night . . . and over-rode and occupied the land of Wessex, and drove many of the people across the sea, and the greatest part of the others they over-rode – except Alfred the king with a small troop went with difficulty through woods and into swamp-fastnesses.

The Danes, despite their promises of peace, had not after all been content to remain in Mercia. They hit Alfred's kingdom in midwinter, just after the Christmas season. This was impeccable timing for a surprise attack; the Vikings used the Christian calendar to their advantage. Alfred, caught unawares, must have despaired as a time of feasting and celebration gave way to terror and bloodshed. He must have wondered what he had to do to rid himself of this pagan scourge once and for all but now, unable to defend his kingdom, he had no choice but to flee along with his countrymen.

Alfred was forced underground, reduced to hiding in the marshes of the Somerset Levels. Asser records:

He had nothing to live on except what he could forage by frequent raids, either secretly or even openly, from the Vikings as well as from the Christians who had submitted to the Vikings' authority.

This is the period of his reign from which emerges the legendary Alfred, the king who burnt the cakes. Hiding in the house of a swineherd, he fails to carry out his appointed task of turning the cakes to prevent them burning and brings down on himself the anger of the swineherd's wife. Another story tells how Alfred smuggled himself into a Viking camp, posing as a wandering minstrel, to gather information on their battle plans. All of these colourful folk tales are later inventions, but their inclusion in the story shows just how bad things had become, and how incredible were the subsequent events that would see Alfred returned to power.

By Easter of 878, Alfred had started to set in motion his plans to regain his kingdom. He established a fortress at Athelney with his men from Somerset and, soon after, set out for Egbert's Stone, where 'all the inhabitants of Somerset and Wiltshire and all the inhabitants of Hampshire – those who had not sailed overseas for fear of the Vikings – joined up with him'.

The West Saxons had somehow got word that Alfred was alive, and began to gather together what troops they could. Now it was the turn of the Vikings to be unaware of events as, a few days later, Alfred was able to mount his own surprise attack and gain revenge for the humiliation of his Christmas defeat.

When the next morning dawned he moved his forces and came to a place called Edington, and fighting fiercely with a compact shield-wall against the entire Vikings army . . . at length he gained the victory through God's Will. He destroyed the Vikings with great slaughter, and pursued those who fled as far as the stronghold, hacking them down.

As if this attack were not enough, Alfred and his men camped outside the Viking defences for a fortnight, until the Vikings were forced to admit defeat. This time it was the Danes, under their leader Guthrum, who were forced to make peace, giving hostages to the Saxons, pledging to leave the kingdom, and assuring Alfred that their king would convert to Christianity. This time the Vikings kept their promises.

Three weeks later Guthrum, described as one of the more honourable of the raiding-army, arrived at a site near Alfred's fortress at Athelney to receive his baptism. After this, the Vikings left Wessex and returned to East Anglia. England was now effectively divided in two: Alfred retained control of Wessex and the West of Mercia, while the Danes kept Northumbria, eastern Mercia, and East Anglia.

This complete turnaround in Alfred's fortunes is not really explained in either the Anglo-Saxon Chronicles or Asser's *Life of King Alfred*. His rapid transformation from a powerless fugitive to a king who can force a Viking leader to embrace Christianity is nothing short of miraculous and may explain why the stories of divine intervention and spying on Viking camps were deemed to be necessary additions.

Behind Alfred's extraordinary success against Guthrum lies one crucial factor, his ability to rally his troops. Even as a fugitive, Alfred was still the King of the West Saxons who, once they realised that their ruler was alive, would have restated their natural allegiance. It must also be remembered that the Danes, although an experienced fighting force, were the occupiers of a foreign country. If Alfred could persuade all his countrymen to fight, they would certainly have the advantage of superior numbers

This mysterious jewel was found in 1693, just a few miles from the site of Alfred's fortress at Athelney. It is probably an æstel – a manuscript pointer used for teaching and formal readings. The inscription reads 'Alfred ordered me to be made'. Alfred is recorded as sending out an æstel to every diocese of his kingdom, along with a copy of his translation of the Regula pastoralis, originally written by Pope Gregory the Great as a guide to bishops.

over the Vikings, many of whom may have been killed in earlier battles. Their intimate knowledge of the countryside may also have helped the Anglo-Saxons to employ guerilla tactics against the Danes.

Guthrum probably saw little advantage in pitting his men in a battle he was not sure that he could win. The Danes already had control over a large part of England, and the Vikings were nothing if not pragmatic. To Guthrum, a treaty by which he had to give up Wessex, but was free to return and settle in East Anglia, probably seemed a comparatively good deal.

It is also possible that the picture provided by the Anglo-Saxon Chronicles of Alfred's miraculous victory is not entirely accurate. The natural bias of the chroniclers in favour of the King of Wessex may have led to the Viking threat being overstated. Historian Richard Abels believes the Great Army may not have been quite the threat we are led to believe and returns to the Old English used in the Chronicles to illustrate his point. The Danes of the Great Army are described using the term *here*, defined by a contemporary legal text as follows:

We say 'thieves' if the number of men does not exceed seven, 'band' for a number between seven and thirty-five. Anything beyond this [we call] a here.

In Anglo-Saxon England, *here* meant a band of raiders while *fyrd* was used to describe an actual army. In the original language the Great Army appears as the *micel here*, perhaps a large band of raiders but most probably not the united force bent on the conquest of England, which makes Alfred's eventual victory seem more impressive.

Richard Abels also wonders if the Viking leaders really were that keen on conquest. The initial reports of the Great Army nearly always show the Vikings taking tribute and moving on. This is typical of their behaviour on the Continent and elsewhere and suggests that the Vikings were not so much interested in ruling the locals, as in what they could get out of them. Their later attempts to take land might have been the result of a realisation that this was a profitable alternative to tribute-taking, rather than any deliberate plan.

Guthrum's willingness to bargain with Alfred is less surprising when viewed in this way; what is more unexpected is Alfred's decision to let Guthrum off so lightly. After all, Alfred clearly had the upper hand and

Jon Goodrum discovered this Anglo-Scandinavian brooch just one hundred yards from his home in East Anglia.

could, if he had wished, have destroyed the Vikings. But Alfred was willing to negotiate so maybe both leaders saw the potential benefits of a truce. For Alfred, there might be the chance of dissuading Guthrum from further incursions while Guthrum may have seen his second chance as an opportunity to establish himself as a leader in the neighbouring kingdoms.

So, following the battle at Edington, Guthrum and Alfred drew up a treaty, dividing the kingdom of Mercia between them. Alfred added the western part to his kingdom of Wessex while Guthrum took the eastern part, merging it with the land he had taken in East Anglia. This division of England would last for many years, with the area controlled by the Danes, including Guthrum's East Anglia and Danish Northumbria, becoming known as the Danelaw.

Today, in the regions of England that were once part of the Danelaw, many tantalising traces of this Scandinavian occupation remain. As in many other places where the Vikings settled, clues are provided by archaeology, place-names and language while Professor Goldstein and his team from UCL hope that their genetics survey will provide a new line of evidence and help to reveal the true extent of Viking settlement in this part of England.

Within the Danelaw, in the village of Fundenhall, near Norwich, lives Jon Goodrum, who has long been convinced that he may have Viking ancestors. His research suggests that his surname probably stems from Guðørmr, the Old Norse for 'battle-snake' or 'dragon', and it has the same roots as the name of the Viking leader Guthrum. Jon was fascinated by the idea that he might be related to Alfred's Danish adversary. One summer's day, about seven years ago, he found firm evidence of the Vikings in his village.

Jon had some spare time and decided to try metal detecting on local farmland. Within a month he had found four or five interesting objects including a small, unusually decorated metal disc that looked quite old. Uncertain as to what it was, Jon took the disc to the Norwich Castle Museum, where it was cleaned up and immediately recognised by the experts there as a Scandinavian-style brooch. The design on the front, a diamond shape with interweaving ribbons around the edge, is typical of the mass-produced brooches that were being made in East Anglia in the tenth century. On the back there is a clear line where a pin was mounted although the brooch must have been reused at some point, because at the top is a small hole, probably made so that it could be hung as a pendant on a necklace.

If Jon and the other Goodrums really are Guthrum's descendants then David Goldstein's genetics lab should be able to find DNA evidence to support this theory. Firstly, the lab can test Goodrum men from across the country to see if they have a common Y-chromosome. This would prove they share an ancestor. If they pass this test, their common Y-chromosome can be compared with the samples taken in Denmark, to see if this common ancestor was Danish. If this result, too, is positive then there is a chance, although we can never be sure, that the Danish ancestor the Goodrum's share was Guthrum himself. Jon is prepared to put his family myth on the line and has found a number of other Goodrums willing to be tested. All he can do now is wait and see what the UCL genetics team discover.

Unfortunately for Alfred, his victory over the Vikings at Edington was not the end of the matter. Soon after his success, a second Viking fleet arrived on the Thames, and set up camp at Fulham. The monk, Asser claims this group joined up with Guthrum's men, but it is just as likely that they had no allegiances with the Vikings already in England and Guthrum's return to East Anglia might actually have been prompted by the arrival of these potential competitors. This second fleet, perhaps discouraged by Guthrum's defeat, left for the Continent, where they would remain for the next thirteen years.

Wessex then entered a sustained period of relative peace, free from the threat of Viking attacks, during which Alfred set about achieving his aims for reviving religion and learning in his kingdom. His thirst for knowledge led Alfred to invite men from far afield to join his court. Asser, later to be his biographer, arrived from Wales, along with monks from Mercia and others who travelled across the Channel from Francia.

In addition to this cosmopolitan gathering of religious leaders, Alfred's court was host to many other visitors, Franks, Welsh, and Irish. But one of Alfred's most famous guests was from a more distant country and, what is more, was a Viking. Ottar (called Othere by the Anglo-Saxons) was the Norwegian traveller whose name I had first heard mentioned in the newly discovered remains of the chief's house at Kaupang in Norway. The stories he told the Wessex court about his Scandinavian homeland were incorporated by Alfred in a history of the world. The history was a paraphrase of a fifth-century manuscript which included a geographical description of Europe. Alfred used Ottar's stories to enhance this section. But, as well as giving us a vital insight into life in ninth-century Norway, Ottar's presence at Alfred's court tells us something of Anglo-Saxon attitudes towards foreigners. Even though he had been involved in bitter conflict with the Danish Vikings, and would become embroiled in many more, Alfred was happy to welcome another of the *pagani* to his court.

Later readers of these ninth-century accounts immediately identified all the Scandinavians as heathens, but Alfred might well have seen the advantage in cultivating friendships with some of them. Indeed, the Icelandic sagas often talk of kings and other powerful leaders inviting visits from Viking leaders, perhaps regarding them as potential mercenaries who might one day be useful in battle. So the visit of Ottar the Norwegian is perhaps not as unusual as it might have seemed, but would Ottar have had such a welcome had he been Danish?

Ottar's is not the only story to have found a voice during Alfred's reign. One reason why Alfred's legend is so prominent in the minds of people today is that the few written records of the time were almost certainly produced under his influence. Alfred set out on a mission to translate Latin works for the instruction of all, insisted that his ealdormen and reeves adopt the habit of regular study, and even translated a number of works into English himself.

His obsession with learning is also reflected in the establishment of a school to ensure that those who entered positions of power in both state and Church would be properly trained. Alfred regarded the Church as an integral part of his kingdom, so those who wished to take religious orders had to learn Latin, and many religious texts were translated into English for the benefit of the less educated. He even founded a monastery at Athelney, the place in Somerset where he had gathered his troops before returning to face the Vikings.

Although this was a time of peace, Alfred must have been aware of a lingering threat from the Vikings settled in the Danelaw and so began to improve the defences of his kingdom. In the 880s settlements across Wessex were fortified, creating a chain of what were known as *burhs*. A unique record of this programme of fortifications survives today in the form of the *Burhal Hidage*, originally produced in Winchester in the eleventh century, although the manuscript we can see today is a sixteenth-century copy. The document lists all the *burhs* that formed part of Alfred's chain of defended settlements. These included refortified Roman sites as well as some that were entirely new, all arranged in such a way as to ensure that nowhere in Wessex lay more than twenty miles from one of these places of safety. The *Burhal Hidage* also describes the men necessary to defend each of these settlements, a total of as many as 27,000 men.

When the construction of all of these *burhs* had been completed, the entire population of Wessex found itself no more than a day's journey from a place of refuge. But the *burhs* functioned as more than just protection from the Danes; they each tended to have a similar, well-ordered layout, often including a market-place: they were places to work, live and trade. The *burhs'* development as trading centres provided a welcome income for the king and the Church in the form of taxes and they also became important administrative centres.

The imprint of Alfred's defensive works can still be seen in the plans of many historic towns within Wessex. In low-lying Wareham in Dorset, the earthen banks of the *burh* still stand for much of their original circuit but in Shaftesbury, where I live today, Alfred's influence is more elusive. My son Barnaby attends King Alfred's School where a statue of the great king proclaims: 'Alfred's name shall live as long as mankind shall respect the past'. Alfred founded the town's great abbey, installing his own sister Æthelgifu as the first abbess and, until recently, Shaftesbury advertised itself as a 'Saxon hilltop town'. But, although obviously well chosen as the site for a *burh*, perched as the town is on the end of a spur of land with sheer drops on three sides, no trace of the actual defences have ever been positively identified. Somewhere there must be a huge ditch and one of these days I am going to find it!

In the years following the Battle of Edington in 878, the Danes, as promised, kept out of Alfred's kingdom while the plans for its protection were put into place. Guthrum appears to have broken his word only once, in 885, when a Viking band including East Anglian Danes attacked Rochester. Alfred punished this betrayal of their treaty by sending a raiding fleet into East Anglia where they won a battle with sixteen Viking ships, but lost to another group of Danes as they returned home.

London had probably been in Viking hands since the Danes settled in Mercia in 877 but nearly a decade later, perhaps as a result of these attacks by the East Anglian Danes, Alfred decided that allowing the Vikings to control London was not such a good idea. He laid siege to the city and eventually captured it, restoring its defences, which included parts of the Roman walls, and putting in place a garrison. Alfred's capture of London ensured that the city would grow up on the site of the old Roman town of Londinium in preference to the site of the trading settlement that had developed further down the river, where it was easier for ships to land. This site had proved far from secure when Viking attacks started up, as all of the factors that made it a perfect place for trading also made it a very vulnerable target. For Alfred, it was far preferable to be safe behind the strength of the old Roman walls.

This campaign marks a turning point in Alfred's reign, after which he is seen as more than just the King of Wessex. According to the Anglo-Saxon Chronicles, he 'occupied London fort and all the English race turned to him, except what was in captivity to Danish men'. It seems as if the Mercians as well as the Anglo-Saxons were now prepared to accept him as their leader in the continuing struggle against the invaders.

Guthrum, the leader of the Danes who had settled in East Anglia, also recognised that Alfred was the man that he would have to deal with and, soon after Alfred took London in 886, these two leaders drew up a treaty.

This is the peace which King Alfred and King Guthrum and the councillors of all the English race and all the people who are in East Anglia have all agreed on and confirmed with oaths, for themselves and for their subjects, both for the living and for the unborn, who care to have God's favour or ours.

RIGHT | *King Alfred and Guthrum divided the country between them.*

This agreement would set the pattern for the administration of England for the next two hundred years, essentially splitting the country into two regions. Appropriately for a culture that relied so heavily on water transport, the agreed boundary was defined mainly by rivers, running along the Thames, up the Lea to its source north of Luton, then straight to Bedford, before running up the Ouse to Watling Street. To the north and east of this border the Danes would take control; to the south and west the English.

The creation of what became known as the Danelaw split the country in two, but at the same time it gave Alfred a kingdom which he could call England. Although previously the rulers of kingdoms had made claims

NORTHUMBRIA

CUERDALE

YORK

LINCOLN

CHESTER

MERCIA

DERBY   NOTTINGHAM
INGLEBY   LEICESTER
REPTON
TAMWORTH   STAMFORD

NORWICH

GUTHRUM'S
TERRITORY

THETFORD

WALES

KING ALFRED'S
TERRITORY

EAST
ANGLIA

WARWICK

MALDON

OXFORD

LONDON

WESSEX

WINCHESTER

CORNWALL

on the lands of others, it seems as if Alfred, for the first time, managed to become a universally accepted leader. Bearing in mind the fact that the written records that hail him as the leader of all the English were probably penned by people who supported him, he may not have been quite as popular as they make him seem. But there is also strong evidence that Alfred was making a genuine effort to be seen to be fair to others.

Having recaptured London from Danish hands, Alfred did not keep it for himself. London had always been a part of Mercia, and although Alfred had effectively annexed this kingdom to his own, he allowed the Mercians a large amount of autonomy. Perhaps as an extra incentive, he gave London to Æthelred, a Mercian ealdorman who would soon be allowed to marry Alfred's daughter.

These attempts to ensure that those outside the West Saxon kingdom would also remain Alfred's loyal subjects paid off when, in the 890s, the Danes began to attack again, Æthelred provided crucial support. With his system of defensive *burhs* and supported by strong and reliable allies, Alfred faced this second Viking onslaught with the expectation of success. His position had vastly improved since the time when the kingdom of Wessex had passed into his hands on the death of his brother.

In 892 Alfred once again found himself facing the Vikings, the same band that had landed briefly on the Thames and then left for the Continent in 879. Another army soon arrived and together, they are said to have made a combined force of 330 ships with additional support provided by the Vikings who had settled in Northumbria and East Anglia. Not all the Vikings were acting together as a united force but, from Alfred's point of view, they might as well have been. With typical Viking timing they would attack simultaneously at sites across the country and, whether they meant to back each other up, or merely take advantage of Alfred's distraction elsewhere, the effect was much the same.

Alfred could not help but find his defences stretched to their limits but he had clearly learnt from his previous campaigns and in many ways now fought like a Viking. He knew of the Vikings' reliance on mobility, and their tactic of retreating to defensive positions may have been the inspiration for his entire system of *burhs*. Having seen how effective quite simple defences could be, and with his *burhs* in place, he was in a position to attack the other Viking advantage, their mobility. This was greatly compromised by the necessity for them to post garrisons at each *burh*, and Alfred also took to mounting some of his men on horseback, allowing them to pursue the Danes across the fields of battle.

Having matched the Vikings' defensive capability and manoeuvrability, Alfred had one more trick up his sleeve. He had not forgotten the importance of unity in the face of a common enemy and the rest of England followed his lead. The West Saxons, the Mercians and even the Welsh collaborated to ward off the Viking threat and in at least one battle Frisians from the north of the Frankish Empire, fought alongside the English forces. The Chronicle adds a note of religious fervour, sometimes referring to all those supporting Alfred as the 'Christians', and perhaps Alfred may have encouraged the unity of these unlikely allies by calling on their common religious beliefs.

But not only did the Vikings teach Alfred about battle tactics, they changed the history of England. Its geographical boundaries were altered with the establishment of the Danelaw, creating a divided country, but the threat posed by the Vikings may have helped to provide Alfred with a reason for the country to unite behind one king. Although perhaps more to do with hindsight than reflecting the feelings of the time, the very idea of Englishness is often said to stem from the time of Alfred's reign.

Eventually Alfred forced the Vikings to retreat back to the Danelaw. The appeal of attacking such a well-defended kingdom must have faded, and those who could not bring themselves to settle down within the Danelaw probably returned to plunder the Continent. But there was still the possibility that the Vikings would attack again, so defences needed to be maintained – at considerable effort and cost. Despite Alfred's great achievements, at his death the Danes still controlled half of England and his Anglo-Saxon descendants would have to continue the fight.

The Danes took over towns like Thetford in East Anglia, barricading themselves in, safe from attack. These Danish defences may have influenced Alfred to begin construction of the burhs.

At the time that Alfred was busy fighting the Danes, we must not forget that another group of Vikings were also active, the Norwegian Vikings who had rounded the north coast of Scotland and entered the Irish Sea. By the end of the ninth century they had not yet established a trading empire in Dublin, but were a regular sight in this region. The initial expulsion of the Norwegian Vikings from Ireland in 902 also produced consequences that were felt in England: the Irish Sea region soon became filled with Vikings in search of a base. While some probably settled on the Isle of Man or returned to raid in Scotland, others began to make surreptitious inroads into the north-west of England.

The richest hoard ever found in England may have belonged to one of these exiled Vikings. It was discovered at Cuerdal near Preston on 15 May 1840 when one of a group of labourers, Thomas Marsden, who had been digging and carrying earth to fill in ground behind a new embankment, struck metal with his spade. Surprised, he dug further into the soil and came across some more metal and silver. His fellow labourers soon joined him and began to fill their pockets with silver coins and arm-bands.

The land belonged to a William Assheton, whose bailiff was fortunately on hand and made sure that the entire treasure did not instantly disappear. He ordered the labourers to empty their pockets, allowing them to keep just one piece each, and the contents of the hoard were then sealed up in a special wooden box to await the return of William Assheton.

But even this prompt action had obviously not secured all of the hoard as, on the very evening of its discovery, a 'Chemist and Druggist' in Preston was sold two coins by one of the labourers. Another local coin collector was also able to include some of the Cuerdale coins in a later catalogue, despite never having officially received any. The temptation to walk off with just a few coins had been too great.

When William Assheton returned to his estate the box was opened and its contents listed. It is claimed that the hoard contained 8,000 coins, 1,000 bars, 1,000 ingots, 1,000 chains, 1,000 rings and 1,000 other articles of silver. These numbers are not entirely accurate, but the overall weight is thought to be in the region of 40 kilograms.

William Assheton decided that he wanted to keep it for himself, as the hoard had been found on his land. But an attorney from Preston put a spanner in the works, informing the Duchy of Lancaster of the find. At this point Edward Hawkins, working for the British Museum, immediately expressed an interest in buying the collection.

The case went to the coroner, who had the power to decide whether the find counted as treasure and could be claimed by the state, just as he would today. The coroner awarded the Cuerdale hoard to the Duchy of Lancaster, on behalf of Queen Victoria, with Edward Hawkins to advise on what should be done with it. In the end the officers of the Duchy

Some of the coins from the Cuerdale Hoard were made into this necklace.

distributed about 6,700 coins to museums and private collectors. One of the officers received twenty-seven of the coins for himself, which were later made into the Teesdale Necklace.

The silver found at Cuerdale was almost certainly a Viking hoard. Not only did the silver come from a wide variety of places – Anglo-Saxon, Scandinavian, Pictish, Carolingian, Irish, Frankish and even Italian objects have been identified – but there was also a large quantity of hacksilver, a classic sign that these objects had been used for trading by Vikings.

Many of the coins also have tiny peck marks on them, most likely the result of someone testing the quality of the silver. Although the popular perception is that biting a coin will tell you if it is genuine (or will break your teeth if it is not), in practice this would not have worked. Instead, it seems that the Vikings used the tip of a sword or knife to make a tiny indentation in the middle or edge of a coin. Determining the quality of the silver from this test would still have been difficult, but with practice the Vikings may have become expert and it is even possible that there were certain people trained for this task, the equivalent of a modern-day jeweller.

The coins come from all across Europe. About nine hundred were actually made in King Alfred's name, some genuine and some Viking copies. There are also a few of his son Edward, some Viking coins struck in York, and some from both Francia and the Netherlands. The most exotic are Kufic coins struck for the rulers of Moslem territories, from Spain to the Middle East.

A hoard of this size must have been buried by someone of great wealth but perhaps not by an individual. It has been suggested that it is the combined loot of an entire army and the date and place of its burial, on the bank of the River Ribble in about 905, would fit with expelled Dublin Vikings trying their luck in England. The Vikings were interested in controlling both York and Dublin, and the River Ribble provided the perfect corridor between these two settlements. Claiming the land near Preston would have been a good tactical move.

So while Alfred is busy fighting off the Danes arriving in the north and east of the country, a second, more subtle Viking invasion has started; the invasion of the Irish Sea Norwegians. By this time it may be more appropriate to call them not Norwegians, but Hiberno-Norse, as many of them may have grown up in the Viking settlements of Ireland or the Northern Isles, rather than in Norway itself. Naturally expanding around the Irish Sea region, they would have been setting up camp on the north-west coast of England and it is in the Wirral, between the River Dee and the River Mersey, that the evidence points to one of their outposts.

Steve Harding, a Wirralonian himself, has always been fascinated by the possibility of Viking connections in his home region. A lecturer in biochemistry at Nottingham University, he enlisted the help of fellow Nottingham lecturer and Viking historian Judith Jesch in his search for evidence of the Vikings. But for this part of the country the written evidence is sparse. The Anglo-Saxon Chronicle is mainly concerned with the activities of the Danish Great Army. The exodus of Vikings from Dublin in 902, reported in the Irish Annals, goes unnoticed. So it is to the Irish sources that Steve has had to look for clues about the Vikings in the Wirral. And there is one story of a Norse settler which contains some evidence of a Viking presence here.

The story of Ingimund is told in the Fragmentary Annals of Ireland, rather ambiguous texts that survive only as a copy of a seventeenth-century copy of the original manuscripts. The possibilities for error are obvious, but Ingimund's story seems to fit into what we already know about the Vikings in Ireland.

Ingimund is said to have led an expedition from Ireland to Anglesey, where he was driven off by the Welsh. He then went to Æthelflæd, Alfred's daughter who had married the leader of the Mercians, and asked her for lands for his Viking troop to settle on. Her husband, Æthelred, is said to have been ill at the time.

Æthelflæd gave him lands near Chester, and he stayed there a long time. The result of this was, when he saw the city full of wealth and the choice of land around it, he desired to possess them.

At first Ingimund decides to address the problem diplomatically and tries to persuade the leaders of the Norsemen and the Danes, together with the Irish who have joined them, that they have a right to the better lands around Chester and a share of its wealth. But there is an alternative strategy discussed at their secret meeting. If they cannot get what they want through persuasion, they will use force.

Somehow Æthelflæd heard of their clandestine meeting. She responded by filling Chester with her forces so that when the armies of the Danes and Norsemen arrived it was quite clear that the Anglo-Saxons had no intention of surrendering. A fight was inevitable and although Æthelred was too ill to join the battle, he and his wife sent advice on the tactics that should be employed.

The Anglo-Saxons are told to begin the battle outside the city gates, through which they are to turn and flee as if in defeat. Hidden just inside the gates will be a troop of horsemen ready to fall upon the Norsemen and trap them inside the city.

The plan worked just as intended and a large number of the Vikings were slaughtered. But they still did not give up, so Æthelflæd and Æthelred embarked on a war of words, sending a message to the Irishmen who were among the pagans, beseeching them to change sides and support the Anglo-Saxon cause. The Irish seem to have been quite willing to abandon the Danes because, as the Annals note, 'they were less friends to them than to the Norsemen'.

While attempts were being made to weaken the power of the Danes, the Norsemen continued to besiege Chester and the Saxons to resist. The Norsemen built structures of hurdles in an attempt to breach the defences but the Saxons hurled down rocks and destroyed them. The Norsemen built them up again, this time stronger, so the Saxons poured boiling water and ale on anyone who attempted to breach the walls. The Norsemen responded by covering their hurdle structure with animal hides to protect themselves. The people of the town resorted to a rather unorthodox means of defence:

What the Saxons did was to let loose on the attacking force all the beehives in the town, so that they could not move their legs or hands from the great numbers of bees stinging them.

This was the final straw for the Norsemen and they left Chester in peace. But not for long, as they are said to have returned soon after to wage war once again.

While no other source confirms this entire story, the Welsh Annals talk of Ingimund's failed attempt to settle in Anglesey and the Anglo-Saxon Chronicle refers to the illness and death of Æthelred, which left Æthelflæd in control. Steve Harding and Judith Jesch had, in Ingimund's story, a clue to Norse settlement in the Wirral – but only if the story does contain some elements of truth. The first clue lies in local place-names that indicate a Viking origin. As a keen Tranmere Rovers supporter, Steve was already familiar with one of the Norse remnants: Tranmere has Norse roots, as do more than eighty placenames in the region. So Steve and Judith set out to collect all the Norse place-names they could find, co-opting Paul Cavill of the English Place-Name Society to their cause. Plot their distribution on a map and the likely boundary of the area settled by the Norwegians can be found.

Right in the centre of this area is Thingwall, one of the Wirral's few place-names of Viking origin that finds its way into the Domesday Book. This is likely to have been the place where the assembly, or *thing*, would meet, its position in the middle of the Norse settlement area obviously chosen with care.

Also in the Domesday Book are several other names with Norse roots. Meols, from the Norse for sandbanks, could well have been their port town, an idea that seems to be supported by the large number of Viking finds collected in the nineteenth century from eroding dunes. Raby, from the Norse for boundry village, lies on the present-day boundary of the Wirral and most probably represents the original boundary between Norse and English.

And Steve and Judith don't just have to rely on place-names to prove their case. There is also evidence of Viking influence in some of the churches in the area. The choice of the Norwegian St Olave as a saint to commemorate one church perhaps hints at the background of its builders and there is a typically Scandinavian hogback grave at the church of St Bridget's in West Kirby. This church is named after the second patron saint of Ireland and may have had links to Christian Viking settlers, or even their Irish allies, honouring the saints of the land from which they had travelled.

So it seems that the Wirral does have some traces of the Vikings who arrived there from the Irish Sea. It is most likely that these Vikings had Norwegian roots, although they may have spent their whole lives in Norse colonies in Ireland, Scotland or the Northern Isles. Their presence in the north of England must have had more far-reaching effects, though, especially among the Danish Vikings who had arrived in the ninth century.

The Wirral in the north-west of England was full of Viking settlements and a number of Scandinavian place names exist to this day.

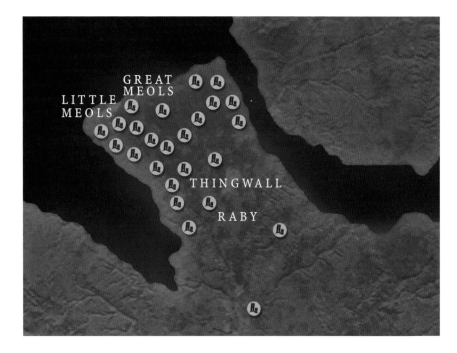

GREAT MEOLS

LITTLE MEOLS

THINGWALL

RABY

The centre of the Danelaw was at York, somewhere else that the Dublin Vikings were interested in controlling.

England at this time had become a cosmopolitan mix of people from many places and with differing cultures and beliefs. The Danelaw was inhabited by a unique mixture of Danes and Anglo-Saxons and while Scandinavian settlers would leave their mark on the land, they would also adopt many English customs. But what about the other side of the divide, Alfred's kingdom? Despite history's rosy view of Alfred and his undoubted prowess as a military leader, the English were left a long way from controlling the whole of England at the time of his death in 899.

CHAPTER 10

A COUNTRY DIVIDED

This is the peace which King Alfred and King Guthrum and the councillors of all the English race and all the people who are in East Anglia have all agreed on and confirmed with oaths . . . First concerning our boundaries: up the Thames, and then up the Lea, and along the Lea to its source, then in a straight line to Bedford, then up the Ouse to Watling Street.

THE TREATY BETWEEN ALFRED AND GUTHRUM

LEFT | *The Cuerdale Hoard was discovered near Preston in 1840.*

On King Alfred's death in 899, England was not yet a recognised kingdom. He had halted the Great Army, gone some way towards uniting Wessex and Mercia, and perhaps sown the seeds of a united England, but the Viking threat was still present. It was his son and grandsons who would have to deal with the Scandinavian settlers and also with internal family conflicts.

Edward, Alfred's son, took the throne but his cousin Æthelwold, the son of Alfred's older brother, was not impressed by this turn of events. As a member of the royal family, he felt he had as much right to lead the West Saxons as Edward. Looking for anyone who might be prepared to fight on his side, Æthelwold approached the Danes who had settled in Northumbria.

The Vikings stationed at York were more than happy to help. The king of the Viking raiding-army in Northumbria ordered his men to follow Æthelwold who, two years later, arrived in Essex with a fleet of ships. While there, he expanded his troops still further, convincing the East Anglian Danes to join him in raiding Mercia and Wessex.

So Æthelwold and the Danes set out for Wessex but Edward reacted swiftly, chasing them back to the Fens. Surrounded by the raiding-army, the Anglo-Saxons fought a bloody battle in which many of their leaders were killed, but the Danes too suffered heavy losses and Æthelwold himself perished. The Vikings maintained control of the battlefield, but the Anglo-

Saxons had achieved their objective. It seemed unlikely that the Danes would be brave enough to attack again.

This family feud demonstrates just how precarious any position of power could be at the turn of the ninth century. Æthelwold was from the West Saxon royal line, and it must not be forgotten that the Mercians too would have candidates they thought would make more suitable kings. Alfred had made a sensible move in marrying his daughter Æthelflæd to the leader of the Mercians. Her marriage ensured her husband's loyalty while he was alive, and on his death she came to rule the region in her own right. Following in her father's footsteps, Æthelflæd established *burhs* at Tamworth, Chester and Warwick and, with the help of her brother Edward, managed to regain some of the Mercian lands which had fallen into Viking hands. When she died in 918, Edward decided it was essential to ensure that the Mercians remained faithful to him, so he seized Tamworth and took Æthelflæd's daughter hostage.

Drastic though this move might seem, it had a political logic. Mercia and Wessex had long been enemies, forced into an uneasy unity only by the Viking threat. Æthelflæd had been a strong leader, capturing Derby and Leicester from the Vikings, and was ready, at the time of her death, to accept the submission of the Danes in York. Without Æthelflæd, it seems that this deal collapsed and the kingdom was officially left to her daughter. But other Mercian ealdormen no doubt had designs on the kingdom and Edward may have feared the possibility of a Mercian alliance with the Vikings in York. Taking no chances, he imposed his own rule, and made official the adoption of Mercia into the kingdom of Wessex.

Before his sister's death, Edward had been making his own inroads into Viking-held lands, at times in response to acts of Viking aggression. In 917 a band had gathered from both East Anglia and Mercia and made an unsuccessful attempt to capture one of Edward's strongholds. Edward's men retaliated by combining forces with troops positioned in *burhs* near to the Viking stronghold at Tempsford and mounting an attack. They killed many Vikings, including the Viking king and two of his *jarls* and, shortly afterwards men from Kent, Surrey and Essex banded together to capture Colchester. The raiding-army in East Anglia soon rallied, and besieged Maldon, but more Anglo-Saxons arrived to assist those in the stronghold and put the raiding-army to flight.

Edward advanced further into East Anglia, until the West Saxon army reached Colchester. Here a group under the control of the Danes, and soon the raiding-army itself, swore allegiance to him. Edward had conquered yet another region, expanding the kingdom of Wessex still further.

Although today it is tempting to cast Edward in the role of saviour of the East Anglians, it is unlikely that all the Anglo-Saxon inhabitants saw him in quite that light. Indeed, a number probably joined the Danes to fight him off. After all, East Anglia had never been a part of Wessex and until 825 had been subservient to Mercia. The Danes were just the most recent in a long line of rulers who claimed this region for their own. The local inhabitants, given the choice, may actually have preferred the rule of the Vikings.

Thinking about what it would have been like to live at this time, I suspect that there was probably very little to choose between Viking rule and that of the Anglo-Saxons. Both could be violent, unpredictable and scheming but, at a practical level, maybe the better trading contacts of the Vikings might possibly have influenced loyalties.

Quite what the relationship was between the Danish rulers in the north and east of England and their Anglo-Saxon subjects is hard to say. History tends to concern itself with what are seen as important events, so whereas Alfred's battles are documented, the scale of the Viking presence in the Danelaw is still uncertain. Even when the Anglo-Saxon Chronicles describe the Danes dividing up the land among themselves, no details are provided as to how this was done. We know that the Great Army travelled extensively, but precisely how many of its members stayed and settled within the Danelaw?

In fact, the term Danelaw makes its first appearance in law books compiled in 1008. Today, it is used to refer to those regions of England which the Danes are thought to have influenced, and in particular the regions they are said to have controlled in the late ninth century. However, the name does not give us any indication of just how these Danes controlled the region, or what the native Anglo-Saxons thought of their new rulers.

Only by answering these questions can we find out what life was really like in the Danelaw. The warriors who settled may have simply taken over positions of leadership, ruling areas without affecting the life of the inhabitants greatly. This is effectively what happened centuries before with the

Romanisation of Britain; a central authority and all the trappings of Empire left the majority of the population largely unaffected. But in the tenth century there is an alternative possibility: that further Danish settlers, arriving in large numbers, changed the culture of the entire Danelaw. The genetic study may provide more conclusive evidence of the size of the Danish influx, but archaeology and linguistics can go some way towards illuminating the picture.

Place-names provide one of the major pieces of evidence for Scandinavian settlement in the Danelaw. As in Orkney and Shetland, there are many names with Scandinavian roots in the north and east of England. In fact, it was the Icelandic saga author Snorri Sturluson who first observed in the thirteenth century that eastern England boasted a number of Scandinavian names. So it seems that some towns and villages in the regions visited by the Great Army adopted Danish names. One might draw the conclusion that these are the areas where Danish people stayed and settled but, unfortunately, the answer is not that simple. The Scandinavian place-names we see today do coincide with the region we call the Danelaw. But while some Scandinavians must have been present for these names to enter common usage, there are several ways in which these places could have acquired them.

We cannot assume that only Scandinavians lived in places with Danish names. Indeed Ingleby, the place near Repton with the Viking cremation cemetery, is a good example of this. Ingleby is a Scandinavian name meaning 'the village of the English', and must have been given as a result of a distinct lack of Danish settlers. But is this proof that no Danes lived there at all, or just of Danish influence?

By taking over key positions of power, members of the Great Army may have enjoyed significant influence over the naming of places, even if they themselves did not live there. The lord of a region might easily decide to rename a settlement, or even establish a new village, despite living some distance away. So, in taking over the running of an area, the Danes may have produced far more apparent evidence of Danish settlement than their actual numbers would deserve.

There is a further complication, the role of fashion. If Scandinavian names became popular, or synonymous with progress or enterprise, there is no reason why they should not be adopted by the Anglo-Saxons. For example, a very common Scandinavian suffix in place-names is -*by* (used

RIGHT | *The extent of Viking settlement in the Danelaw can be traced through cities, towns and villages with names of Scandinavian origin.*

in names like Grimsby or Whitby) which, judging by its distribution, may well have been used by Danish rulers. Anglo-Saxons living in or near these places might then have adapted their own place-names using this suffix or even taken it with them to a new region.

So, without being sure who was responsible for initially coining a name, it is difficult to draw any conclusions about the people settling in the Danelaw. Not only might Anglo-Saxons have taken the names with them as they moved around, but Scandinavian naming conventions may have persisted long after the Danes had gone. Some places might even have received Danish names long after the end of the Viking Age.

But, even with all these problems of interpretation, there are some interesting patterns to be seen in the place-names of the Danelaw. There are, for example, far more that involve a person's name within this part

This picture of Garbold the Dane comes from a 1930s family history which suggests he was the founder of Garboldisham. He is probably a mythical character.

of England than there are in Denmark. In the region called the 'Five Boroughs', which included Derby, Leicester, Lincoln, Nottingham and Stamford, the number of places ending in -*by* that include a person's name is 68 per cent, as opposed to 10 per cent in Denmark. There are also a large number of places which use Danish personal names with an English ending, such as *Grimston*, the *tun* (or village) of Grim.

Perhaps these towns named after Scandinavians were those founded by members of the Great Army whose place-naming traditions might then have spread to nearby areas. Or alternatively, these other places with Scandinavian names may also have been inhabited by Danes. Although it is almost impossible to be sure which is the case, one thing is certain: the Scandinavians left their mark on the towns and villages of England and we still use many Scandinavian place-names today.

In East Anglia, not far from Thetford, lies Garboldisham, a town which bears the name of a famous Viking. The story of Garbold the Dane is similar to that of many other Vikings. Returning from raiding in the Mediterranean with lots of treasure, he hears tell of similar wealth to be had in England and sets sail with forty ships. Garbold makes his home in this distant land, until one day he has a dream that foretells his death. Eager to put all his affairs in order before this dream comes true, Garbold distributes his land and ships between his three sons but hides away some of his treasure, riches that are only to be used in times of great need. The treasure is to remain hidden as long as the family's fortunes remain intact, its location known by only three totally trust-worthy people. And with that, the story stops. The exact location of the treasure is never revealed, and if Garbold's family have continued to prosper, it could still be there today awaiting that time of great need.

The story, a local myth, is quite possibly a Victorian fantasy but David Corbould believes that he too, like the town, carries the name of Garbold. His father passed on a book to him that recounts the legend of Garbold the Dane and describes the Corbould geneaology. It traces the family line back to the first occurrence of the name, in 1395 in the village of Occold, just ten miles from Garboldisham. So it is quite possible that these first Corboulds really are the descendants of Garbold.

This oval brooch was found in a female burial at Santon Downham, Norfolk.

The place-names in north and east England clearly demonstrate links with Scandinavia and seem to be backed up by finds of 'Anglo-Scandinavian' brooches in East Anglia and Northumberland. But, as was pointed out to me by more than one museum curator, owning one of these brooches would not have made you Scandinavian as they could just have easily been traded. So, although these items of jewellery can be interpreted in different ways, and at times are not even very easy to date, they do provide, in their hybrid style, clear evidence of the cultural mixing that was to become such a feature of life in the Danelaw.

Many aspects of what tends to be collectively known by archaeologists as 'material culture' show the influence of new styles previously unseen in Anglo-Saxon England. The influences are not just Scandinavian either. Carolingian styles, from the Frankish Empire, appear in the metal-work and thrown pottery, steatite bowls are introduced from the Shetland Islands or Norway, while Byzantine silk and pottery from the Rhineland have also been found. The Vikings are doing what they seem to do best: not simply trading but assimilating a wide variety of cultural influences from the areas with which they are in contact.

All of these different influences came into play in the Danelaw where an exciting cultural mix soon developed. Before the ninth century, the kingdoms of England had evolved differing styles of metalwork, with the products of Wessex craftsmen very different from those of their counterparts in Northumbria. But during the Viking period, styles from Winchester and Wessex are found moving into the north. There are several possible explanations for this. Scandinavian settlers have taken the spoils of battle with them into the Danelaw, copying southern designs, or even bringing craftsmen from other regions with them as they settled. Whatever the case, the metalwork in the Danelaw shows a vitality of design that transcends old cultural boundaries and for which we must thank the Vikings.

This image of the Vikings as easy-going travellers, keen to adopt new traditions and styles, is not one that we may be used to and, yet, adaptability has always been one of their strengths. At this time the Anglo-Saxons within the Danelaw also begin to adopt many of the customs and fashions of their new compatriots. Of course they may have been persuaded to do so by force as the Danes had effectively conquered their kingdoms, but they also owed no loyalty to Wessex. Their kingdoms may well have been just as much at risk from an expansionist Wessex as from colonising Danes so perhaps, at times, the East Anglians and the Danes were quite happy to work together. There are hints, though, that sometimes the relationship may have been more complex, and not always peaceful. A good example is the story of St Edmund.

Edmund was the King of East Anglia when the Great Army arrived. Later manuscripts describe how, in 870, the raiding-army, under their leader Ivar, over-wintered at Thetford. Here, unlike other leaders who had agreed to rule on behalf of the Vikings, Edmund would not let himself be reduced to the status of a puppet king and he also resolutely refused to deny his Christian faith. As a result he was killed and his kingdom seized.

Edmund's brutal death at the hands of pagans no doubt contributed greatly to his later acceptance as a saint. The first mention of his sainthood occurs on a memorial coin minted in East Anglia, some time around 895. About two thousand of these coins have since been found, with well over half coming from the Cuerdale Hoard, buried near Preston in about 905.

But minting coins was not a Scandinavian practice. Payment was by weight and the Vikings used any convenient piece of silver as currency: a coin was no more or less useful than a brooch. Yet it seems that several East Anglian mints may have been producing coins in the name of St Edmund the King around the turn of the ninth century. So, at the very least, the Scandinavian settlers were allowing the Anglo-Saxons to carry

King Edmund of East Anglia is bound to a tree and bombarded with arrows.

on with this practice. But, even so, St Edmund might be thought a rather unusual choice for a Viking kingdom to commemorate, considering they were the ones responsible for his violent death only a couple of decades earlier. There may, however, be a reason for this unusual choice.

After Edmund's death, the East Anglians had been ruled by locals in the Vikings' name, until Guthrum returned in 880. Although they appeared to accept Danish rule, it is possible that Edmund's successors were biding their time and, when Guthrum died in 890, the Danes may have seen trouble brewing. The cult of their martyred king would have made a powerful rallying point for the Anglo-Saxons of East Anglia so perhaps the Danish leaders, aware of this, decided to hijack St Edmund for their own purposes. Issuing coins in his name might be interpreted as atonement for his death, at least partially countering the voice of those who sought revenge. As ever, the Vikings could be pragmatic when required.

To the archaeologist, coins are extremely useful artefacts as they usually carry the name of a ruler and, in many cases, a date. They offer clear evidence of trade and a coin in a particular layer on a site can often indicate its date with far greater precision than would be possible by using a method such as radiocarbon dating. As dating evidence coins must, however, be used with caution. A date of 905 on a coin does not mean that it was lost or buried in 905, and does not automatically date the layer within which it was found to 905. What it means is that the layer cannot be *earlier* than 905, but could be a lot later. Consideration must be taken of factors such as how worn the coin is and how long it might therefore have been in circulation. Nevertheless, the appearance of Viking coins is welcome and provides hints of the other side of the cultural exchange: the adoption by the Vikings of Anglo-Saxon traditions.

During the early period of Viking raiding, the quality of Anglo-Saxon silver had diminished considerably so that by the time Alfred took the throne, many supposedly silver coins contained only 25 per cent of the precious metal. Although the Viking raids probably did not help the declining standard of the coins, they cannot be held responsible for it. It was not simply an English problem either: in Francia, Charles the Bald also found his coins declining in quality. The problem may simply have been one of a general lack of silver.

In 864 Charles the Bald decided to improve the standard of his empire's coinage and, a decade later, Alfred followed suit. Wessex underwent a complete currency exchange in which five old pennies could be swapped for one new one in which the silver content had been increased to about 90 per cent. Alfred also increased the weight of each coin at this time, clearly following the Carolingian lead and concerned that any kingdom worth its salt ought to have good-quality coins.

A Viking copy of a King Alfred coin (right). A coin of Halfdon, Danish King of York (left).

Before the arrival of the Vikings, York had been a bit of a backwater, and the coins issued in Northumbria were of base metal by the mid-ninth century. But once the Vikings had taken control of Northumbria and East Anglia, things began to change. The first Viking coins were copies of Alfred's, some even using his name, and were of high quality silver. However, these Viking copies were of the coins issued prior to Alfred's monetary reforms and so adhered to the English standards that moneyers in East Anglia would have used before the arrival of the Vikings.

These, the earliest Viking coins, cannot have been intended as counterfeits as, even though they use Alfred's name and designs, they are obviously of a different weight and size to the official issues. Mark Blackburn, of the Fitzwilliam Museum, Cambridge, believes that they were intended to be used as currency, part of a process devised by Viking leaders to create an official economy, along the lines of those they saw in the Anglo-Saxon and Carolingian kingdoms. But old Scandinavian habits appear to have persisted and for years a dual economy existed in the Danelaw. In some regions the new Anglo-Scandinavian coinage was accepted as currency, while in others the bullion system, using a mixture of foreign

King Alfred issued many coins during his reign. The Vikings used his coins as a template for their own.

and Anglo-Saxon coins and hacksilver, still persisted. Much of this bullion shows the tell-tale peck marks produced by the tip of a blade used to test the quality of the silver, and many Anglo-Saxon coins which ended up in Viking hands, like those found in the hoard at Cuerdale, are peck-marked. It is interesting to note that the coins being produced by the Vikings in East Anglia and York were considered to be of a good enough standard that they did not need to be checked in this way.

Mark considers that the Vikings, having fought against Alfred, were now beginning to adopt the trappings that they felt were necessary for a powerful kingdom. Coinage was a way of impressing upon their Anglo-Saxon neighbours the fact that they, the Vikings, were here to stay.

Confidence soon increased and, after a few tentative years of producing Alfred copies, the Danes began to put their own names on the coins. The first to do so was Guthrum, although the coins do not bear this name but actually say Athelstan-Rex, the Anglo-Saxon name he took at his baptism. His contemporary in York, Guthfrith, also produced coins, although only one of these has ever been found. Coins have also been found bearing the name of Halfdan, the leader of the band of Danes that first settled at York in 866.

These early coins are interesting for a number of reasons. The Vikings write their names in roman script, not in the runes they used in Scandinavia, and on the reverse of the coins is the name of the moneyer, the person responsible for producing them. Remarkably, none of these names are Scandinavian. A few are Anglo-Saxon, but most are those of Franks. The Vikings had little experience of minting coins in Scandinavia, and it seems that when they decided to establish mints in the Danelaw, they brought over a number of skilled moneyers from the Continent. These men established families who for generations dominated the production of coins in eastern England.

Mark Blackburn believes that all of these coins were intended as much for an Anglo-Saxon and Carolingian audience as a Danish one, the intention being to demonstrate Danish power in a way which the English would clearly understand. Similarly, the adoption of Christianity was perhaps motivated by pragmatism rather than by any great change in belief – yet another way to become part of the system.

The Danish leader Guthrum was perhaps the first to see the value of adopting Christianity. Having fought with Alfred, and realising that he was incapable of conquering the whole of Wessex, he decided to enter into a deal as part of which he was baptised, changing his name to the Anglo-Saxon Athelstan. Not all Viking leaders went quite as far as Guthrum, but they must also have recognised the importance of religion to the Anglo-Saxons. In the mid-990s, the Alfred-style coins were replaced by new, distinctive issues that celebrated the independence of the Danelaw kingdoms and promoted a strong Christian message. As well as the coins produced to commemorate St Edmund in East Anglia, a fascinating series minted in the northern part of the Danelaw honoured the kings of York. These coins display crosses, excerpts from psalms, and references to the 'Lord God Almighty' while later examples carry the name of St Peter, the patron saint of York Minster.

In fact, these coins minted in the Danelaw often carry a stronger Christian message than their contemporary Anglo-Saxon or Carolingian counterparts. Perhaps as part of a political decision, the Vikings have grasped the importance of religion and are setting about demonstrating that, in their new-found faith (whether sincere or not), they can out-Christian the Anglo-Saxons.

It is often assumed that the Church suffered under Scandinavian rule but the truth is that although the Vikings threatened the Church, in the long run it survived. They certainly raided many sites, and even took over some important locations such as Repton. But these were natural targets, especially as the Church was closely linked to the positions of power. The Vikings do not seem to have harboured any hostility to Christianity itself and were quite happy to use it to their advantage when necessary.

The Middleton Cross shows a warrior, complete with sword, shield, axe and spear.

We can see evidence for Christian beliefs mixing with the pagan traditions of the Scandinavians at several sites in the north of England, including the stone cross found in St Andrew's Church in Middleton, North Yorkshire. This cross shows a warrior in a helmet, with a knife, seated on a stool or throne. The sculptor has included a shield, sword, axe and spear, probably to represent the power of this warrior.

To have a warrior on a cross is unusual, but another sculpture shows the mixing of Scandinavian and Christian beliefs even more clearly. In the churchyard at Gosforth, in Cumbria, a large cross takes pride of place. The cross at the top of this huge sculpture is Celtic in style, but the four panels include both Scandinavian and Anglo-Saxon designs. The Crucifixion is intermingled with scenes from Ragnarök. This is a Scandinavian myth describing the destruction of the world, when the pagan gods are over-thrown by the forces of evil.

This cross, erected in the tenth century, demonstrates how the inhabitants combined pagan and Christian beliefs. For the incoming pagan Scandinavians, it was easy to adopt Christ as just another god. Thor's hammer and the Christian cross are remarkably similar! But there is also evidence that the Scandinavians were using the Christian traditions to establish themselves in England.

Archaeologist Dawn Hadley believes the Vikings adopted Christian traditions to convince the Anglo-Saxons of their own importance. During the Viking Age there seem to be many more churches and religious monuments popping up in East Anglia, Yorkshire and Lincolnshire. Previously, most of the sculpture had only served to mark out sacred places. There might be a single consecrated object in a church, perhaps a cross, or perhaps a monument to a saint. But under the influence of the Scandinavian settlers in the tenth century, we find more sculpture at already existing sites, perhaps an increase of as much as ten times in some areas.

Dawn Hadley thinks the increase in sculpture occurs because society was changing at this time and, perhaps due to the Scandinavian influx, there was increased competition for power. As immigrants to the region, the Vikings had to bring their family history with them, and they would probably want to make their mark. One of the best ways to claim nobility for their family name would be to have a monument erected. This sculpture of the tenth-century shows the Scandinavians yet again adapting perfectly to local society, quickly realising the best way to state their importance.

The region we call the Danelaw was a complex place in the tenth century. A complete Scandinavian culture that would be recognisable to those in their homelands did not persist. Instead, the Vikings adopted from the Anglo-Saxons what they needed to make their kingdoms appear successful. In doing so, they also found some of their unique style rubbing off on the Anglo-Saxon natives. The result is a hybrid known today as Anglo-Scandinavian.

This Anglo-Scandinavian style is apparent in the sculpture and the metalwork found in the Danelaw. It also suggests that the Anglo-Saxons in this region were happy to co-operate with the Vikings, even if they resisted them at first. Despite the image we are given through the Anglo-Saxon Chronicles – of England as a nation fighting for its independence from the Danes – it is not surprising that the inhabitants of Northumbria and East Anglia were happy to embrace the varied culture which was emerging in the Danelaw. Alfred may be referred to today as the man who created England, but his contemporaries in the other Anglo-Saxon kingdoms would not have seen it that way. Wessex had hijacked Englishness for its own political advantage.

The Danish leaders in York and East Anglia had adopted many Anglo-Saxon customs. But how did Edward, King of Wessex, treat the Scandinavian settlers when he began to claim back these 'English' lands? At the Fitzwilliam Museum in Cambridge, Mark Blackburn has archaeological evidence which suggests that the English too could be tolerant of other customs.

Recently, a small and classically Viking hoard containing coins from a wide range of places was discovered at Thurcaston, about five miles from Leicester. There are Viking pennies decorated with battle swords – five in the name of Sihtric Caech, 'the one-eyed' – which may have been minted at Lincoln, and two from York commemorating St Peter. Three of the coins are Anglo-Saxon, minted for Edward the Elder and of a different size and weight to those minted by Vikings.

Also included in the hoard are cut pieces of two Islamic dirhams. These Islamic coins are always extremely useful finds, as it was the practice of the moneyers to put the name of the Caliph, the local ruler, the location of the mint and the date on each coin. The two found in Leicester came as far east as Samarkand in Central Asia, and date from between 913 and 915.

From the dates on these and the other coins, Mark thinks the hoard must have been buried in 924 or 925, certainly no earlier than 923. The presence of the Islamic dirhams, minted no more than twelve years earlier, shows just how quickly goods could travel once in Viking hands. These coins had passed through many hands in their journey from Central Asia, across Russia and Scandinavia and finally to England.

But this collection of coins tells us about more than Viking trade; it tells us something of Leicester at the time of its burial. Leicester was re-conquered from the Danes by Edward's sister Æthelflæd in 918 so by the time this hoard was buried, Leicester had been part of the Anglo-Saxon kingdom again for at least five years. Mark thinks its very presence indicates that the Anglo-Saxon rulers were as tolerant of a multicultural community as the Danish leaders were before them. At the very least, they must have turned a blind eye to persisting Viking traditions, like the use of foreign coins as bullion.

This tolerance also allowed Danish influence to flourish long after their rulers had been defeated. Coin hoards, sculpture, brooches and other artefacts are the material side of the Scandinavian settlement and in the Domesday Book, compiled some two hundred years after the arrival of the Great Army, we find many Scandinavian names. But as well as the Scandinavian personal names and place-names recorded in the Domesday Book, many Old Norse words found their way into the English language. Almost all of them are ordinary, everyday words still in use today, words that describe the family, such as husband and sister, foods such as eggs, and a wide variety of others, including happy, anger, thrive and law. And the Scandinavian influence was not limited to these words; the grammar and structure of the English language also altered.

The effect which the Scandinavian settlers had on the English language suggests that their influence may have extended over a long period of time, and beyond the boundaries of the Danelaw. In the same way, Anglo-Scandinavian sculpture shows that Scandinavian taste affected more than just the immediate area of the Danish settlements. Although much can be found in the region of York, other examples are found outside the conventional boundaries of the Danelaw. These massive sculptures are not as easily dated as coins, but they do have the advantage over metal-work and other highly portable objects in being very difficult to move. As such, the place where we find them today is likely to be where they were originally intended to be.

Many examples of this Anglo-Scandinavian sculpture are found in the north-west of England, not a part of the country that was taken over by the Danish Vikings based in York. These sculptures show the influence of the Hiberno-Norse Vikings from the Irish Sea region, perhaps those who were looking for new land to settle after their expulsion from Dublin in 902. There was no love lost between Dane and Norseman; they were rivals and if at any time they did work together it was for mutual benefit, not through any cultural loyalty. The Danish inhabitants of York saw no reason to share anything that they had gained with these dispossessed Norsemen but were soon to feel their threat.

York was not a healthy place to be in the early years of the tenth century. The town was attacked and controlled by various leaders: the Danish Vikings; Edward of Wessex; Ragnald, the Irish-Norse Viking leader; Ragnald's brother Sihtric. When Sihtric died in 927 York was once again ripe for the picking. Sihtric's son Olaf was in York, and his brother Guthfrith travelled from Dublin, whether to aid his nephew or to wrest the town from his kinsman's grasp is impossible to tell. But Olaf had another uncle who would foil the plans of the Dublin Vikings to rule both York and Dublin. By this time the Anglo-Saxon King Edward was dead and his son, Athelstan, was on the throne. Aware of the strategic importance of York, Athelstan had married his sister to Sihtric, at the time that he was king of York. So Olaf Sihtricsson was Athelstan's nephew too.

Olaf's two uncles, the Dublin Viking king and the Anglo-Saxon king, each decided to lay claim to the prosperous city of York. But even the combined Viking forces of Guthfrith and Olaf would prove no match for the army Athelstan brought from the south of England and once again the kingdom of Northumbria found itself ruled by Anglo-Saxons.

The Dublin Vikings, originally from Norway, and the Danes of the Great Army clearly felt that York was a prize worth fighting for and Athelstan too seemed determined to rule this kingdom even if it did mean some military losses. Today, archaeological excavations are revealing just what this truly Anglo-Scandinavian town was like in the tenth century. What is emerging is a trading centre, as valuable a place as Viking Dublin.

York was originally the Roman town of Eboracum, but after the occupying army withdrew shortly after 400 AD, the town was effectively abandoned, its remaining walls protecting only a wasteland. In the seventh century, the Anglo-Saxons began to reuse these defences, a cathedral was built and bishops took up residence. York became an important regal and ecclesiastical centre, but was not necessarily densely populated. Northumbria was still something of a backwater in Anglo-Saxon England, and York was nowhere near the bustling city it would become by the time of Domesday. It is the Viking take-over that began the expansion of the town.

Between 1976 and 1981 the York Archaeological Trust carried out a huge archaeological excavation at Coppergate, an excavation that has revealed Viking Age York in astounding detail. For about four hundred years after the Romans had departed, the archaeology reveals very little, but in the mid-ninth century, just when the Great Army was arriving in England, there are signs of renewed activity.

By the tenth century, clear plot boundaries have become obvious and the town appears to be flourishing. Towards the end of that century the simple wattle-and-daub structures which characterised the early Viking town are replaced by sophisticated two-storey timber buildings. According to Richard Kemp, the director of the Jorvik Centre that now occupies the site of the Coppergate dig, this 'high-rise' development made Jorvik, in 975, 'probably the tenth-century equivalent of Hong Kong or New York!' The reason why it is possible to study houses in such detail and why so much evidence for everyday life has survived for over a thousand years, is due to a happy twist of fate, and the habits of York's Viking inhabitants. Organic soils can, under the right burial conditions, provide a protective, oxygen-free environment for the objects buried in them. The remains of twigs, thatch, straw and other plants, as well as human and animal waste, all help to produce this unique type of soil.

The residents of Viking Age York produced a lot of rubbish in the course of their everyday lives. Leftover wood from house-building, straw or heather used as bedding, and the waste created when woodworking, tanning or manufacturing textiles all had to be disposed of in some way.

York was a bustling settlement in the Viking Age, with both Anglo-Saxon and Viking rulers. These gravestones come from York Minster.

Due to the increasing numbers of people living in York, the rubbish grew faster than it could be broken down by natural processes. So this accumulation of organic rubbish acted a bit like a bog, trapping moisture inside it, reducing the oxygen content of the soil and killing the bacteria that cause decay. This soil produced the perfect conditions to preserve many organic materials, providing archaeologists with a treasure trove of artefacts.

Only Viking Age York benefited from these organic soil conditions. The Romans, whose stone walls and tiled roofs meant that little building waste could contribute to this organic melting-pot, were also better at rubbish disposal than their Viking Age counterparts. And the earlier Anglo-Saxon inhabitants were simply not numerous enough to produce the quantities of rubbish required.

Thanks to the dubious quality of the waste disposal system in tenth-century York, we can see a huge range of objects made of organic materials such as leather, cloth, and wood today. Combs survive with the remains of head lice still trapped between the teeth, while the contents of cesspits provide a veritable treasure trove of information. Not only do they show precisely what had been eaten prior to a visit to the pit but also contain moss and strips of old clothes, Viking toilet paper! The picture painted by these finds is of a town not unlike Viking Dublin, a prosperous and bustling centre with trading links to the rest of the Viking world. Most of the artefacts are simple domestic items, such as cooking pots and wooden cups, and when jewellery is found, it is not the elaborate gems buried with Scandinavian rulers in their homelands but simple, mass-produced brooches which would have enabled every inhabitant to have their own piece of silver.

Although York, like the rest of Danelaw, has a preponderance of Anglo-Scandinavian goods, there is a real difficulty in pinpointing any purely Scandinavian artefacts. The small number of burials which have been uncovered do not clarify the picture much either. In excavations during the early 1960s a few skeletons were found in the churchyard of St Mary Bishophill Junior. Two were buried with grave goods, something that was not typical of Christian burials at the time. A woman was wearing a silver arm-ring of Anglo-Scandinavian style, dated to the late ninth or tenth century, while a man was found with a silver penny minted in York, an iron knife, and a whetstone. Also found in the man's grave was a bronze buckle, which he had probably been wearing at his waist at the time of his burial.

Two graves are not a lot to go on, but they may provide yet another clue to the way these two cultures intermingled. These are not people

This jet cross pendant was found during the excavations of Viking-Age York.

This bronze buckle was probably worn as part of a belt. It was found in a grave discovered during excavations in Viking Age York.

buried with all their worldly goods nor are these objects particularly valuable. So perhaps they are Scandinavians who, although nominally Christian, have not quite abandoned their old beliefs and whose possessions retain just a glimmer of the tradition that finds its ultimate expression in the splendour of Viking homeland burials like that from Oseberg.

Life in the town of York must have been good, trade and manufacture brought prosperity, and yet there must always have been the uncertainty of when the next attack would come and who would be the next leader. Perhaps in these circumstances it is not surprising that people chose to be buried in a way that would hopefully appease both the old gods and the new one. Prayers and a Christian burial might provide for the afterlife but it was better to take along a few possessions as well, just in case the final destination was Valhalla rather than the kingdom of heaven.

The lack of objects from York in a purely Scandinavian style is yet more evidence for the integration of Danes, Norwegians, and Anglo-Saxons. Perhaps this cultural blending also made it easier for the inhabitants to accept leaders from differing cultural and political backgrounds. The people of York seem quite happy with Athelstan as their new king when he drives out Guthfrith and Olaf in 927, and go on to accept both Scandinavians and Anglo-Saxons as future leaders.

After his conquest of York, Athelstan had effective control of all of modern-day England. He became a powerful king who, for most of his reign, went unchallenged, but in 937 several important leaders decided to unite against him.

Athelstan faced a coalition consisting of Olaf Guthfrithsson, who had become King of Dublin on his father's death, Constantine II, the King of the Scots, and the Britons of Strathclyde, a Welsh-speaking kingdom in what is now south-west Scotland. The Vikings had a vested interest in reclaiming part of the lands they had once held, and Athelstan had antagonised the Scots by raiding in Scotland just a few years before. Both the Scandinavian and Scottish kingdoms were no doubt feeling threatened by Athelstan's advances to York, and the Britons of Strathclyde must also have felt they were next on the list for a take-over.

The two armies met at Brunanburh and the ensuing battle is described in a poem inserted in the Anglo-Saxon Chronicles. It tells us little of the circumstances leading up to the conflict but it does seem that Olaf was probably the ringleader. Dublin was a powerful Viking base by this time, and Olaf was perhaps the most important Viking leader in the British Isles. It appears to have been his decision to oppose the King of the English, and enlisted the help of others he thought would be threatened by the expanding Anglo-Saxon kingdom. The battle of Brunanburh was to be violent and bloody.

Viking leaders also issued coins in their own names. This one comes from the reign of Olaf Guthfrithsson.

With chosen troops,
throughout the day,
the West-Saxons fierce
press'd on the loathed bands;
hew'd down the fugitives,
and scatter'd the rear,
with strong mill-sharpen'd blades,
The Mercians too
the hard hand-play
spared not to any
of those that with Anlaf
over the briny deep
in the ship's bosom
sought this land
for the hardy fight.
Five kings lay
on the field of battle,
in bloom of youth,
pierced with swords.
So seven eke
of the earls of Anlaf;
and of the ship's-crew
unnumber'd crowds.
There was dispersed
the little band
of hardy Scots,
the dread of northern hordes;
urged to the noisy deep
by unrelenting fate!

The West Saxons lost many men, but Olaf's army was torn apart and he himself barely escaped the battlefield. Five Norse kings were killed, as well as the son of the King of the Scots, Constantine II. The Norse and their allies escaped to their boats.

Brunanburh served to reinforce Athelstan's position not only as 'King of the Anglo-Saxons and the Danes', but as 'King of the English'. Although today we remember Alfred 'the Great' more clearly than his grandson Athelstan, this may be largely due to the benefits of a sympathetic biographer and the support of the Anglo-Saxon Chronicles. Looking back at the battles of the ninth and tenth centuries it is easy to see Alfred as the saviour of England, but it is probably Athelstan who was more impressive to his contemporaries and who should rightly be regarded as the first king of all England. In the Anglo-Saxon period, Alfred's biography was paid little attention and it was Athelstan who claimed the glory.

Once again the lack of documentary evidence makes it difficult to confirm this idea, but there is one story that seems to offer some support. At the end of the tenth century, Æthelred, Alfred's great-great-grandson, chose to name his eight sons after previous West Saxon kings. The first-born is given the honoured name of Athelstan, with the second son being named after Alfred's grandfather Egbert who had defeated the Mercians in 825, and become the first West Saxon king to lay claim to Mercia, East Anglia and Northumbria. The next five of Æthelred's sons took the names of Athelstan's successors, up to and including Æthelred's own half-brother. Finally, when it came to naming his eighth and final son, Æthelred has to resort to using Alfred, his great-great-grandfather's name.

Later eleventh-century sources do list Alfred as an important king, but he is not given any special position. Ultimately, Alfred had held firm against the Danes, but he had been forced to compromise. His successors, who drove the Viking leaders from the country, might naturally have been regarded as more obvious national heroes.

It was Athelstan who effectively won back the Danelaw from Viking control and although later skirmishes see York changing hands, the rest of the country remains English. But was this a truly united country? Within the area that had been the Danelaw, cultural differences had developed during the period of Scandinavian rule that would not simply disappear. Here the way of life and even the legal system were different from those enjoyed in regions that had remained steadfastly Anglo-Saxon.

There were still strong elements of Danish culture in this newly united England in the tenth century and the cultural mix seemed to be working. But not all of Athelstan's successors would be such strong leaders and, before long, cultural tensions would begin to flare. The external threat from the Vikings had not disappeared either; they had simply left the country for a while, to regroup and gather their strength. For while England was getting used to being a united country, Denmark was growing in strength. The Danes who returned in the eleventh century had built up an empire of their own, and would be keen to exert more than just a cultural influence on their Anglo-Saxon neighbours.

CHAPTER 11

THE FINAL STAND

The English, indeed, were the more bold at first, and cut down the Danes with terrible slaughter, to such an extent that they nearly won the victory . . . [the Danes] forthwith showed in battle how dangerous a thing is desperation. For . . . they raged on against the enemy with such madness, that you would have seen not only the bodies of the dead falling, but also of the living as they avoided the blows.

CNUT RETURNS TO TAKE ENGLAND, FROM *ENCOMIUM EMMAE REGINAE*

LEFT | *The Jelling Stone, Jutland, Denmark, was erected by the Danish King Harald Bluetooth, commemorating his mother and father and celebrating the conversion of the Danes to Christianity.*

After defeating the combined forces of the Norse, the Scots and the Britons at Brunanburh, Athelstan was in control of all of England. He was a powerful king who married his half-sisters into royal houses across Europe and his contemporaries regarded him as one of their greatest rulers. Yet, despite his achievements, Athelstan never married or produced an heir and so, on his death, the throne passed to his half-brother Edmund.

The Dublin Vikings had still not given up all hope of expanding their kingdom and, although they had decided not to take on Athelstan again, when he died they saw their chance. Olaf Guthfrithsson led an army back to York and took the city. He then expanded his kingdom further south, taking back the region of the 'Five Boroughs' – Lincoln, Derby, Nottingham, Leicester, and Stamford. Intent on continuing the Norse dynasty in York, his cousin, Olaf Sihtricsson took over the kingdom on his death.

King Edmund decided he must recover some of this lost land, if he was to live up to the reputation of his predecessor. In 942 he retook the Five Boroughs, and by 944 the Dublin Vikings had been ejected from York, leaving its inhabitants with yet another new leader.

The last Scandinavian ruler of York is also one of the most famous Vikings, largely due to his fearsome name. Like Olaf, Erik Bloodaxe was a Norwegian, but he did not come to England from Dublin. His father,

Harald Fairhair, was one of the greatest kings of Norway, described in legend as the first Norwegian leader to unite the entire country.

Having united his own country, Harald is said to have divided the Norwegian kingdom between his sons, giving the largest proportion to his favourite, but not eldest, son Erik Bloodaxe. When Erik took over the kingdom on Harald's death he was quick to eliminate any competition, killing his two brothers.

Erik is one of the main characters featured in *Egil's Saga*. The saga's hero is Egil Skalla-Grimsson who was, like many of the characters in Icelandic sagas, a complex mixture of warrior, farmer, poet, and merchant. His adventures take him to most of the lands under Viking control, and more than once he crosses the path of Erik Bloodaxe. Although modern scholars think Egil himself probably never met Erik, the story tells us something of how Erik was perceived, and may also be the source of his violent nickname.

Erik Bloodaxe first enters the saga when Egil has a clash with one of his servants and kills him. Egil is a berserker, a Viking warrior who works himself into a trance-like rage before going into battle. While Erik may have killed his brothers, Egil is said to have killed a playmate when he was only six years old. The two are both violent men, and the saga celebrates their aggression. The feud between the two Vikings escalates when Egil kills one of Erik's sons. For several years after this, Egil survives as a pirate, keeping well away from Erik. But eventually Egil finds himself shipwrecked on a trading voyage to England and is brought before Erik, now King of York.

Egil is sentenced to death, but in a dramatic twist, he composes a poem that so honours Erik Bloodaxe, that he cannot demand that Egil dies. So his poetic skills, praised throughout the saga, enable him to escape once again, and to continue with his adventures. But, when not being forced to celebrate Erik's virtues, Egil pens a more truthful poem, telling of Erik's violent nature and calling him a Bloodaxe.

Egil Skallagrimsson is the hero of a Scandinavian saga. He was a violent warrior, but also a talented poet.

As *Egil's Saga* was written long after the events it describes we cannot rely on its factual accuracy, but it does seem that Erik Bloodaxe managed to control York. Despite, or perhaps because of, executing both his brothers, Erik soon found himself ejected from the Norwegian kingdom. He was not a well-liked ruler and when, in about 936, his half-brother

Hakon challenged him, Erik was forced to abdicate. He was reduced to travelling the Scottish Isles, raiding to support himself, but soon saw an opportunity to develop a new kingdom.

Quite how Erik managed to install himself at York is not clear, but by 948, the Anglo-Saxon Chronicles report that the Northumbrians had taken him for their king. This was only to be a brief rule, however, as Olaf Sihtricsson of Dublin also had his eye on York and took over the following year. The inhabitants of York had yet another change of leadership, the sixth in fifteen years.

The attitude of those living in York towards their rapidly changing rulers is impossible to know, but we can gain a glimpse of the uncertainties that they might have felt from the story of the Archbishop of York. Wulfstan had been appointed Archbishop by Athelstan, but he seems to have been quite happy to alter his loyalties as required. When Olaf Sihtricsson first takes charge in 941, it is Wulfstan who stands by him, and eventually helps negotiate a peace deal with the English king. But when the inhabitants of York come under Anglo-Saxon rule again, Wulfstan declares his loyalty to King Edmund. Edmund's successor Eadred took the throne in 946, and by 947 Wulfstan was up to his usual tricks. He and the Northumbrians accepted Erik Bloodaxe as their king, but within a year Eadred had forced him out again.

Erik Bloodaxe had obviously made some friends during his brief stay in York because when, in 952, the Northumbrians forced Olaf out, they invited Erik back to be their king. Archbishop Wulfstan no doubt had a part to play in this coup, as King Eadred almost immediately had him arrested. Wulfstan was taken to a fort near Lindisfarne, where he was held until Erik left the country.

Coins like these were issued in the name of Eric Bloodaxe when he was the ruler of York.

The loss of his main ally must have been a blow to Erik and although he was in York long enough to mint some coins in his name, he was soon expelled once again, this time by King Eadred. He left, intending to travel to Carlisle but was ambushed and killed at Stainmore. Erik Bloodaxe was the last Viking ruler in York, and after his death Northumbria became a permanent part of the English kingdom. For about the next thirty years the Viking attacks abated and three generations of English kings were left in relative peace.

During this time the Danes who had settled in England continued to mix with the local population. An Anglo-Scandinavian culture developed, and it would have been difficult to distinguish between the two groups at an everyday level. But the Danelaw was still distinct from the rest of England in many ways, most notably in regal, trading and ecclesiastical practices.

In the 960s or 970s King Edgar issued a law code, in which the English and the Danes were given separate identities. Some rules applied to the entire nation, while in particular areas the Danes were allowed to decide others for themselves. The freedom granted to the Danes might have reflected their loyalty to King Edgar, but if Edgar was unsure about his ability to control the Danes, an ideal way of appearing to remain in control was to grant them the 'freedom' to rule themselves.

Edgar's son, Æthelred, also issued law codes, and once again different rules applied to Danes and English. The Woodstock code applied to regions following English law, but rather than let the Danes devise their own laws, Æthelred drafted the Wantage code, designed to be used in the area of the Five Boroughs and Northumbria.

It seems that the inhabitants of the Danelaw were to be regarded as different to those of the rest of England. Distinctions were also made between Norsemen, usually of Norwegian descent, and often from Viking settlements in Ireland or the Scottish Isles, and Danes. When King Edmund won back the Five Boroughs from the Dublin Vikings in 942, the viewpoint of the Anglo-Saxon Chronicle is that he has freed these Danes from the clutches of the Norsemen.

The Anglo-Saxon Chronicles regularly cast the Vikings in the role of a pagan enemy. Several times the Chronicles refer to 'Christians' winning battles when Welsh and English forces have combined against Vikings. But despite these cultural differences, the blending of Anglo-Saxon and Scandinavian styles and traditions suggests that in everyday life both groups of people were quite tolerant.

During the period of respite from the Viking raids, the cultural exchange in the Danelaw continued. The inhabitants must by this time have been a very mixed bunch and, although they were often referred to collectively as 'Danes', they probably bore little similarity to those whose homeland was Denmark. Then in 980, two years after Æthelred took the throne, the Vikings began to attack again.

For several years the attacks were just isolated raids, inconvenient for those at the receiving end but not a threat to the kingdom as a whole.

But then, in a marked escalation of the scale of the attacks, Olaf Tryggvason and Svein Forkbeard appeared on the scene, two characters whose entangled lives were to have a profound effect on Æthelred's fortunes and those of his kingdom.

Olaf Tryggvason was a Norwegian Viking, the grandson of King Harald Fairhair, who first appeared at Folkestone in 991 with a fleet reported to consist of ninety-three ships. He raided with some success and was bought off with ten thousand pounds in Danegeld but there was a certain inevitability that he would be back for more.

Svein Forkbeard was a Danish king, the son of Harald Bluetooth, perhaps the most famous member of the Jelling dynasty that restored the power of Denmark after a period of relative weakness. During Harald's reign the country was fortified, roads and bridges improved and regions of Norway brought back under Danish control. But as well as securing his country from attack and expanding its claims abroad, Harald, after his own conversion, is said to have Christianised all the Danes.

Harald Bluetooth did not attempt to cross the North Sea himself in search of conquests. Instead it is his son, Svein Forkbeard, who appears first as a raider in the late tenth century. He too may have participated in the raids of 991 but, despite the rivalries that were eventually to surface over the question of Norway, in 994 Svein teamed up with Olaf Tryggvason to carry out a new campaign of raiding in England.

This joint Viking army put Æthelred in a similar position to that in which Alfred had found himself a century earlier. But although Alfred had made peace with the Great Army, he had never made the mistake of trusting them entirely. Yet now, even as the English nobility continued to pay them off, Svein and Olaf made their way along the coasts raiding at will.

They attacked in Northumbria and then along the south coast of England. In return the English allowed them to make a winter camp at Southampton, gave them provisions, and paid them 16,000 pounds. While the Viking army was camped at Southampton Olaf, who was clearly regarded as a considerable threat, was invited by Æthelred to become his well-paid mercenary. Olaf served Æthelred for some time before returning to Norway where, with his new-found wealth, he was able to put in a bid for the Norwegian kingship. Æthelred had almost certainly counted on this when he made the deal with Olaf. He cannot have expected the

Norwegian to protect him for ever, but his eventual return to Norway must also have been in English interests.

Æthelred may not at times have been the most astute leader but he was sensible enough to take advantage of the rivalry between Norway and Denmark when faced with Svein's raids on England at the end of the tenth century. Svein still saw himself as overlord of Norway, so when Olaf began to emerge as a strong local leader, Svein was forced to take action. For the next few years Æthelred's kingdom was left in peace as Svein battled it out with Olaf and the Norwegians. Eventually, at the Battle of Svold, Olaf fell. This left Svein free to return to England.

But even during the period that Svein was distracted in Norway, and while the protection of the Vikings at Southampton had been paid for, there was no lasting peace. Soon the raiding-army resumed its travels. Finally, and far too late, the English did make some attempt to fight back but they never managed to mount any credible resistance. In 998 the Anglo-Saxon Chronicles report:

Here the raiding-army turned eastward again . . . And an army was often gathered against them, but then as soon as they should have come together something always started a retreat, and [the raiders] always had the victory in the end.

Æthelred does not seem to have had Alfred's powers of leadership and time and again the Vikings attack, steal horses, and travel where they will. At one point Æthelred even decides to build a new fleet of ships to aid in the defence of his kingdom.

But when the ships were ready, there was delay from day to day, which distressed the wretched people who lay on the ships . . . and they always let their enemies' strength increase. And then in the end the ship-army achieved nothing, except the people's labour, and wasting money, and the emboldening of their enemies.

Æthelred's extreme bad luck in his dealings with the marauding Vikings led to him being nicknamed 'the Unready'. This was not a name used by his contemporaries but, in retrospect, it seems highly appropriate as the name actually stems from the Old English word, *Unræd*, meaning ill advised.

Compounding his mistakes in dealing with the Viking raiders, Æthelred

LEFT | *This eleventh-century manuscript shows Viking warriors arriving by boat.*

agreed to pay them off once again in 1002. This time the sum was increased to 24,000 pounds of silver and inevitably led to the Danes returning whenever they were in need of a bit of extra cash. By 1012 the payments had escalated even further and the English were forced to raise a whopping 48,000 pounds to keep the peace.

This increasing pressure from the Danes on Æthelred's kingdom led to internal tensions as not all the noblemen agreed with Æthelred's tactic of paying off the Danes and they were dismayed at the military failures. Some Anglo-Saxons may even have expressed their frustration by carrying out individual attacks on Danes living in England.

This necklace was discovered at Saffron Waldon, in the grave of a well-to-do pagan woman.

In the village of Hadstock, not far from Saffron Waldon, lies a small church, a peaceful setting for a gruesome tale. Saffron Waldon is in East Anglia, and would have been part of the Danelaw. A pagan burial discovered in 1876 was probably that of a Danish settler, and the region is peppered with finds of Anglo-Scandinavian jewellery.

The wooden door of Hadstock church is thought to date from Saxon times and, according to legend, once displayed a grisly warning to the Danes in the region. In 1791 a small piece of skin was removed from the door and eventually found its way into Saffron Walden Museum, where it can still be seen today. The piece of skin, only a few inches long, was described in the museum catalogue of 1845 as human skin. By 1883 the label on the specimen reports that it is not only human skin, but that of a Dane. The story goes that a sacrilegious Viking, who had attempted to steal from the church, was killed and his flayed skin was mounted on its door as a warning to other potential robbers. Similar discoveries were made at Worcester and Copford, so it seems as if this grisly means of crime prevention may have occurred in more than one place in Viking Age England.

A more modern analysis of the skin had suggested that it was either pig or human skin, so we decided to run some DNA tests to find out. The museum were happy for us to take away a very tiny piece of skin – no more than one centimetre square. Ancient DNA expert Alan Cooper of Oxford University, was called in for this delicate task. But when the

A wooden door of this church, in the village of Hadstock, was covered with leather rumoured to be the skin of a Viking.

moment came to cut the skin, it turned out to be too tough for his slender scalpel! However, he persevered and was eventually able to obtain a suitable sample.

Alan managed to find some surviving DNA but as the results of the analysis came through we realised that they were not going to back up the original story. The skin was not human, but that of a cow. This had been a great success for the DNA extraction techniques, but a bit disappointing for those of us on the Viking trail.

Even if the villagers of Hadstock did not flay an errant Dane, there is evidence elsewhere for conflict between the Danes and the English. In 1002, King Æthelred took a similarly aggressive stance and on St Brice's Day, 13 November, he ordered the slaying of all Danish men who were in England.

Æthelred is said to have feared for his life. Concerned that the Danes in England might decide to join forces with those arriving from their homeland, he sent out a decree that 'all the Danes who had sprung up in this island, sprouting like weeds amongst the wheat, were to be destroyed by a most just extermination'.

Note the terminology, it was a 'most just extermination'. The massacre is not well documented, apart from the details given for the slaughter in Oxford. Here the Danes broke into a church, hoping to find sanctuary but, in this case, the sanctity of a religious establishment was conveniently overlooked by the Anglo-Saxons. The people attacked the church, burning it to the ground with the Danes still inside.

This brutal massacre did nothing to raise Æthelred's standing in the kingdom. He had been using Vikings as mercenaries, fighting for him against other bands of Viking raiders, but had perhaps realised that their loyalty could not be relied upon. Consequently any more recently settled Danes who were not currently in Æthelred's pay also became victims of the St Brice's Day massacre.

This attack on the Danes seems to be the action of an increasingly desperate and beleaguered king. Æthelred turned to the Duke of Normandy for help in confronting the Vikings and even married the Duke's daughter Emma in 1002. This attempt at political manoeuvring was, however, an out-and-out failure as the Duke of Normandy continued in his alliance with Svein Forkbeard. Emma was to go on to play a prominent role in English politics, but not always in her husband Æthelred's favour.

Svein Forkbeard returned to raid in 1003–4, according to some later sources to avenge the death of his sister who had been killed in the St Brice's Day massacre. He also returned in 1006–7, on both occasions being bought off with huge payments of Danegeld, but by 1012 had realised the weakened state of the English. The next time he returned, in 1013, he was not simply coming to collect tribute, he was determined to take the kingdom.

King Æthelred's response to this new threat was to levy a tax upon his subjects and use the money to hire Danish mercenaries. The leader of this mercenary army was Thorkell the Tall, a Dane who had arrived in 1009 and quickly overrun a large part of southern England. This resulted in a huge payment of 48,000 pounds of silver and yet, in 1012, he agreed to lead forty-five ships in Æthelred's name. Of course, there was a fee involved and for shifting his alliance Thorkell received a further 12,000 pounds of silver.

Svein Forkbeard attacked in earnest in 1013. Most of the country fell rapidly, but with Thorkell's help London held out against the Danish king until Æthelred fled to Normandy. London too then gave in and Svein Forkbeard became King of England.

A number of weapons that date from this time, and that could have belonged to some of Forkbeard's men have been unearthed in London over the years. In the 1920s battleaxes and spearheads were found in the Thames near London Bridge, along with a small axe and a grappling hook. As with many archaeological finds made some years ago, there are no records of exactly how the weapons were discovered. So working out exactly how they ended up in the Thames involves a degree of speculation. One suggestion is that the weapons were being carried in a boat that sank. But there was no mention of timbers or other boat remains being found with them. The weapons are made in a Viking style, but we cannot even be sure that they belonged to Vikings as the Anglo-Saxons soon adopted the Scandinavian weapons, and are portrayed wielding battleaxes, the classic Viking weapon, on the Bayeux Tapestry. So the weapons found in the Thames might also have belonged to the English defenders of London.

Maybe these weapons were captured during a battle, and dumped into the River Thames; but would the victors waste perfectly serviceable weapons? An alternative explanation is that these weapons were sacrificed, deliberately thrown into the river as an offering, in the hope of ensuring the aid of the gods in battle.

Other Viking swords have also been found throughout London. One discovered in Putney is engraved with a single word – *Ingelrii,* one that along with *Ulfberht* is one of the most common names to be found on Viking weapons. We can safely assume that all the blades that carry the name of *Ingelrii* did not belong to the same warrior so it seems that this

These swords and axes were discovered in the Thames in the 1920s. They may have belonged to Vikings.

must be the signature of a craftsman. But one sword has even been found with *Ingelrii* on one side and *Ulfberht* on the other. Maybe this is the work of a forger who thought that if one signature increased the value of the weapon, then using both would make it extremely easy to sell!

So where did *Ingelrii* and *Ulfberht* come from? The swords may have belonged to Vikings, but these weapons came from the Rhineland where the quality of the iron was much better, and the smiths were highly skilled. One of their inscribed blades would have been the prized possession of any Viking warrior.

So perhaps these superior weapons were those used by Svein and his warriors when they took London in 1013. This seemed like the end for Æthelred, who was forced out of the country. His marriage to Emma of Normandy may not have provided reinforcements against the initial Viking threat as he had hoped, but it did give him a safe place to hide.

Æthelred's exile did not last long as Svein died in 1014 after the remarkably short reign, even in these turbulent times, of just five weeks. Svein's son Cnut was chased out and yet again England was plunged into turmoil. This gave Æthelred the opportunity to return but again he justified his epithet of 'ill-advised'. Not long after his return, he conspired to murder two leading noblemen from the Danelaw but, not wanting to dirty his own hands, he entrusted the task to Eadric of Mercia.

The murders were all to do with the question of succession, no doubt a topic of considerable interest in the kingdom. The two murdered noblemen were supporters of Æthelred's son, Edmund, who had a claim to the throne. In response to the noblemen's deaths, Edmund married one of their widows, and took control of the Five Boroughs. Æthelred's plan backfired on him as he was now facing not only the Danish threat, but out and out rebellion from one of his own sons.

Whether by fate or design, the Vikings once again timed their attack with great precision. With the country divided, Cnut returned from Denmark to stake his claim on the land won by his father just a few years earlier. Æthelred's ill health meant he had to leave the control of his army to Eadric of Mercia, while Edmund gathered together his own warriors.

These two English contingents proved quite incapable of working together and, divided by politics, the English again fell to the Danes.

Æthelred was fading with each passing day and Eadric realised that he might be left in a rather awkward position. His best chance seemed to be to change sides, and so he defected to Cnut's side with part of Æthelred's fleet, probably those ships that belonged to Thorkell. The country was now divided into three – Æthelred's immediate entourage retained control of London, Edmund still held the Five Boroughs and East Anglia, while Cnut now controlled Wessex and parts of Mercia. And this was the country that, not that many years earlier, had been united under Athelstan.

Edmund Ironside, as he is now known, fought long and hard against Cnut. In the autumn of 1016 Eadric obviously thought that the tide was turning, as he defected yet again, this time to Edmund's side. This should have provided Edmund with much needed reinforcements but, in the end, he must have cursed the arrival of his former adversary. At the crucial Battle of Ashingdon, the English found themselves facing the bulk of Cnut's army.

Then Ealdorman Eadric did as he so often did before, first started the flight – and thus betrayed his royal lord and the whole nation. There Cnut had the victory and won himself all England.

After this disaster, Edmund was forced to come to terms with Cnut. They divided the country, although Edmund was allowed to retain only Wessex. But soon even this would be in Danish hands as, by November of this year, Edmund was dead, and Cnut ruled the whole of England.

In the wake of his victories, and following Edmund's death, Cnut replaced many of the English ruling classes with his own men. The numerous battles had seen the deaths of a large number of those who had been in positions of power, and Cnut also needed to select those noblemen he thought would serve him loyally. Interestingly, two men who had supported Æthelred also found themselves in positions of power in Cnut's court.

The Viking Thorkell had been a loyal mercenary to Æthelred, fighting off Cnut's father, and keeping London in English hands when many other regions were surrendering. Yet in 1020, when Cnut returned to Denmark to ensure that he became king there on his brother's death, Thorkell was effectively left in charge of England.

Earl Godwine also managed to survive the transition from an English to a Danish kingdom, although he did not end up with quite such a prestigious position. He had been a loyal supporter of Edmund Ironside, and a bitter enemy of Eadric, the ealdorman who deserted at the Battle of Ashingdon. Unlike Eadric, who was willing to switch allegiance with every new turn of events, Godwine had stood by Edmund's side until his death.

It might be expected that this loyalty to the English Crown would ensure that Godwine met a less than happy end once Cnut gained power. But strangely, Godwine's name also finds its way on to the lists of new nobles. It seems that, above all, Cnut was impressed by loyalty. Maybe Godwine's unswerving belief in Edmund convinced Cnut that he too might benefit from the Earl's loyal nature. So Godwine survived the purge, while the turncoat Eadric was executed.

Another of Æthelred's supporters ended up in a position of influence, this time through marriage. On Æthelred's death, his wife Emma of Normandy had taken their two sons back to her homeland to ensure their safety. When Cnut took the throne he already had two sons by Ælfgifu of Northampton but, to maintain the potentially useful links with Normandy, Cnut married Æthelred's widow Emma. They came to an agreement that only their own sons could inherit the kingdom, thereby excluding Ælfgifu's two sons, as well as Emma's sons by Æthelred. However confident they were that their wishes would be obeyed, problems would later arise from this complicated arrangement and from the large number of potential successors.

Before the arrival of Cnut London had been an important city, the richest and most populous in England, but it was not yet the English capital. Wessex was the home of the monarchy and therefore Winchester was the most important political centre.

The Danish attacks during Æthelred's reign focused on the Thames Valley, not least because of the wealth of this region, and London became a specific target. This forced Æthelred to select it as his main military base, from which point its power and influence grew rapidly, mainly due to its astonishing resistance to the Danes. The inhabitants of London were

A contemporary manuscript shows Cnut and Emma, his queen, presenting an altar cross to New Minster, Winchester.

loyal supporters of Æthelred and then his son Edmund, until, at his death, they were forced to accept Cnut as their leader.

So when Cnut took over the throne, he had to keep a close eye on the city of London. It was an ideal base for his powerful navy of Scandinavian mercenaries and the network of roads established by the Romans provided good communications with the rest of the kingdom. From 1016 onwards the city appears to have been under military occupation, with pockets of Danes garrisoned at sites across it. Many of the locations of these Danish enclaves are still identifiable, thanks to the churches that carry the names of Scandinavian saints. Six London churches are dedicated to St Olaf, the future king of Norway who had fought at Æthelred's side. St Clement Danes, on the road to Westminster, may have been used by mercenary sailors, camping close to their ships.

These garrisons would all have needed paying, and Cnut, like previous kings, relied on taxing his subjects to meet such bills. In 1018 a special *geld*, or tax, was levied across England, raising a total of seventy-two thousand pounds, of which ten-and-a-half thousand pounds came from London itself. The extra burden on this emerging capital city might be regarded as a punishment for its resistance to Cnut's conquest, or it may just realistically reflect the wealth of this trading centre compared to the rest of the country.

It was during Cnut's reign that the monetary system also became very important. Cnut wanted coins minted in England to be easily traded with other parts of his empire and so, as the Scandinavians were still primarily concerned with the weight of the silver, it was crucial to have a standard that was based on a fixed weight. This new standard, applicable across the whole of Cnut's empire, was given the mark of the Husting of London and London became the centre for coin production and the distribution of dies to moneyers.

Cnut's reign was unusual in the history of England as he was a foreigner, not linked in any way to the previous rulers of Wessex. His power was

Like most Anglo-Saxon and Viking rulers, Cnut and his son, Harthacnut, issued coins in their names.

founded on conquest and military might, which gave him the freedom to choose exactly where to locate his headquarters. London's position made it ideal for naval forces and it was the ealdormen of London who began to play a role in the succession of kings, something that would have been unheard of as recently as the reign of Athelstan less than a century earlier. After Cnut's rule it became clear that anyone who wished to control England had first to control London.

As well as ruling England for nearly twenty years, Cnut is likely to have been recognised as overlord by the Welsh and the Scots, and also controlled Denmark and Norway for some of that time. But he ruled in Denmark through regents and in Norway through one of his sons. First and foremost he was an English king, with an English power base. Today we would call Cnut an Anglophile. The Scandinavian styles and traditions which had already found their way to England probably regained favour during his reign, but Cnut was just as interested in exporting English ideas back to Denmark. The trappings of Anglo-Saxon culture that he found most interesting, as had the leaders of the Danelaw before him, were coins and Christianity.

Although Denmark had officially adopted Christianity during the reign of Cnut's grandfather Harald Bluetooth, the English were concerned about his potential paganism. His many gifts to the Church, and even his visit to Rome for the coronation of the Holy Roman Emperor, Conrad II, were no doubt intended to assure his subjects that he took Christianity seriously, despite his relatively recent pagan ancestry.

Due to Cnut's religious leanings, the Church in Denmark also came under renewed English influence. Harald Bluetooth had decided that Denmark would become a Christian country not least because of the threat from the German empire to the south. But although Harald remained in control, it was the archdiocese of Hamburg-Bremen that provided religious leadership until Harald's son, Svein Forkbeard, drove out the German bishops and replaced them with English clerics.

This policy was continued by Cnut who upset his southerly neighbours by appointing several English bishops in Denmark. His reconciliation with Emperor Conrad II was brought about when Cnut travelled to Rome to attend his coronation. During this trip Cnut agreed to marry his daughter to the emperor's son, and negotiated customs reductions for pilgrims and traders from England and Scandinavia. After this, Hamburg-

This gravestone was found in the churchyard of St Paul's Cathedral in the nineteenth century. The artwork is Scandinavian, suggesting that an important Danish figure may have been buried here in the eleventh century.

Bremen took a more favourable view, despite the consecration of at least three Danish bishops at Canterbury.

As well as developing a church based around English officials, Cnut introduced a system of coinage into Denmark, based on what he had learnt and developed in England. The English moneyers would license the right from the king to strike coins at as many as fifty mints across the country. Old coins were regularly exchanged for new issues, for which the moneyers would require new dies. These could be obtained on payment of a fixed sum, effectively working like a tax.

From the mid-tenth century, only one official currency had been used at any given time with each type of coin usually lasting about five years, before being reissued. It is thought that certain costs, like taxes, could only be paid in the most up-to-date currency. This would deter people from using old coins in some transactions and may explain why so few of these coins are found in hoards in England. They would be out of date, and declining in value, almost as soon as they were buried.

Most surviving coins from this period have been found in Scandinavia,

The tenth-century fort at Trelleborg, Denmark, indicates the emergence of a powerful Danish kingdom. It was built during the reign of Harald Bluetooth.

where they were still used as bullion, and therefore did not depreciate in value. But in Denmark, too, the foundations for a true currency were being laid. Svein Forkbeard had been the first Danish leader to have coins struck in his name, but only eight of these coins have been found, all made from the same die. Cnut issued a whole range of coins, mimicking Anglo-Saxon examples, and by 1028 there were two new national coinages in circulation. Coins weighing one gram were minted in eastern Denmark while in the west the coins weighed about twenty-five per cent less.

By the end of Cnut's reign at least eight mints were in operation, producing coins that bore both his name and that of his son Harthacnut. Local styles had begun to develop, although the moneyers continued to look to England for inspiration. But it seems that despite the intentions of the administration to develop a currency unique to Denmark, coins imported from England and Germany were much more popular. Imported in vast numbers, these foreign coins would have been treated like bullion and exchanged by weight.

Cnut was a powerful force to be reckoned with in eleventh-century Europe. His reign ensured that the Danish influence on Britain would not disappear, but today his story is not well known. To most people he is known only as the King Canute who, in order to demonstrate that his powers were not absolute, sat on the shore and unsuccessfully commanded the sea to obey him. In part, Cnut's comparative obscurity is because he was not as lucky as Alfred in having an official biographer to ensure that his name went down in history. But it is also because events after his death would later cast the lives of Cnut and his contemporaries as minor characters in the build-up to what would be the most famous invasion in British history.

Much of what we know about Cnut's life comes from the *Encomium Emmae Reginae*. This work was commissioned by Emma after Cnut's death and its name suggests that it is Emma's story, but the author clearly intended to glorify her second husband, and makes no mention of her previous marriage to Æthelred. The most likely purpose of this eleventh-century book was to aid Emma in her quest to maintain her own importance, this time in the role of mother, rather than wife, of the King of England.

On his father's death, Harthacnut, Cnut's son by Emma and the heir they had agreed would succeed him, took over in Denmark. But in England, hardly surprisingly in view of the sheer number of potential candidates, the succession became a far more complicated issue. Cnut's son by his English mistress, Harold Harefoot, was in England ready to make a claim. To make matters worse, Emma's sons by Æthelred were waiting in Normandy, itching to get their hands on the throne. In these circumstances the united empire Cnut had built up was hardly likely to last.

Harthacnut should by right have taken over the throne of England, but was forced to return to Denmark. The Norwegians had thrown off the yoke of Danish authority and then gone one step further, invading

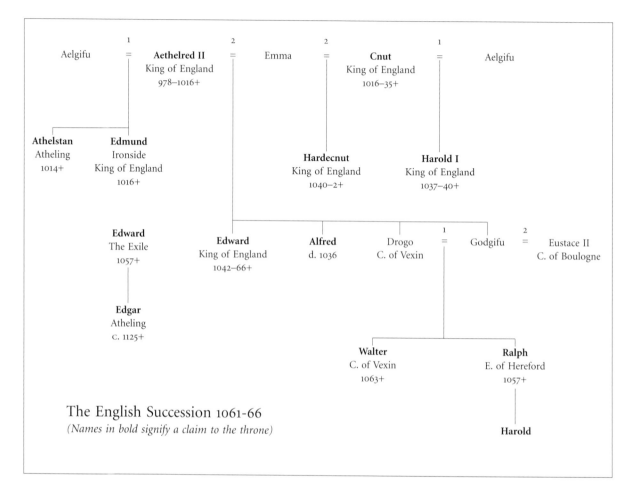

The English Succession 1061-66

(Names in bold signify a claim to the throne)

the country that had controlled them. Harthacnut's half-brother, Harold Harefoot, saw his opportunity and took over.

But in England one of Cnut's loyal earls maintained a foothold for Harthacnut and protected his widow Emma who was hiding at Winchester. This was the same Earl Godwine whose loyalty to Æthelred had been rewarded by Cnut not with execution but with a position of power. If Cnut truly wanted his son, with Emma, to succeed him, then the loyalty he prized in Godwine paid off. Godwine could not, however, expect much support from Harthacnut who was having trouble dealing with the situation in Denmark. The earl was left out on a limb as Harold began to win support in Wessex, and even stole some of Cnut's treasure from Winchester. Emma, until now Godwine's firm ally in support of

Harthacnut, decided that she could not afford to lose her influence by allowing the son of Cnut's mistress to take control and summoned Edward and Alfred, her children by Æthelred, back from Normandy.

No one in England was too impressed with this unnecessary complication to an already confused succession and both sons failed in their attempts to secure power. Edward intended to join his mother at Winchester but was forced back when he landed near Southampton, and never reached her side. Alfred hoped to reach Harold Harefoot's base in London, but was arrested by Godwine at Guildford. It seems that Godwine handed his prisoners over to Harold, who had Alfred blinded. Soon after, Alfred died.

This attempt by Emma to alter events made allies of Godwine and Harold. A deal was worked out by which Godwine would be allowed to retain control of Wessex, if he recognised Harold as king. Queen Emma was forced to flee to Normandy.

For a couple of years Godwine must have breathed easily; he had chosen the winning side, and England now had a new ruler. But when Harold died in 1040 he found himself in the middle of another crisis as Harthacnut returned from Denmark. He lost no time in digging up his half-brother's body and throwing it into the Thames and presumably wanted an explanation from Godwine as to why the normally loyal earl had betrayed his, Harthacnut's, interests.

Godwine was in an extremely awkward position but a peace-offering in the form of a magnificent ship seems to have done the trick, at least for a while. Harthacnut was not popular, no doubt partly due to his taxation of the English to fund his fleet. But as a concession, he employed the Scandinavian custom of sharing the kingship, and invited Edward back from Normandy to sit at his side.

This must have compounded Godwine's feeling of vulnerability, as he had played a key role in the death of Edward's brother. But he could not risk antagonising Harthacnut again, and was obliged to keep silent. Godwine must have thought his troubles could not get much worse but before long Harthacnut was also dead, and Godwine found himself offering another equally rich ship to Edward as he took the throne. Amazingly, considering past events, this gesture paid off and before long Edward had married Godwine's daughter, reinstated him to the richest earldom of England, and given minor earldoms to both of his sons.

And so the stage was set for the events of 1066. Harold Godwinson became Earl of Wessex on his father's death, and continued to expand his sphere of influence. Edward did not have a son and heir and so, on his death on 5 January 1066, Edward's kingdom passed to Harold Godwinson.

This decision was accepted by the majority and there was none of the controversy that had raged over Cnut's succession. But support from his countrymen was not enough for Harold Godwinson. King Edward had also sought to ally himself with the Normans and Harold, as an earl, had been his right-hand man. While in Normandy, Harold had been forced to swear an oath that he would help its king, William, to obtain the English throne on Edward's death. It is entirely possible that this oath was given under duress, when he was effectively a captive in William's court. Harold had subsequently been bequeathed the kingdom of England by Edward on his deathbed and he had no intention of giving it up. But William of Normandy felt that he had a legitimate claim to the English throne and, King Harald Hardrada of Norway saw a chance to expand his fledgeling empire to the west.

Harald Hardrada had travelled across the Viking world, before winning joint kingship of Norway from Magnus the Good. On the death of Magnus, Harald became sole ruler and fought unsuccessfully for several years to control Denmark too. Looking around for other conquests, Harald hit upon England, a rich kingdom, and one to which he had inherited a legitimate claim. Cnut's son Harthacnut had signed a treaty with Magnus back in 1036, agreeing that whoever lived longest would inherit the other's kingdom. Magnus had not chosen to take up this claim on England, but when Edward died in 1066 Harald decided that his kingdom was ripe for the picking.

Harald put together a massive fleet of longships and set out across the North Sea. Sailing up the River Ouse, heading directly for the northern power base of York, he took the English completely by surprise. He then went on to Fulford where, on 20 September, he was met by a hastily gathered force of English earls. Although some of the Northumbrian and Mercian troops might have had previous battle experience, the Norwegian warriors had spent the past sixteen years fighting the Danes. They were far more experienced and ruthless than the English, and the result was complete carnage.

As with many of the events in this period, finding evidence in support of what is recorded in the Anglo-Saxon Chronicle is difficult. But excavations at York have revealed a number of burials that could shed light on the battles of 1066.

The York Archaeological Trust has excavated over four hundred Anglo-Saxon skeletons from the cemetery belonging to the church of St Andrew in Fishergate. These burials took place over a period of about five hundred years, with different parts of the cemetery representing differing elements of the community. One area seems to have been reserved for members of the monastic community, while, in contrast, other areas include the burials of young children and even infants.

The skeletons can also tell us something of the lifestyle of the people of York at this time. One benefit of a largely sugar-free Anglo-Saxon diet seems to have been relatively good dental health, the only sugars these people probably ate being those that occur naturally in fruit and honey. But the most interesting find to emerge from the analysis of the skeletons was the large number that exhibited signs of serious injury. The skeletons of twenty-nine men show the marks of cuts made with sharp implements, and the injuries show no evidence of having healed. These are evidence of multiple injuries, the sign of violent death.

Closer investigation of the marks reveals that many of them are consistent with the slicing or thrusting action of a sharp-edged weapon such as a sword. Others display a completely different type of injury, one likely to have been inflicted by a pointed weapon such as an arrowhead. In addition, many of the men showed signs of skull injuries, these wounds suggesting that they had not been wearing any protective headgear, rare during the Viking period.

The most likely explanation for the injuries sustained by these men is that they were the result of a serious battle, one that resulted in large numbers of casualties. The injuries can also tell us much about how the battle might have been fought. There are almost twice as many blows to the left side of the body as to the right, while a large number of blows to the side and back also indicate a less formalised type of fighting. There are a number of decapitations, which, along with stabbing injuries to the lower back, may have occurred when the victims were lying on the ground. A number of similar strikes to the back of the thighs suggest that this area of the body might have been a deliberate target, perhaps in an attempt

These skulls may be of members of the Anglo-Saxon army, defeated by the Vikings at Fulford.

to slash the leg muscles. Other blows may have been inflicted by men on horseback.

The position and date of the burials suggest that at least half of the casualties died as a result of one event. As York suffered from unrest throughout the ninth and tenth centuries – both Anglo-Saxon leadership disputes and Viking attacks from both Norwegians and Danes – there are clearly a number of possible events that can be suggested. But these skeletons date from the mid-eleventh century, making it a distinct possibility that they are casualties from the Battle of Fulford.

After the battle was over, the Norwegians entered York. The victims of the slaughter were probably gathered up by their comrades and brought into the centre of the city for a Christian burial. The Northumbrians, their army in tatters, and with no real hope of immediate aid, surrendered to Harald and his men. The stage was now set for the battle between Harald and Harold. In the north was Harald Hardrada, his confidence bolstered by his recent victory over the Northumbrians. In the south was King Harold Godwinson, anxiously keeping an eye on the south coast for any signs of aggression from William of Normandy. He had been warned of the impending Viking threat as soon as ships were sighted and, swiftly raising an army, had set off for York.

The speed with which Harold was able to raise his army is a testament

The battles of 1066 would change the course of British history.

to the loyalty of his subjects. His march north began before the blood-shed at Fulford, but even with horses, it would take his men about a week to reach York. On 25 September, five days after the Battle of Fulford, Harold surprised the Vikings at Stamford Bridge. They were completely unprepared for his arrival, perhaps expecting that it would take him longer to march up from the south, or maybe that he would be so preoccupied with the threat of Norman invasion that he would abandon the Northumbrians to their fate. Whatever the reason, the Vikings found themselves trapped in a river valley, where they could easily be cut off from their ships.

This is just what Harold's men intended. But even with the element of surprise on the side of the English, the battle lasted all day. The English had already trekked some two hundred miles from London to reach the battle site, and must have been exhausted by the time Harald Hardrada was slain. At this the Norwegians broke ranks and attempted to flee, but were pursued by the English right to their ships. Of the 330 ships Harald is said to have brought from Norway, only 24 were said to have been needed to carry the survivors home.

And so the last of the Viking invaders were chased from English soil. But King Harold had no time to savour his victory as, just then, the wind changed direction. The northerly winds that had carried the Norwegians to York had also effectively trapped William of Normandy's ships on the other side of the Channel. But on 27 September the weather changed, and William was quick to take advantage of it.

The Normans crossed the Channel overnight, and landed at Pevensey where William then had seventeen days to dig in his troops. When the news reached Harold, he had been allowing his men to rest and regain their strength but, having seen off one potential invasion, he knew he could not give up now. He assembled what reinforcements he could and headed back down south.

The English gathered in London, where they had a couple of days to regroup, before a three-day march to Hastings. The Bayeux Tapestry tells the story of a battle that lasted the whole day, a battle in which both the Normans and the English gained minor advantages. Then suddenly King Harold fell and without their leader to rally and inspire them, the English broke ranks and allowed the Normans in for the kill.

So the army that had so successfully stopped the Norwegian invasion just a few weeks earlier fell to William of Normandy. What could have been a Scandinavian take-over had become a Norman conquest, bringing to an end the Viking Age in England.

Today we can see the remnants of the Viking Age across Britain and Ireland. The Vikings left their mark in the place-names and the language, the archaeology and the historical tales. And we see in the genes of today's British and Irish population the legacy of those Norwegians and Danes who not only invaded but made their homes here. But the final irony lies in the Norman invasion itself.

The Normans were not Scandinavian. But their ancestors were Vikings.

In 885 a Viking army arrived on the Seine, where its leaders were eventually given land. Rollo the Viking was granted land around Bayeux, and became the first leader of Normandy. By the time William the Conqueror became Duke of Normandy, those who lived in the region had completely adopted French culture but nothing could hide their Viking ancestry.

So where do the Viking genes which remain in the British and Irish populations of today really come from? Some may have come from the Vikings themselves, the raiders and then settlers who have provided such a strong cultural legacy. But some may have come from the very people who are seen to have brought an end to the Viking Age in Britain – not Norsemen, but Normans.

CHAPTER 12

THE VIKING LEGACY

What an amazing bunch the Vikings were: raiders, traders, farmers, settlers, fearless adventurers and ultimately adaptable. I wouldn't have trusted a Viking as far as I could throw him but in a scrap, I know whose side I'd rather be on . . .

JULIAN RICHARDS, 2001

LEFT | *This eleventh-century manuscript illustration shows the Vikings leaving English soil in 880, heading off to raid on the Continent. But although the Vikings eventually left Britain for good, their legacy lives on.*

Over the last year I have travelled thousands of miles in the footsteps of the Vikings, on a journey that started with only the most basic understanding of their culture and achievements. Even at this stage I had some inkling that there was going to be more to the Viking story than pillage and horned helmets, but I had no real idea of what my journey was to be, and of how much I would learn along the way. At the end of it, my overriding memory is one that seems very appropriate to the Vikings. It is of water, the dark stillness of the Norwegian fjords, the windswept buffeting seas around Orkney, the sparkling light on the magical lakes and rivers of Ireland.

There have been some very powerful moments along the way. Wondering what stories a Christian relic from Northumbria could tell of its journey to Norway in Viking hands. The power and intimidation embodied in a Viking boat compared to the delicacy of its carved decoration. Sitting cosily by the fire in a Viking house as the streams froze outside. Trying to imagine the last moments of the people whose twisted bodies lay in a ditch in Anglesey.

So what have I learnt after all these travels, after picking the brains of every archaeologist, historian, scientist and potential Viking that I have met?

Firstly, treat history with caution. History is written by people with an agenda. On the other hand, if you are aware of this agenda then you can pick out the facts from the legend and political spin. Then history becomes an incredibly useful tool, particularly when the archaeological evidence is sparse. But never, ever, take it at face value.

Secondly, archaeology will continue to provide more answers (and inevitably pose more questions), whether they come from major discoveries like Tarbat or from the occasional find of a Viking brooch in a Lincolnshire field.

And, finally, genetics could be about to answer some of the really big questions, like: 'Just how Viking are we?'

My journey has taken me from the Viking homelands and the first raids to the Norman invasion that effectively ended the Viking Age in England. I now feel personally very much more enlightened, but what did the Vikings leave behind and how does this affect our lives today?

Perhaps one of the most enduring legacies is the popular image of the Vikings given to us by the written records. Not only did these historical stories aid in the creation of the Viking image, they also provided tales for future generations. Without the Vikings, Saxo Grammaticus might never have written his *Gesta Danorum* and without that we might never have had Shakespeare's Hamlet (Prince of Denmark, remember?). The Vikings also provided one of England's most celebrated kings with a worthy enemy, and would history have turned out the same without King Alfred? The very beginnings of Englishness itself are often traced back to his reign, and while this might be more due to the influence of later historians, it does raise an interesting question. If the Vikings had never attacked, would we still be living in a united kingdom, or in smaller individual kingdoms – home rule for Wessex?

In Ireland, too, the Vikings' historical role has been that of the wicked pagan enemy, there to enhance the reputation of Ireland's kings; but they played their part in the complex politics of Ireland for many generations and had a major role in the foundation of Dublin. I am sure that those canny Viking traders would approve of the booming economy of the 'Celtic Tiger', but would maybe wish for a little more recognition of their part in its history.

To me, the places where the Viking legacy seemed strongest were the islands: the Hebrides, the Isle of Man, but most of all the Northern Isles of Orkney and Shetland. Maybe it all started with the preliminary results of the DNA survey from Orkney which showed the survival of a Viking gene, but these were the places where I felt a real Viking 'presence'. These islands are places of wind and sea, the elements that transported and drove the Vikings on their epic journeys.

There is a practical reason for this lingering Norse feel in the Northern Isles: simply that Norwegian contact continued here until much later than elsewhere in Britain. In fact, both Orkney and Shetland were under Scandinavian rule until the fifteenth century. The earls of Orkney acknowledged the Norwegian Crown, but acted as independent rulers of their own kingdoms and, in an interesting twist of fate, at one stage Orcadian dissenters even spent their summers raiding Norway. I do wonder how the Norwegians liked having the tables turned on them, especially when it was their own countrymen doing the raiding. But eventually Norwegian influence began to wane and in 1266, when the Isle of Man and the Hebrides were given to Scotland, Shetland and Orkney were the only remaining Norwegian lands off the coast of Britain.

By the fourteenth century, the Norwegians were still treating the Northern Isles as just another Norwegian province, but Scottish influence was growing and in 1379 a Scottish earl, Henry Sinclair, took control of the islands on behalf of the Norwegian king. Finally, in 1468, Orkney was given to the Scottish Crown as a dowry when Princess Margaret of Denmark married King James III of Scotland. Orkney was effectively pawned, held as a pledge redeemable by a cash payment, but when no payment had appeared by the end of the year, the Shetland Islands were added to the pledge. It soon became clear that no money was likely to be forthcoming, so both Orkney and Shetland were annexed to the Scottish Crown.

From the moment the Sinclairs took control, Norse customs began to disappear. One of the first was the Norse practice of dividing up land between all the male children in a family, which was gradually replaced by the inheritance of the eldest son. But many Norse traditions appear to have continued, including the collection of wadmal. While Orkney and Shetland were under the control of Norway, the islanders had to pay tax to the Norwegian king and in Shetland they paid their taxes in wool. Wadmal was the special name given to the cloth used for these payments – cloth that was also used to pay rent on the islands. Shetland archivist Brian Smith has traced the history of this unusual tax from its earliest reference in the 1320s almost to the present day. Even though it was a specifically Norwegian tax, when the Northern Isles became part of Scotland the Scottish king decided to continue collecting it from the Shetlanders. The kings could also pass this right to collect tax on to their representatives and so it continued, appearing on inventories from the sixteenth and seventeenth centuries. As late as this date some of the cloth was still being sent back to Norway, probably for making clothes for servants although even they were getting tired of the poor quality. Brian has found records of seventeenth-century Norwegian peasants complaining about the wadmal cloth they were receiving.

Owing to the difficulty of keeping the cloth in good condition, after about 1650 the Shetlanders paid the equivalent in cash to the Scottish and then the British Crown until the 1740s. The right to levy the tax was then passed to the earls of Morton, who sold it on to the Dundas family in 1766. In 1820 the Dundas family took pity on the Shetlanders and allowed many to exempt themselves from the annual charge with a one-off payment. But not all Shetlanders could afford this. Brian Smith says his aunt still paid the equivalent of 2s 9d to the Dundas family until about twenty years ago, and there are a handful of Shetlanders who still pay the Viking wadmal tax!

But links between the Northern Isles and Norway survived long after the payment of wadmal had ceased. After all, with Bergen only about 180 miles to the east of Shetland, Norway is almost as close as the Scottish mainland.

Perhaps the most convincing remnant of Norse culture in the Northern Isles, and the one that is most apparent today, is the language. Nearly all the place-names of Shetland and Orkney that are still used can be traced back to some sort of Norse roots. But more than just names, until the eighteenth century people would also have been speaking a Viking language. The original Norwegian settlers of Orkney and Shetland probably spoke Old Norse, the language of early Viking Age Norway, but as the decades passed a new spoken language grew up from these roots. Norn was spoken in the Northern Isles for centuries, but it is difficult to know exactly what it would have sounded like. There are few written records from the period of Norse settlement and these tend to be expressed in more formal terms, not in the language that was in everyday use.

However, some pieces of Norn have survived. There is a copy of the Orkney Lord's Prayer published in 1700 which reads:

These are the records of a Wadmal collector in Shetland in the seventeenth century. One of his letters describes how it was difficult to store the material, and rats managed to eat away most of one of his shipments.

Favour i ir i chimrie,
Helleru ir i nam thite,
gilla cosdum thite cumma,
veya thine mota vara gort
o yurn sinna gort i chimrie,
ga vus dad on da dalight brow vora,
Firgive vus sinna vora sin vee
Firgive sindara mutha bus,
Iyv vus ye i tumtation,
min delivera vus fro olt ilt, Amen.

Some words seem familiar, but it is not really recognisable to a modern-day English speaker!

People were searching for traces of the Norn language as early as the eighteenth century. In 1774 a researcher called George Low discovered an old man on Shetland who, refreshed with gin, could repeat Norn poems and songs. It is difficult to decipher from Low's writings exactly what this old man was saying: some of it looks like French, but this may simply be a language that Low was familiar with. Is this the language of the Vikings or simply the gin talking?

As Norn gradually died out with the Scottish take-over of Shetland and Orkney, we will never know if George Low's investment in gin really paid off. In the 1920s Jakob Jakobsen published an etymological dictionary, where he brought together all the Norn words he had collected during several trips to Shetland. He found 10,000 words that he considered to be of Scandinavian origin but recent investigation has revealed that only about a tenth of these are still recognised in Shetland today. The Viking influence may be fading but some traces of this ancient language still remain in the local Shetland dialect. Norn words are used for types of animals, plants, food, weather, and tools; the practical vocabulary of a practical people.

So Shetland, closest to the Viking homelands, still has its language and any visitor in late January, during the festival of Up-Helly-Aa, would think that they were witnessing a celebration of these Viking roots, the continuation maybe of a thousand-year tradition. But they would be wrong. The festival itself dates back to the years immediately after the Napoleonic Wars when, as it has been put, 'soldiers and sailors came home with rowdy

The roots of the festival of Up-Helly-Aa, in which a Viking ship is burned, are not really Norse at all. It was invented some time in the nineteenth century.

habits and a taste for
longship and squads of
Guizer Jarl's Squad' –
appeared between the 1880s
but, even if the Vikings are a
addition to a not very ancient fe
I am sure that their ancestors w
approve of this wild midwinter ce
bration.

Another island where Viking influ-ence has survived is the Isle of Man. The Viking presence can be seen in its wealth of artefacts, stone crosses, silver hoards and rich burials. Coins were minted in the names of its leaders. But it also has a living Viking legacy in the Tynwald, or Norse parliament.

When the kingdom of Man controlled the Hebrides, representatives were sent from each of five districts in the kingdom to an annual assembly where administrative decisions were made. Holding assemblies of freemen called things was a common Viking practice. Each district had their allthing, which everyone could attend, and then district representatives would go to larger assemblies, called landsthings in Denmark, or lögth-ings in Norway. At these meetings the Vikings made new laws, held court proceedings and performed public transactions before witnesses. The most important assemblies could pass or reject new laws suggested by the king.

The kingdom of Man was lost to Scotland in 1266, one year after the last Viking king, Magnus Olafsson, died. But the tradition of the Norse thing lives on. Each year on Midsummer Day, 5 July, an assembly meets at the Tynwald, the site of the Norse parliament on the Isle of Man. Today the annual meeting is held on an artificial mound, Tynwald Hill, and in the open air, just as a Norse thing would have been. Following a church service, the officials and dignitaries assemble on the hill to read, in English and in Manx, the new laws that have been enacted in the past year.

So the Northern Isles have wadmal and Norn, the Isle of Man has the Tynwald, but what is the Viking legacy in other parts of the British Isles?

It is there, but in a more subtle form, one that we make use of all the time. Right across England there is strong evidence for place-names that have both Norwegian and Danish origins. As far back as the eleventh century the saga writer Snorri Sturluson first noticed that places in eastern England had distinctly Scandinavian names and today we can spot them across the whole country.

On the Isle of Man, the Tynwald gathering has Norse roots. Each July, all the laws passed on the island are read out in this public ceremony.

Within the Danelaw, the region of north-east England created by the division of the country after the arrival of the Great Army, thousands of town and village names have a hidden Danish heritage. At home in Nottingham, just as I had no idea of the Viking connections on my first dig, I did not realise that many of the names that I was familiar with shared the same links. The nearby town of Derby, the villages of Bleasby, Tithby, Granby, Harby – all end in -by, the Danish word for farm or town. We also use the same Danish word in the phrase 'by-law', meaning a law which applies to a particular town or village. And there are plenty more endings that come to us from Danish. Owthorpe, Sibthorpe, Stragglethorpe share the ending -thorp, meaning village, while -thwaite means an isolated place and -toft a piece of ground.

These are descriptive names, but there are plenty more that include the personal names of Scandinavians who once had influence in the area.

Nottingham is not one of them: here the person with the most influence was obviously not a Dane, but a Saxon with the unfortunate name of Snot. However, places like Grimsby do contain Scandinavian personal names and a whole category of place-names has been created after the town of Grimston. Grim is a Viking name but -ton was the Anglo-Saxon word for town or village. Presumably Grim took over an Anglo-Saxon settlement, and the town then took his name, creating what in place-name terms is knows as a 'Grimston hybrid', a Viking name with an Anglo-Saxon ending.

As well as creating brand-new names for places, the Scandinavian occupation also affected the existing names of towns, villages and farms. Some had their Anglo-Saxon names translated into a Scandinavian equivalent: Churchton becomes Kirkby, from the Scandinavian kirkja for church. Other names were simply altered to make them easier for the Scandinavians to pronounce, with Shipton becoming Skipton and Chesswick, Keswick.

Surnames too can show a Scandinavian naming tradition, such as those that end in -son, like Thompson or Harrison. In Scandinavia, children would take their father's name, with the suffix -son added for a boy and -dottir for a girl. So people would effectively be called John, Tom's son, or Anna, Harry's daughter. This tradition is still used in Iceland today, a country whose Viking roots are completely unambiguous.

But if you don't live in Grimsby, and your name is not Johnson, have the Vikings really affected anything about your life today? As it turns out, the answer is yes, because the Vikings didn't stop at naming places and people. The unique combination of Anglo-Saxons and Scandinavians in the Danelaw helped to create the English language that we speak today.

As they stack the kegs
My sister with the freckles
And the meek odd fellow
Get the dregs – rotten muck
In the seat by the window
The sky glitters in the harbour
The rotten keel drags in the dirt
As they take the reindeer for slaughter

Good poetry it may not be (I wrote it) but, with the exception of the odd 'in', 'the', 'for' and 'as', all of these words have Scandinavian roots. Reindeer may not be a word that is used on a daily basis but window, sky and sister, together with others like call, dirt, flat, guess, race, skirt and want, certainly are. Even personal pronouns like they, them and their, replaced their Old English equivalents and Scandinavian influence on the English language extends even further than this.

Before the Danes arrived there would have been a number of different Anglo-Saxon dialects in use, varying from one kingdom to another, but written documents of the ninth to eleventh centuries are almost exclusively West Saxon. These allow us to track changes in Wessex, Kent and southern Mercia relatively well but because there are few written records elsewhere, there is little information about Anglo-Saxon dialects in the regions that became the Danelaw. Our first inklings of what might have happened there come from twelfth- and thirteenth-century documents that use markedly different forms of English than earlier manuscripts. These are what may give a clue as to how the Scandinavian settlers changed the language of the Danelaw.

Old Norse, the language of the Vikings, and Old English were already relatively similar and it is likely that these two different cultures could understand each other in much the same way as Spanish and Italian speakers can today. Living together within the Danelaw, both Danes and Anglo-Saxons would soon begin to merge their languages. Scandinavian words that were less ambiguous than their Anglo-Saxon counterparts would come into use, and new words would be created.

But it is not only the loan words that altered the language. The mixing of Old Norse and Old English, both of which were more like modern German than modern English, produced a whole new grammatical structure. From languages which depended on the endings of words to give meaning, came one in which the order of the words in a sentence became more important. This 'Danelaw English' brought the language one step closer to the English we speak today.

The answer to the question of how this new form of language became so widely used most probably lies with the people of what is now the East Midlands. In the thirteenth and fourteenth-centuries many of them would have migrated to London, in search of trade and jobs, and taken their own spoken and written words with them. So when Standard English was developing in the fourteenth and fifteenth centuries, 'Danelaw English' would have been used by many Londoners and would have provided a strong influence. This is a period in which we begin to see people commenting on regional differences in language. The people of York are said to speak very badly, while those of Mercia and East Anglia speak a dialect that allows them to communicate easily with those from both the north and the south. As Standard English became recognised as a convenient and easy dialect for communication with English speakers throughout the country, the Scandinavian influences within it would have spread. And this is why we find many traces of Viking language in the original Standard English, and consequently in the English we speak today.

In my search for the Vikings' legacy, the extent to which their language became embodied in the way English is spoken today seems clear evidence of their lasting influence. It shows a people that came not simply to raid and trade, but settled, farmed, married and became a part of the complex mixture that is today's society in Britain and Ireland. And it therefore seems most appropriate that the final place where we can seen their legacy is in our genes. The remnants of the Norwegian Y chromosome survive strongly in Orkney, and there are traces of Celtic blood in Iceland, an icy windswept place to which the Celts would probably never have travelled if they had not lived alongside Irish Vikings.

At intervals over the past year, as my search for the Vikings continued, I had checked up on the progress of the DNA survey at University College London. I had seen the contacts made with groups of volunteers from all the different sample locations, seen the mouth swabs taken (and given one myself) and visited the laboratories to talk to David Goldstein and Jim Wilson about how things were going. Some of the preliminary results started to come in, in particular for the Goodrums and the Corboulds who had been tested. Unfortunately, Jon and the other Goodrums did not seem to have a common Y-chromosome. So it looked as though they couldn't all have descended from the same Danish Viking settler. But it seemed as if the Corboulds, who considered themselves descendants of Garbold the Dane, did share a similar Y-chromosome. They seemed to have a common ancestor but was this ancestor a Danish settler?

The disappointing answer was no – it seems that the Viking legend in the family is just that – a legend. The Corboulds can still hold out some hope however – it is possible the 'Corbould' marker might come from an area of Denmark not tested by the survey, and so was not picked up as part of the Danish marker. But the lab did notice that the results from the Corbould family, whose more recent ancestry lies in Norfolk, fitted very well with the random sample they had taken from that county. So the preliminary indications were that regional variations were going to be identifiable.

As an archaeologist I am often told that I must have great patience, necessary to spend days slowly trowelling away the soil a teaspoonful at a time. But like most archaeologists I am not really that patient and would happily use a mechanical digger if it would do the job properly. I knew that I would have to be patient with the DNA survey and, as I finish this book the analysis is still going on. I know that the results will only come through when all the samples have been processed and that it is all about groups rather than individuals. That is why groups of people from specific areas, all of whom can trace their ancestry back over several generations in that area have been sampled. That is why groups of people back in Norway and Denmark have been sampled to provide the Viking Y-chromosome signatures. Only when group can be compared to group will we be able to say what genetic legacy the Vikings have left us.

For a while my most persistent question to David's team was 'have you processed my sample yet? For some reason I wanted to know whether I had that Viking marker and I suspect that I hoped that the answer was yes. But then it was patiently explained to me that as an individual the results would not really be that significant. Not having the genetic marker would not necessarily mean that I had not got any Viking ancestry. The study only looks at the Y chromosome and my Viking ancestry might be hidden in another part of my DNA; it could have been on my mother's side of the family (which knowing my dear late Mum seems much more likely!). Equally even if I did have the marker, it might not have come from the Vikings. After all, our 'Viking marker' is found in most of the present day Norwegian population too, so it may have come from a more recent Scandinavian ancestor. For example, finding a 'Viking marker' in Australia would not mean the Vikings had travelled there one thousand years ago. These types of genetic studies only work alongside history and archaeology, and these tell us it is far more likely that a recent European sailor could have brought a 'Viking marker' to Australia. Unless of course, the Vikings were more adventurous than the sagas tell!

With or without the genes – I'm convinced we're a pair of modern day Vikings.

I have come to the conclusion that I do not really mind whether I have the genes or not. Initially I wanted to feel a part of the Viking tradition of my childhood, the sea rovers with their flaxen hair and horned helmets. But perhaps this was just me wanting to be taller, blonder and braver. I have now realised that there is much more to the Vikings than this image suggests. They were adventurous, brave to the extent of being reckless at times, highly adaptable and pragmatic, practical in their farming and settling and yet wonderfully artistic. In many of the places that I have visited I have seen the evidence of a Viking past and seen their skills and character in the people of today. Their legacy does not simply belong to a few, it lies within the common heritage that belongs to us all. The Vikings played a part, a crucial part, in the history of our islands and I am now convinced that in *all* of our veins runs just a little bit of the blood of the Vikings.

POSTSCRIPT

After the hardback edition of this book had gone to press, the results of various scientific tests came through, and this paperback edition gives me a chance to outline some of the fascinating results.

An extraordinary catalogue of injuries was identified in the skeleton of the Viking warrior from Repton (p.153). In addition to sustaining a previously identified axe wound to the groin, this man had been stabbed twice through the left eye, probably with a spear; part of his lower jaw and the upper part of his left arm had been sliced away, presumably by a sword blow; his feet had been mutilated by repeated axe blows and finally he had been disemboweled. These injuries could not all have been sustained on the battlefield, so perhaps this Viking was a victim of Saxon revenge.

Near York we were able to shed new light on Harald Hardrada's Viking army (p.226). After sailing up the River Ouse Harald arrived at Riccal and it was also from here that the battered remnants of his army disembarked after their final defeat. There has long been speculation that skeletons excavated from fields close to the river at Riccal were Harald's men. The proof came from oxygen isotopes contained in teeth taken from six separate burials. This showed categorically that these people had grown up in Norway. We had found the last Viking army ever to set foot on English soil.

But for all of us involved in this project, it was the results from the genetics survey carried out by Professor Goldstein and his team at University College, London that were most anxiously awaited. The basic principle was simple - to try to identify a 'Viking' signature in the modern male populations of Norway and Denmark and then see if this signature could be identified in sample male populations taken from testing sites within Britain and Ireland. A strong Norwegian Viking signature could be identified in the Northern Isles of Shetland and Orkney (60% of those tested), the very northern tip of Scotland and down through the Hebrides (30%) and the Isle of Man (15%). This follows clearly the 'Sea Road' but surprisingly there was no trace of Norwegian ancestry found in Ireland where there is historical evidence for Viking settlement. Here, as with North and South Wales, the DNA samples were almost entirely Ancient Briton ('Celtic') - the signature of the indigenous population.

Within the majority of England, southern Scotland and the Welsh borders, we hoped to identify the signature of the Danish Vikings who had invaded from the 9th century onwards. However, their signature was indistinguishable from that of the Angles and Saxons who, from the 5th century, had also invaded and settled England. Geographically and genetically close, these two groups could only be considered together as 'invaders' and their combined signature mapped out. This showed that their influence decreased as the test sites moved towards the south coast and Cornwall and that mainland Scotland was not appreciably more 'Celtic' than southern England.

The survey, which has generated results that will continue to be studied and discussed for many years, has identified a new type of Viking legacy, one that runs deep in the veins of many of us. But beyond this it has served to re-emphasise our extraordinary diversity and the complexity of a culture that has been enriched over thousands of years. The Vikings certainly played their part.

Julian Richards April 2002

ACKNOWLEDGEMENTS

Over the last year or so it has been a real pleasure working with the BBC production team involved in making the Blood of the Vikings series. Paul Bradshaw, Liz Tucker, Gerald Lorenz, Julia Jay, Alom Shaha and our executive producer Caroline van den Brul have all helped me to become immersed in the world of the Vikings and, in doing so, have helped to shape this book.

For me, the series has been a genuine voyage of discovery, in the course of which I have been positively encouraged to indulge my curiosity. I offer my sincere thanks to all the archaeologists, historians, archivists, genetic scientists and Viking experts who I have met along the way and who have shown me so much patience and enthusiasm. Thank you for so willingly sharing your expertise and a special thanks to all those in Norway, Denmark and Sweden who had to cope not only with my incessant questions but also with my almost total lack of any Scandinavian language.

Thanks to all at Hodder & Stoughton, including Janette Revill for her imaginative design, Juliette Brightmore for finding some great pictures, and Julia Cassells and Rachel Grimes for their expertise in the production and editing of the book.

I would especially like to thank Rupert Lancaster, my editor at Hodder, who has not only been tremendously encouraging and incisive but has also shown remarkable patience with the inevitable interruptions caused by filming. A special thanks is also needed for acknowledging my need for a quick family holiday even when the deadline loomed nearer.

Sue and Barnaby – thanks once again for being patient with a preoccupied husband/Dad. It won't happen again (until the next time).

Finally, and most importantly, I would like to thank Nicola Cook, without whose efforts this book would, quite simply, not have been written. I cannot overstate the value of Nicola's meticulous research, the contributions she has made to structuring this volume and her amazing ability to find the answers to even my oddest and most obscure questions. Thanks, Nicola.

SOURCES

CHAPTER 1: p7 – 'They were like England in the nineteenth century', Oxford Illustrated History of the Vikings; CHAPTER 2: p11, 15 – 'Here terrible portents came about', The Anglo-Saxon Chronicles; p15 – 'And Billfrith, the anchorite, wrought the ornaments', British Library online information server, http://www.bl.uk/index.html; CHAPTER 3: p31, 33 – 'He said that the land of the Norwegians was very long', Othere's Account to King Alfred, Anglo-Saxon Prose, Michael Swanton (ed.) (J. M. Dent, 1975); CHAPTER 4: p51 – 'He preferred to go west across the sea to Scotland', Laxdale Saga, (The Temple Classics, 1899); CHAPTER 5: p75 – 'In a word, although there were an hundred hard-steeled iron heads', Cogadh Gáedhel re Gallaibh, taken from Viking Expansion Westward by Magnus Magnusson (Bodley Head, 1973); CHAPTER 6: p93 – 'A great raiding ship-army came over here . . .' Anglo-Saxon Chronicles; CHAPTER 7: p105 – 'there shall come great tempests', Old Irish text, Epistil Isu, from 'Cáin Domnaig', J. G. O'Keeffe (ed. and trans.), Eiru, 2 (1905); p109 – 'Guthfrith, grandson of Ímar, with the foreigners of Áth Cliath', The Annals of Ulster, Séan Macairt and Gearóid Mac Niocaill (ed.) (Dublin Institute for Advanced Studies, 1983); p123 – 'When a chief has died his family asks his slave women and slaves', The Cultural Atlas of the Viking World; CHAPTER 8: p131 – 'Here the raiding-army went from East Anglia . . .' Anglo-Saxon Chronicle, as above; p134 – 'And the same year a great heathen raiding-army came', ibid; p135 – 'It was late in the year when they turned to making war against the raiding-army', ibid; p140 – 'But Alderman Osric, with the command of Hampshire', ibid; p141 – promised money therewith; but under the security of peace, ibid; p141 – 'Since the pagans, protected by the defences of the fortress, refused to give battle', ibid; p144 – 'And four days later King Æthelred and Alfred, his brother, fought on Ashdown', ibid; p152 – 'In this year the army went from Lindsey to Repton and took up winter quarters there', ibid; CHAPTER 9: p157, 164 – 'When the next morning dawned he moved his forces', Alfred the Great, Asser's Life of King Alfred and Other Contemporary Sources; p163 – 'Here the raiding-army stole away in midwinter after Twelfth Night', Anglo-Saxon Chronicle; p163 – 'he had nothing to live on except what he could forage' Alfred the Great, Asser's Life of King Alfred and Other Contemporary Sources, as above; p170 – 'This is the peace which King Alfred and King Guthrum', ibid; p76 –

'Æthelflæd gave him lands near Chester, and he stayed there a long time', *Fragmenta Tria Annalium Hiberniæ I*, Bibliotheque Royale, Brussels, MS., trans. Prof. I. L. Foster, Jesus College, Oxford. Reproduced in *Ingimund's Saga*; p177 – 'What the Saxons did was to let loose on the attacking force all the beehives', ibid; CHAPTER 10: p181 – 'This is the peace which King Alfred and King Guthrum', *Alfred the Great, Asser's Life of King Alfred and Other Contemporary Sources*, p201 – 'With chosen troops' *Anglo-Saxon Chronicle*; CHAPTER 11: p205 – 'The English, indeed, were the more bold at first', *Encomium Emmae Reginae*, Alistair Campbell (CUP, 1998), p211 – 'Here the raiding-army turned eastward again', *Anglo-Saxon Chronicle*; p211 – 'But when the ships were ready, there was delay from day to day', ibid; p217 – 'Then Ealdorman Eadric did as he so often did before', ibid; CHAPTER 12: p237 – 'Favour i ir i chimrie', Orkney Lord's Prayer, reprinted from Wallace 1700:68–9 in *The Norn Language of Orkney and Shetland* (Shetland Times, 1998).

PHOTO ACKNOWLEDGEMENTS

Ashmolean Museum, Oxford: 164. Bibliothèque Nationale de France, Paris: 210. © Martin and Birthe Biddle, Oxford: 153. Bodleian Library, University of Oxford: 18 (Ms Laud Misc. 636). British Library, London: 29 (Add. Ms 39943), 219 (Ms Stowe. 944). British Museum, London: 106, 137, 175, 180 photo Michael Holford, 190, 191, 220 photo Michael Holford. © Mike Caine, Isle of Man: 239. Douglas Campbell: 4. Chicago Historical Society: 8. Nicola Cook: 167, 212, 213. © Corbis/photo Hubert Stadler: 127. Master and Fellows of Corpus Christi College, Cambridge/The Parker Library: 161 (CCC Ms 26). Delaware Art Museum, Wilmington, USA (detail of stained glass by Sir Edward Burne-Jones) photo Bridgeman Art Library: vi. Derby Museum and Art Gallery/photos Eric Mathews: 151, 154, 155. Dúchas, The Heritage Service, Dublin: 112. English Heritage Photographic Library, London: 30 © photo Skyscan. Mary Evans Picture Library, London: 5, 158. Field Archaeology Specialists Ltd, University of York: 27. Gotlands Fornsal, Gotland's Historical Museum, Sweden/photo Raymund Hejdström: 150. Historic Scotland, Edinburgh: 58, 64, 65. © Doug Houghton, Orkney: 61, 72, Eryl Rothwell Hughes, Anglesey: 101 bottom. Hunterian Museum, Glasgow University: 207. Kobal Collection, London: 2. Kunstindustri Museet, Oslo: 136. Arni Magnússon Institute, Reykjavic, Iceland: 50, 206. Manx National Heritage, Isle of Man: 94, 103, 105. Museum of Danish Resistance 1940-1945, Copenhagen/photo Kit Weiss: 10. Museum of London: 216, 221. National Archives of Scotland, Edinburgh: 236. National Monuments Record, English Heritage: 198. National Museum of Denmark, Copenhagen: 80, 85, 204, 222. National Museum of Ireland, Dublin: 83, 116, 117, 118, 124. National Museums of Scotland Picture Library, Edinburgh: 56, 57, 66, 74. Nordiska Museets Bildbyrå, Stockholm: 7. Norfolk Landscape Archaeology, Norfolk County Council Cultural Services: 134. Norfolk Museums and Archaeology Service, Norfolk County Council Cultural Services: 135, 187. Pierpont Morgan Library, New York/photos Art Resource, New York: 16, 130, 138, 159, 173, 189, 232. Private Collections: 21, 186. Julian Richards: ii, v, 24, 25, 32, 36, 37, 39, 43, 45, 46, 48, 67, 70, 76, 81, 82, 88, 89, 92, 98, 100, 101 top, 102, 149, 152, 156, 244. Royal Library, Stockholm: 142. © Roger Scruton, N. Yorks: 193. Shetland Islands Tourism, Orkney/© photo Charles Tait: 238. Smithsonian National Museum of Natural History, Washington DC/photo Peter Harholdt: 23. Statens Historiska Museum, Stockholm: 52 photo Michael Holford, 143. Board of Trinity College, Dublin, Ireland (*Book of Kells* Ms 58 folio 114r)/photo Bridgeman Art Library: 12. Liz Tucker: 109. © University Museum of Cultural Heritage, University of Oslo: 40. © York Archaeological Trust: 199, 200, 201, 228.

Maps by Skaramoosh, London: 15, 34, 55, 78 with additional information by permission Donnchadh Ó Corráin, 171, 179, 185, 229.